NORTH CAROLINA

OFF THE BEATEN PATH®

Help Us Keep This Guide Up to Date

We would love to hear from you concerning your experiences with this guide and how you feel it could be improved and kept up to date. Please send your comments and suggestions to:

editorial@GlobePequot.com

Thanks for your input, and happy travels!

OFF THE BEATEN PATH® SERIES

ELEVENTH EDITION

NORTH CAROLINA

OFF THE BEATEN PATH®

DISCOVER YOUR FUN

SARA PITZER

Globe
Pequot
Guilford, Connecticut

917.56
OFF
2017

For the good friends and neighbors who encourage
me and offer help when I need it.

All the information in this guidebook is subject to change. We recommend
that you call ahead to obtain current information before traveling.

Globe Pequot

An imprint of Rowman & Littlefield
Off the Beaten Path is a registered trademark of Rowman & Littlefield.
Distributed by NATIONAL BOOK NETWORK

Copyright © 2017 Rowman & Littlefield
Maps: Equator Graphics © Rowman & Littlefield

British Library Cataloguing in Publication information is available

ISSN 1539-7769
ISBN 978-1-4930-2757-6 (paperback)
ISBN 978-1-4930-2758-3 (ebook)

∞™ The paper used in this publication meets the minimum requirements of American
National Standard for Information Sciences—Permanence of Paper for Printed Library
Materials, ANSI/NISO Z39.48-1992.

Contents

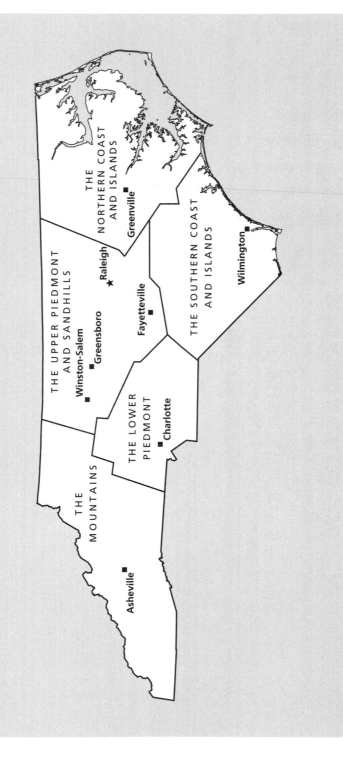

THE MOUNTAINS

Asheville

THE LOWER PIEDMONT

Charlotte

THE UPPER PIEDMONT AND SANDHILLS

Winston-Salem
Greensboro

Raleigh

Fayetteville

THE NORTHERN COAST AND ISLANDS

Greenville

THE SOUTHERN COAST AND ISLANDS

Wilmington

Introduction

I was lost—again—somewhere around Raleigh, but nowhere near the place I wanted to be. I'd already pulled into the entrance of a large industrial park, where an executive stopped on his way out to ask if he could help me. I'd already walked along the sidewalk in front of North Carolina State University, where a professor leaving campus gave me detailed instructions on getting out of the city in the direction I wanted to go. And I was pretty sure I was going to get it right, if I could just find the beltway. Seeing that the car in the next lane had both windows down as we waited for a light to turn, I called across to the driver, "Is this road going to take me to the beltway?"

"Where do you want to go?" he yelled back. I told him. "Follow me," he shouted, and when the light changed, he took off in a cloud of exhaust. I followed him nearly 10 miles. At the proper entrance onto the beltway, he blinked his turn signal and also pointed emphatically with his left hand, just in case I missed the signal. I turned. He was already gone, leaving me with a grin and a wave.

And that's how people in North Carolina are.

I have seen many changes since I moved here in 1983. What does not change is the friendliness of people who live in the state, always ready with a smile and a greeting, even if they've never seen you before, and quick to lend a hand if you seem to need help.

A North Carolina saying has it that if you don't like the weather, wait a minute. But while it does change year-to-year and day-to-day, the sky inevitably turns that clear, bright color known here as Carolina blue. Quite apart from the sky, we have a lot to be proud of here, a lot for visitors to enjoy.

Barbecue, Pottery, Wine & Beer

Take the barbecue, for instance. Two authors writing an article on Southern barbecue for *Cook's* magazine traveled through several states looking for the best barbecue restaurants, but they were not able to get to North Carolina. They apologized in their article, because, they said, in comparison, nothing else is barbecue at all. (North Carolina barbecue is always pork cooked over a wood fire, never prepared in a sauce, and usually served with slaw and hush puppies.)

Then there's the pottery. This state has scores and scores of potters, working in the historic old production styles and in contemporary studio modes, producing such a variety of work that a personal collection could easily crowd everything else from a room.

Wineries are catching on, too, more opening every year, with vineyards thriving in the sunny climate. In fact, before Prohibition, North Carolina was a successful wine-producing state, and it's returning to that heritage all across the state. North Carolina has 143 wineries as of this writing. For a current list and map, check ncwine.org.

Craft brewing is the newbie. Cities of all sizes have their own breweries and brewpubs. The mountain town of Asheville, with 10 breweries, was once voted "Beer City USA" in a newspaper survey, but since then many towns have opened local beer breweries. Hard cider, also produced in the state, has a growing fan base too.

Rich History

Historically important, North Carolina, one of the 13 original colonies, played key roles in the Revolutionary War, the Civil War, and World Wars I and II. The area is rich in Native American history; blacks made many early significant advances here; and the Moravians created a historic settlement at Old Salem. The Wright brothers first accomplished powered flight in North Carolina, on a site that is popular today with hang gliders more interested in playing than in setting records.

The Shape of the Land

As for topography, North Carolina has some of the oldest mountains in the world, the largest natural sand dune on the East Coast, and some of the most unspoiled beaches and islands in the country. The rich soil of the Piedmont and foothills grows apples, vegetables, Christmas trees, cotton, and tobacco, a problematic crop with much historic significance.

Each of the three major geographic areas of the state—the mountains, the Piedmont, and the coastal plain—differs radically from the others. It's almost like traveling through three smaller states. The nature of each region influenced the kinds of commerce that flourished historically and that continue to flourish, and also left a mark on the people. As you travel you'll hear fascinating changes in the music of the accents of people native to each region.

The mountains make up the smallest part of the state, but they compensate in interest and beauty for what they lack in area. Some of the highest mountains in the Appalachians are here. As anyone who drives in the mountains knows, transportation is difficult. In earlier times it was nearly impossible; hence the development of small pockets of civilization separated by stretches of wilderness, creating those tough, independent, resourceful, self-sufficient folks—mountain people. This kind of early self-sufficiency and distance from major metropolitan areas made the growth of all kinds of crafts almost inevitable. The mountains are still the richest source of handcrafts in the state.

In the Piedmont, which makes up almost two-fifths of the state, you'll find mostly rolling hills and red clay. Although the clay is harder to work than the sandy soil of the coast, it seems to have held its fertility better against some pretty bad early farming habits. (Wherever they are grown, cotton and tobacco are notorious for wearing out the soil.) Since the Piedmont doesn't have many large stretches of flat land, it didn't invite the huge plantations that used to be worked with many slaves. Smaller family farms were often worked by the people who owned them, perhaps with some hired help. The historians Hugh Talmage Lefler and Albert Ray Newsome point out in their classic *The History of a State: North Carolina* that the narrow, swift streams of the Piedmont, which weren't worth much for transportation, were great for generating power. And that, along with the presence of hardwoods and other resources, accounts for the great number of manufacturing activities that used to flourish in the Piedmont before most of it went offshore. Probably because of the past concentration of moneyed manufacturers and merchants, you'll also find rich lodes of cultural attractions and arts here.

The coastal plain accounts for about another two-fifths of the state's area. The North Carolina coast has been considered dangerous since the first settlers tried to cope with its ever-changing beaches, currents, and waterways. There was no guarantee that just because you had safely sailed into a particular port once, you would find it safe, or even open, the next time you tried. That's at least one reason why English colonization shifted up toward the Chesapeake and why North Carolina was settled more sparsely and slowly than some other colonies were. Even today you'll find areas that are remarkably sparsely settled compared to most states' coastal regions. For vacationers the main activities and sightseeing highlights are related to the same activities that have long supported the area economically—fishing, boating, and beach going.

Although tourism and technology have homogenized somewhat the state's regional populations, you can still find lots of those tall, thin, rangy people. It remains a pretty good joke in the Piedmont for a young woman marrying outside the area to claim she's found herself a mountain man.

Recreation & Travel

As a place to play, the state offers hiking and whitewater rafting, waterskiing and snow skiing, freshwater and saltwater fishing and boating, athletics, auto racing, horseback riding, and golf on some of the most famous courses in the country.

Good Sense about Driving in North Carolina

- North Carolina law requires drivers to move over to the next lane or reduce speed for stopped emergency vehicles, including those with amber lights, on the shoulder of the highway.

- If you have a fender-bender accident with no injuries where both cars are able to be driven, move over to the shoulder of the road. Not doing so could result in a $250 fine plus court costs.

- It is illegal to text while driving in North Carolina.

- Take the speed limits seriously. State troopers are vigilant on interstates, but you're even more likely to get busted for exceeding speed limits in small towns. If the sign says 35 miles per hour, believe it. A local sheriff may be waiting in any open space along the road. (Ask me how I know.)

- Watch out for critters. The deer population continues to grow, and especially in the evening and early morning, they may leap from any grassy area along the road, both on rural roads and Interstates. Squirrels, raccoons, opossums, skunks, and the occasional cow or horse may wander onto the road. In eastern North Carolina, bears are frequently spotted beside or on the road.

Face it—you're not going to be able to do it all or see it all in one trip, or even in ten trips. Don't try to squeeze too much into a single trip, or you'll end up driving a lot and not doing much else. But the driving you do shouldn't be unpleasant if you avoid the interstates around major cities at rush hour and accept the fact that the two-lane roads tend to be well maintained but slow, since there are few good places for passing slow drivers and tractors. To understand the roads and decide when to travel on a major highway and when to get onto secondary roads, you'll definitely need a state map. The best one is the North Carolina transportation map, issued by the North Carolina Department of Transportation and the Division of Travel and Tourism (800-847-4862). You may pick one up free at a welcome center, request it online (ncdot.org/travel/mappubs/statetransportationmap), or receive it by writing to the North Carolina Division of Travel and Tourism, 430 N. Salisbury St., Raleigh 27611.

If you or those traveling with you are in any way physically challenged, you should also request a copy of the book, *Access North Carolina: A Guide to Travel Site Accessibility*. This is a remarkably good book published by the North Carolina Department of Human Resources, the Division of Vocational Rehabilitation Services, and the Division of Travel and Tourism. It briefly describes historic sites, state and national parks and forests, and general-interest attractions, focusing on their accessibility of parking, entrance, interior rooms, exterior areas, and restrooms. The book is free. Call the aforementioned tourism number, or check the website: http://dvr.dhhs.state.nc.us/DVR/pubs/accessnc/accessnc.htm.

More Stuff to Read

A state with so many resources inevitably becomes the subject of many books. Depending on your interests, you may find several of them useful along with this guide. The University of North Carolina Press publishes *Turners and Burners: The Folk Potters of North Carolina,* by Charles G. Zug III, the most complete explication of the subject available. The press also publishes many books about North Carolina history. For further information, write University of North Carolina Press, P.O. Box 2288, Chapel Hill 27514.

If you are a devotee of back roads, you may enjoy Earl Thollander's *Back Roads of the Carolinas,* devoted entirely to "nonhighway" drives along roads that often aren't on regular maps. Thollander designed the book, lettered the text in calligraphy, and drew the maps and wash illustrations himself. Often Thollander suggests a dirt road or other obscure route from one historic point to another, which you could use as a much, much slower alternative to the routes I suggest. It is published by Clarkson N. Potter. Finally, the North Carolina publisher John F. Blair offers several books about the history and ecology of the North Carolina coast. It's especially fun to read such books ahead of time and then carry them with you to consult, because the material comes alive as you see the subject matter firsthand.

NORTH CAROLINA GENERAL WEBSITES

North Carolina Division of Tourism
visitnc.com

African-American Heritage
ncculturetour.org

Golf in North Carolina
visitnc.com/golf

Native American Culture
cherokeeheritagetrails.org

North Carolina Association of Festivals and Events
ncfestivals.com

North Carolina Crafts
discovercraftnc.org

North Carolina Ferry Division
ncferry.org

Sports in North Carolina
nccommerce.com/sports

Good People

With or without the books, though, North Carolina comes alive when you travel here because of its people. Significant history, appealing countryside, even good food can be part of any well-planned trip. Adding helpful, friendly, almost uniformly cheerful people changes the mix from plain cake to an angel food celebration. In the years I've been traveling almost continuously around the state, I've not had a single unpleasant experience with a North Carolinian. Unless you carry a chip the size of one of Mount Mitchell's ancient trees on your shoulder, you won't either. And if you're in that bad a mood, don't come. If you can't have fun in North Carolina, you can't enjoy yourself anywhere. Might as well stay home.

Rapid Growth

Maybe I shouldn't have talked so loud. Maybe I shouldn't have been so enthusiastic. Maybe I shot myself in the foot, big time, because North Carolina has been discovered. It happened fast. Not long ago the state was pretty much all off the beaten path, except for development around Raleigh and Durham, Greensboro, and, more recently, Charlotte. But in recent years, North Carolina has been among the fastest growing states in the country, attracting people from the colder areas of the Northeast as well as many people who've decided they don't like life in Florida anymore. Housing developments and shopping malls circle not only the major cities but many of the smaller towns as well. Suddenly there's a Wendy's and a car wash at every intersection. Ever-widening highways cover great expanses that used to be woods or farmland or fishing holes with concrete and macadam. Let's face it, we're talking about sprawl here, just as it's happened, for instance, in places like parts of California; around Atlanta, Georgia; and in the Pocono Mountains of Pennsylvania. That's the bad news.

But it's the good news, too, because with the rush of growth, some people are getting worried about losing what makes this place special, and they're acting decisively to preserve some of it. Two examples come to mind at once: the little town of Hillsborough, up near the Virginia border, and the city of Salisbury at the center of the state. In places like these and in other communities, residents are emphasizing historic preservation and working to keep their downtowns vital.

A Changing Population

Along with this development, another new dimension has changed North Carolina—the immigration of Hispanic and Asian people as well as people from

NORTH CAROLINA WELCOME CENTERS

North Carolina Welcome Centers
4324 Mail Service Center
Raleigh 27699-4324
(800) 847-4862
visitnc.com/resources/view/nc-welcome
-centers/
This is strictly a call center, not a place
to visit. But by calling ahead you can ask
for maps and other Information to be
sent to you. It typically takes a couple of
weeks for the packet to arrive.

I-26 East
Columbus
(828) 894-2120

I-26 West
Mars Hill
(828) 689-4257

I-40 West
Waynesville
(828) 627-6206

I-77 North
Dobson
(336) 320-2181

I-77 South
Charlotte
(704) 588-2660

I-85 North
Norlina
(252) 456-3236

I-85 South
Kings Mountain
(704) 937-7861

I-95 North
Roanoke Rapids
(252) 537-3365

I-95 South
Rowland
(910) 422-8314

European countries, a result of the evolving global economy. Many Hispanics have come to find jobs better than those at home. They've often started out in the jobs nobody else seemed willing to do, like the hot, heavy work of making bricks and quarrying granite and cleaning shopping malls. But as their hard work pays off and their children move up in school, the Hispanic population is becoming a force in the state. Mexican restaurants and stores selling the kinds of ingredients with which Hispanics cook dot most communities, while supermarkets try to keep up with the new customers, too. Similarly, Asian immigrants have brought their influence, reflected in Thai, Vietnamese, Korean, and Chinese restaurants, even in smaller towns. Add to that the influence of transplanted Yankees with their demands for bagels and Philadelphia cheese steaks, Italians who like their prosciutto and salami, and vegetarian Muslims, and you've got the core of a surprisingly sophisticated population in an area that once consisted almost entirely of down-home Southerners. Their shops and restaurants have become part of the state and worthy of off-the-beaten-path status.

What this means is that even if you've been here before, visiting North Carolina now is a whole new experience.

North Carolina has state parks and recreation areas that are visited by millions of visitors every year. Many have camping, fishing, and hiking. Some offer special educational programs. Some are developed, while others remain wild. For full details, check the website: ncparks.gov.

North Carolina State Parks

IN THE MOUNTAINS

Burnsville
Mount Mitchell
(828) 675-4611

Connelly Springs
South Mountains
(828) 433-4772

Jefferson
Mount Jefferson State Natural Area
(336) 246-9653

New River
(336) 982-2587

Nebo
Lake James
(828) 652-5047

Roaring Gap
Stone Mountain
(336) 957-8185

Sapphire
Gorges
(828) 966-9099

IN THE PIEDMONT & SANDHILLS

Albemarle
Morrow Mountain
(704) 982-4402

Apex
Jordan Lake State Recreation Area
(919) 362-0586

Danbury
Hanging Rock
(336) 593-8480

Durham
Eno River
(919) 383-1686

Henderson
Kerr Lake State Recreation Area
(252) 438-7791

Hillsborough
Occoneechee Mountain
(919) 383-1686

Hollister
Medoc Mountain
(252) 586-6588

Kings Mountain
Crowders Mountain
(704) 853-5375

Lillington
Raven Rock
(910) 893-4888

Orrum
Lumber River
(910) 628-9844

Pinnacle
Pilot Mountain
(336) 325-2355

Raleigh
William B. Umstead State Park Crabtree Creek—north side of park
(919) 571-4170

Reedy Creek—south side of park
(919) 571-4170

Seven Springs
Cliffs of the Neuse
(919) 778-6234

Southern Pines
Weymouth Woods
(910) 692-2167

Troutman
Lake Norman
(704) 528-6350

Wake Forest
Falls Lake State Recreation Area
(919) 676-1027

AT THE COAST

Atlantic Beach
Fort Macon
(252) 726-3775

Carolina Beach
Carolina Beach
(910) 458-8206

Creswell
Pettigrew
(252) 797-4475

Elizabethtown
Jones Lake
(910) 588-4550

Gatesville
Merchants Millpond
(252) 357-1191

Kelly
Singletary Lake
(910) 669-2928

Kure Beach
Fort Fisher State
Recreation Area
(910) 458-5798

Lake Waccamaw
Lake Waccamaw
(910) 646-4748

Nags Head
Jockey's Ridge
(252) 441-7132

Pine Knoll Shores
Theodore Roosevelt
Natural Area
(252) 726-3775

Swansboro
Hammocks Beach
(910) 326-4881

Washington
Goose Creek
(252) 923-2191

Wineries

The wine industry in North Carolina has taken off. Every year more wineries open across the state, often in remote places, as grapes begin to replace tobacco as a crop, and cotton mills as businesses. By 2010, the number of North Carolina wineries had topped more than 140. Many of the wines produced are sweet, from scuppernong and other Muscadine grapes, which have historically done well here. But growers and vintners are also beginning to make such dry wines as Cabernet Sauvignon and Pinot Grigio, as well as such specialties as blueberry wine. Some of the wines are available in grocery stores and wine shops; others are sold mainly out of the winery's shop, often at the vineyard. Wine tours and tastings are becoming an increasingly popular activity. For the most current offerings, check visitncwine.com as you travel.

The Ben Long Frescoes

Benjamin F. Long IV has become one of North Carolina's best-known artists. Although he grew up in Statesville and studied at the University of North Carolina at Chapel Hill, he went on to the Art Students League in New York and later lived in Florence, Italy, as an apprentice under the fresco master Pietro Annigoni. The fresco technique was the method Michelangelo used to paint the Sistine Chapel. In more than 30 years working with frescoes, including commissions in France and Italy, Ben Long had created 11 of these large works in North Carolina, beginning with *Mary Great with Child* for St. Mary's Episcopal Church in West Jefferson. The Blue Ridge National Heritage Area has sponsored a program to create a map and illustrated trail to provide information about each site as well as the fresco process for students and tourists. Visit benlongfrescotrail.org. For greater detail about the process, see pages 49 and 52.

FRESCO TRAIL ARRANGED CHRONOLOGICALLY

St. Mary's Episcopal Church, West Jefferson; (336) 982-3076
Mary Great with Child, 1974
John the Baptist, 1976
The Mystery of Faith, 1977

Holy Trinity Episcopal Church, Glendale Springs; (336) 982-3076
The Last Supper, 1980

Bank of America Corporate Center, Charlotte; (800) 231-4636
Untitled Space, 1992

Charlotte-Mecklenburg Law Enforcement Center, Charlotte; (704) 353-1000
Untitled, 1996

Transamerica Square, Charlotte; (704) 388-8230
Continuum, 1997

Montreat College Chapel of the Prodigal, Montreat; (828) 669-8012
Return of the Prodigal, 1998

First Presbyterian Church, Charlotte; (704) 331-5123
The Good Samaritan, 2001

Statesville Civic Center, Statesville; (704) 878-3493
Images at the Crossroads, 2002

St. Paul's Episcopal Church, Wilkesboro; (336) 667-4231
St. Paul's Conversion, 2002
St. Paul Writing His Epistles, 2002

City of Morganton Municipal Auditorium (CoMMA), Morganton; (800) 939-7469
The Sacred Dance & the Muses, 2004

The Crossnore School, Crossnore; (828) 733-4035
Suffer the Little Children, 2006

A Word about Prices

They change, usually going up, but not always. Here are some guidelines for notations in the places to stay and places to eat listed at the end of each chapter.

Restaurants—the price of one entree excluding beverages, dessert, tax, or tip

Inexpensive	less than $10
Moderate	$10 to $20
Expensive	more than $20

Accommodations—the rate of a one-night stay in a standard room excluding tax during high season

Inexpensive	less than $100
Moderate	$100 to $200
Expensive	more than $200

However, it is important to know that accommodation rates may vary with the season, day, week, or occasional special event. They may go up when demand is greater in the area and be reduced as "unsold inventory" as a weekend approaches with many rooms still not taken. This is especially true of larger chains.

The Mountains

The Western Mountains

Whatever you plan in the North Carolina mountains, allow about twice as much travel time as usual. Narrow roads wind through woodland and countryside, up hills so steep you sometimes feel as though your car will peel off the road backward, from hairpin turns into switchbacks followed by more curves. The squiggles don't all show up on the maps, and the maps can't allow for the time it takes if you get behind a big truck with no place to pass for 50 miles. Decide ahead of time not to hurry; relax and absorb the peerless scenery.

One way to enjoy the panoramic views of mountains and valleys is by driving some part of the *Blue Ridge Parkway.* It stretches from Shenandoah National Park in Virginia along the Blue Ridge Mountains into the southern part of the Black Mountains, through the Craggies, the Pisgahs, the Balsams, and into the Great Smokies, a total of 469 miles. The maximum speed limit along the parkway is 45 miles per hour, but in reality, traffic is often slower. It doesn't take much arithmetic to figure that it would take a long time to cover the entire length of the parkway at 30 or 40 miles per hour. The best way to

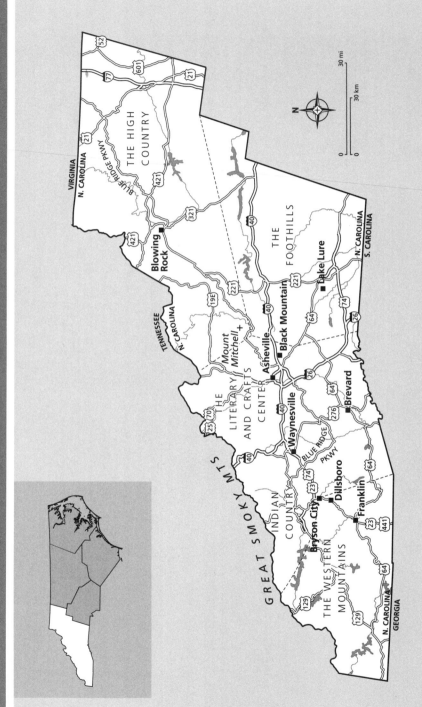

plan a trip is to alternate stretches of the parkway with drives on the roads you can reach by turning off along the way. Crossovers from the parkway are marked with mileposts that are numbered and named.

To take in some of the rugged mountain scenery without driving the winding roads, you might board the *Great Smoky Mountains Railroad* (800-872-4681; gsmr.com) at the depot on Depot Street in *Bryson City.* The tracks were first laid in the 1890s, and rail transport made it possible to establish a vigorous logging industry in the mountains. Eventually highways replaced trains, and by 1988 the state of North Carolina had taken over the tracks in this region and leased a 53-mile stretch to the Great Smoky Mountains Railroad, which runs a variety of excursion trips through the mountains. The *Scenic Model Railroad Museum* (100 Greenlee St., Bryson City; 866-914-5200; smokymtntrains .com), next to the Great Smoky Mountains Railroad Depot, honors the area's railroading history with a 24-by-45-foot model layout, with more than a mile of track on three levels over which six trains run at once. The layout has a working roundtable with roundhouse and a 5-foot waterfall. The model includes a freight yard with at least 400 cars, a dozen animated scenes, and more than 60 buildings made by hand, not assembled from packages. This collection has

ANNUAL EVENTS IN THE MOUNTAINS

ASHEVILLE

Annual Spring Herb Festival
(early May)
www.ashevilleherbvestival.com

BANNER ELK

Blowing Rock Independence Day Festival
(July 4—the Saturday closest to July 4)
(828) 295-7851

Black Mountain Sourwood Festival
(Second weekend in August)
(828) 669-2300 or (800) 669-2301

Woolly Worm Festival
(third full weekend in October)
(800) 438-7500

DILLSBORO

Dillsboro NC Easter Hat Parade
(last Saturday before Easter)
(800) 962-1911

Western North Carolina Pottery Festival
(first Saturday in November)
(800) 962-1911

GRANDFATHER MOUNTAIN

Scottish Highland Games
(second weekend in July)
(800) 468-7325

VALLE CRUCIS

Valle Country Fair (Annual Apple Festival)
(third full weekend in October)
(828) 963-4609

7,000 Lionel engines, cars, and accessories. A plus for true enthusiasts is that some of the displays have switches allowing the viewer to start the action. A retail store is attached to the museum, as well as an activity center for children. Days and hours of opertion change seasonally. Admission is free to purchasers of a Great Smoky Mountains Railroad trip.

From Bryson City, drive 9 miles southwest on US 19 to **Nantahala Outdoor Center** (888-905-7238; noc.com) at the **Nantahala Gorge.** The website gives full details about all the restaurants and programs. The outdoor center attracts the outdoors crowd, especially rafters, hikers, and bike riders. This is a congenial place to hire a guide and all the equipment you need for a whitewater rafting trip down the Nantahala River. It's also great for fishing, picnicking, and hiking or walking. Part of the fun is watching the serious rafters, who, as one observer put it, seem to have a continuing contest to see who can show up in the most worn, mismatched, clothes-don't-matter outfit. **The River's End Restaurant** (13077 Hwy. 17 West) right by the river has been a popular eating place with hikers and rafters for years. Some of the most popular recipes have been bound into a cookbook, *River Runners Special,* with each recipe listed for difficulty (Class I, II, III, and so on) like the rapids on the river. Vegetarian lentil mushroom soup is Class II; amaretto cream pie is Class IV.

At River's End you'll feel perfectly comfortable in your mismatched hiking clothes and down vest, sitting at a rustic table looking out over the river while you gobble a hearty serving of spicy beef stew with the restaurant's special herb bread. Just across the river, **Slow Joe's Cafe** is the place for quick meals and snacks despite the contradiction in name and service promises. **Relia's Garden,** near the center of the property, has a view of the mountains rather than the river. This restaurant sits in a field on the hill across from the garden, landscaped with terraced gardens of herbs, unusual vegetables, and exotic

The Wolf Chooses You

Among the most popular excursions on the **Great Smoky Mountains Railroad** are the gourmet dinner train rides, which include full meals with wine and formal service. On one trip, a couple celebrating their anniversary requested boxes to pack up the remains of generous servings of duck they were too full to finish. The woman said she would take it home to feed her wolves. She kept a dozen in a fenced field behind the house, she said. These were wolves that had sprung from dog-wolf unions. As other guests in the car began contributing their leftovers to Operation Wolf Feed, the woman went on to explain that she didn't go out to acquire wolves, they came to her house. "You don't choose the wolf," she said. "The wolf chooses you."

It Was Inevitable

In his younger years a good friend of mine spent most of his free time at the **Nantahala Outdoor Center** (they call it NOC). Several of his brothers were river guides over the years, and they finally convinced their mother, a good-natured Pittsburgh lady, to venture onto the river on a raft. She listened to the lecture about keeping her feet pointed downstream if she fell off, but she didn't take it very seriously. And she buckled into her life vest without protest but didn't take it very seriously either. She listened to the paddling instructions without getting especially serious. But she did know what to do if the raft dumped her off.

It did. And that nice lady ended up floating rapidly in icy water, with her feet pointed downstream, buoyed by her flotation vest, shouting to her sons at the top of her lungs, "I'll never forgive you for this."

plants. A walk through the gardens crushes fragrant bits of mint and thyme underfoot. This is the upscale restaurant in the area. **The Pourover** is a live music venue by the river that some people call "the best open-air bar west of Asheville."

The restaurants do not have listed telephone numbers. And River's End Restaurant is the only restaurant with an address on a public road. It makes sense when you remember that Slow Joe's is across a river connected with a footbridge, and Relia's is in the center of a garden.

Staff members of the Nantahala Outdoor Center, from guides to cooks, tend to return year after year, as do visitors. The Appalachian Trail, crossing right through the center, brings many serious hikers. Moreover, the presence of the family that started the center is still much in evidence. Relia's Garden, for instance, is named for Arelia, wife of the founder and for many years director of food service. Her plants fill the terrace gardens. Spending time here feels like being part of an extended family or a close community. It is special. The center, its lodging, restaurants, and programs operate from roughly mid-March to November 1, depending on the weather. For information about operating hours when you plan to be here, check the website or call the toll-free number.

Indian Country

Picking up the Blue Ridge Parkway at Cherokee brings you to some decisions about the kind of tourist you mean to be. The town, in the **Qualla Boundary Cherokee Indian Reservation,** where US 441 and US 19 meet, maintains several features dedicated to preserving and explaining the history of the Cherokee nation, which was nearly wiped out by the infamous "Trail of Tears" forced walk in 1838, when the US government tried to relocate all Indians to west of the Mississippi River. Some of the Cherokees escaped the march by hiding in the hills.

Eventually they were able to return to this area, where they were once the powerful Cherokee nation. Their story is told in **Unto These Hills,** an outdoor drama played by a cast of 130 people, beginning between 8 and 9 p.m. nightly, except Sun, from mid-June through late Aug, in an outdoor theater that seats 2,800 people. The program is presented by the Cherokee Historical Association with support from the Theatre Arts Section of the North Carolina Arts Council and funds appropriated by the North Carolina General Assembly. The story begins with Spanish explorer Hernando DeSoto's arrival in 1540 and climaxes with the Trail of Tears exodus. Many of the players are descendants of the Cherokee who lived the story. Moderately high admission fee. The story and performances are frankly moving; it's not uncommon to see people in the audience cry (866-554-4557; cherokee-nc.com).

Unfortunately, activities of this caliber are surrounded by the tourist-tacky pseudo-Indian concessions that seem to plague the areas around Indian populations across the country. The matter is further complicated by the addition of ***Harrah's Cherokee Casino*** (800-427-7247; Harrahs.com) several years ago. The casino, which has 60,000 square feet of electronic gambling area with 2,800 video machines, 3 restaurants, and a 1,500-seat theater, attracts people by the busload. The area now has at least 100 motels, hotels, cabins, and campgrounds, all pretty much one right next to another. Harrah's is an enterprise of the Cherokee tribe. Trying to sort out the authentic from the merely exploitative can be depressing. You can count on quality at the ***Oconaluftee Indian Village,*** sponsored by the Cherokee Historical Association. The village is on the Cherokee Indian Reservation. It is a living replica of a 1750s Cherokee village

AUTHOR'S FAVORITE PLACES
IN THE MOUNTAINS

Asheville	Carl Sandburg Home National Historic Site
Folk Art Center	
New River State Park	Mount Mitchell State Park
Hot Springs	Sylva
	Waynesville

and shows you Indians practicing their historical crafts of basket making, pottery, canoe building, food preparation, and weaponry and, perhaps even more important, explains the culture within which these activities proceeded. Tours begin every 15 minutes, but you are not locked into them, and there is plenty of time for exploring, photographing, and questioning. Open daily from 9 a.m. to 5:30 p.m., May through Oct. Moderately high admission charge (828-497-2111; cherokee-nc.com).

Qualla Arts and Crafts Mutual, Inc., the most successful Indian-owned-and-operated craft cooperative in the country, representing 350 Cherokee crafters, at the entrance of the *Unto These Hills* theater on US 441, offers you an opportunity to buy genuine Indian beadwork, baskets, wood carvings, pots, masks, and the like. Cherokee work is displayed in separate rooms from that of other tribes. Open daily 8 a.m. to 4:30 p.m. These hours may vary. It's a good idea to call ahead (828-497-3103; cherokee-nc.com).

Finally, the *Museum of the Cherokee Indian* displays traditional arts and crafts and offers a video on the history of the nation, along with displays of tools and various accounts of the Trail of Tears journey. Computer-generated images and holographic imaging bring scenes to life. Open Mon through Sat from 9 a.m. to 5 p.m., later during the summer. Moderate admission charged. Closed Thanksgiving, Christmas, and New Year's Day. For full information about attractions, call (828) 497-3481; cherokee-nc.com/museum.

The *Cherokee Visitor Center* on the reservation is a good source of information about the village, crafts co-op, and museum (800-438-1601; visit cherokeenc.com).

Cherokee is considered the gateway to the Great Smoky Mountains, and it seems important to mention, however briefly, the *Great Smoky Mountains National Park,* established in 1934 partly with money donated by John D. Rockefeller. The park merits a full book in itself: Elevations climb as you move along the northeast; plant life, wildlife, and scenery invite superlatives; the bears and the weather are unpredictable. About half the park falls in Tennessee, but North Carolinians, figuring there's plenty for all, forgive that. Staying on the North Carolina side, you'll find enough hiking, fishing, and camping to last most of your life without being repetitive. There are several visitor centers in the park. For information, call (865) 436-1200 or check the website: nps.gov/grsm. The park is said to have attracted more than 10 million visitors annually in recent years, mostly in the summer, although with about 500,000 acres to explore, there'd seem to be enough room for everyone. Admission is free. You'll probably enjoy your visit more if you avoid the peak summer season.

Southeast of Cherokee and Bryson City, where US 23/74 and US 441 come together, the little town of *Dillsboro* stretches along the banks of the

Mountain Greenery

Jackson County Green Energy Park is getting something good from a former landfill: methane gas for blacksmith forges. The *Blacksmith Village,* in Dillsboro, has three forges, the only ones in the United States fired using methane gas from a land-fill. Blacksmithing courses and studio spaces are offered for blacksmiths of all experience levels. For more information, call (828) 631-0271 or visit jcgep.org.

For the artisans living and working by a landfill at the base of the Black Mountain Range in western North Carolina, the methane is free energy. *Energy Xchange,* a nonprofit corporation formed in 1999, supports craft studios, greenhouses, cold frames, and a public gallery in Burnsville with methane gas trapped rather than released into the environment as the energy source. Potters, glassblowers, and artists using recycled and reclaimed objects are among the artists working here. The facility is open to the public Mon through Fri 10 a.m. to 4 p.m., Sat 9 a.m. to noon (66 Energy Xchange Dr.; 828-675-5541).

Tuckasegee River. Culturally, this area is influenced by the river, which is popular for trout fishing, rafting, kayaking, and canoeing and has the advantage of being gentle enough, at least in areas, to be appropriate for young children and beginners who'd like to try rafting. The main fish in the river are rainbow and brown trout, which are stocked, as well as catfish and smallmouth bass near the dam at Dillsboro.

In addition to its natural resources, Dillsboro, with a population of only a couple hundred residents, is working actively to develop awareness of its history and to offer visitors local arts and crafts. More than 50 shops sell pottery, handmade jewelry, unusual gifts with a regional theme, wood carvings, metalworks, and paintings. In the off-season, some of the businesses won't be open, but your experience will be much more off the beaten path. One place you can count on any time of year is *Tree House Pottery,* a gallery at 148 Front St. (828-631-5100; treehousepotterync.com), owned and operated by Joe Frank McKee and Travis Berning, who met in graduate school at the University of North Texas. This is a working studio, as well as a nice gallery, and part of the fun of stopping in is the chance to talk with one or both of these potters. These guys can chat while they work, and they seem to enjoy it. They feature functional raku and horsehair pottery, both of which are more complicated to make than a simple clay pot. If you're interested in pottery, they'll teach you a lot. In addition to their own work, Frank and Travis carry pottery, woodwork, photography, and glass from other crafters. The shop is open year-round, Mon through Sat 10 a.m. to 5 p.m., Sun 11 a.m. to 4 p.m.

The Dillsboro Inn (146 N. River Rd.; 828-586-3898 or toll-free 866-586-3898; dillsboroinn.com) is just a short walk from the historic Dillsboro craft shops and studios, but the star of the place here is the Tuckasegee River. There are 7 suites on the waterfront, from which you can hear the river. It's taken innkeepers T. J. and Terry Walker more than 10 years to build and renovate the Dillsboro Inn to their satisfaction. The Walkers came to North Carolina via Florida and New York. T. J. says, "It's my experiences as a little kid at summer camp that brought me back here." But summer camp was never like this, except for the rustic location and nightly campfires with marshmallows. The suites are spacious, furnished with a hint of luxury and an emphasis on privacy. It's a good place to get away and rest, not a gather-round-the-breakfast-table hostelry. "We're not a bed-and-breakfast," T. J. says. The continental breakfast is delivered to the suites. All suites have private baths with hairdryers, kitchenettes with microwave and refrigerator, WiFi, cable TV, and heat if the weather gets cold. The spacious yoga room, designed to be especially peaceful, has a deck with a view of the river. The best way to spend time here, the Walkers say, is quietly, letting troubles float downstream. Two rooms are pet friendly and there's a playground in the adjoining park where kids can wear off extra energy. The inn also has a 6-person outdoor hot tub, which seems a bit out of character for a place emphasizing privacy and calm. Hiking is an obvious activity in the area, and the Tuckasegee is recognized as a first class river for fishing. A special feature of the Dillsboro Inn is that you make reservations either by telephone or e-mail, not an online reservation service, giving the innkeepers a chance to learn a little about you, including whether or not your visit will be to mark a special occasion.

Another nearby lodging with a different approach is *the Chalet Inn* (285 Lone Oak Dr.; 828-586-0251 or 800-789-8024; thechaletinn.com), a few miles

Western North Carolina Fly Fishing Trail

Some fly-fishing enthusiasts in Jackson County have put together a listing and map of 15 of the best fly-fishing waters in North Carolina, with a variety of options for catching brook, brown, and rainbow trout. The map describes streams by category: hatchery supported, wild trout, delayed harvest, wild trout with natural bait, and catch and release with a single hook and artificial lure. The map also tells you how to find each site. Fishers are asked to take the trail pledge, promising not to litter, trespass, or intrude on the rights of property owners, and to leave streams in better condition than when they found them. The map is available in a convenient paper version as well as online at *flyfishingtrail.com.*

west of Dillsboro on US 74/441. Owned and operated by George and Hanneke Ware, the Chalet is on 22 acres of wooded mountainside, surrounded by perennial gardens, streams, a waterfall, and pond. The grassy areas are groomed for lawn games, and you can follow hiking trails of varying difficulty through the woods. Since opening the inn in 1993, after renovating an existing building to give it the feel of an Alpine Gasthaus the Wares have continued to improve the gardens and trails on the property and to provide information about other nearby mountain possibilities. International travelers like the Chalet Inn because its European style feels familiar. Each room has its own balcony and is angled for privacy. George and Hanneke play up the European theme by serving breakfasts that include fresh, homemade European-style breads, whole-grain breads, cheese, and German cold cuts along with standard American egg dishes. Breakfast is served by candlelight in the dining room outside on an open, but heated, patio. You can pretty much communicate in your language of choice here. Hanneke was born in the Netherlands and George served in the army there at NATO headquarters. In addition to German and Dutch, they manage a little French. When Hanneke knows guests with foreign backgrounds are coming, she takes the trouble to learn at least a few phrases to greet them. The inn is between Bryson City, Dillsboro, and Cherokee, about 15 minutes away from the beginning of the Blue Ridge Parkway, the Nantahala River Gorge, and Great Smoky Mountains National Park.

People go to **the Jarrett House** (100 Haywood St.; 828-586-0265; jarrett house.com) to eat, but the old inn also has 18 guest rooms, each with private bath. Jarrett House is famous for its food, which includes a variety of entrées accompanied by unlimited amounts of old Southern classics—green beans, slaw, pickled beets, baked apples, potatoes—and heaps of little light biscuits. The vegetables are served family style. Jarrett House, standing on the corner in the center of town, has been an inn since back in the 1800s. It opened as the Mount Beulah Hotel in 1884 and was a stopping place for trains of the Western North Carolina Railroad traveling between Asheville and Murphy. The inn's name came from Frank Jarrett, who bought the place in 1894, when tourists began coming to the area to get away from summer heat in the lowlands. The building has been kept fastidiously clean, white on the outside, with such antiques as old sewing machines and oak pieces inside in the halls upstairs. The inn is open May through Dec; the dining room is open Apr through Dec.

Just 15 or 20 minutes farther east via US 23/74, the town of **Sylva,** which once would've been only a quick stop on the way to other attractions, has become the kind of community where people wish they could live, and it's full of quirky and interesting spots, beginning with the historic downtown area, which has been in the process of revitalization since about 1998. On Main

Street, a variety of thriving shops—outfitters, bookstores, music stores, and specialty shops—attract both local and tourist traffic. When you get into the downtown area, park. Traffic tends to be slow because the streets are narrow, and you can walk the town easily, to see more with less aggravation.

Two old structures hold special interest, and you'll have no trouble seeing either one. First is the **Hooper House** (773 W. Main St.; 828-586-2155; mountain lovers.com), where offices of the Jackson County Chamber of Commerce, the Jackson County Travel and Tourism Authority, Sylva Partners in Renewal, and the **Jackson County Museum** are headquartered. The building is open Mon through Sat from 9:30 a.m. to 5:30 p.m. and Sun from 1 to 4 p.m. This Queen Anne Victorian structure was designed from plans that came from Sears, Roebuck & Company. Completed in 1906, the building became the home of Dr. Delos Dexter Hooper, one of the first medical doctors in Jackson County.

It had fallen into disrepair and was scheduled for demolition when a group of local citizens in 1999 began a drive to raise money for its restoration, which cost more than $347,000. Much of the passion for the project came from Julie Spiro, the chamber's director and a great-niece of the doctor. She not only worked on fund-raising but also did much of the physical work on the building herself. Renovation involved scraping away 14 layers of old paint, analyzing and duplicating the colors of the original coats, and removing more than 800 nails from the walls.

On a hill above Main Street, the **Jackson County Courthouse** attracts photographers and fitness nuts. It's a 1913 neoclassic revival building that sits so high above the town it appears on a foggy day to be floating. If you want to climb from the street to the entrance, you've got 107 steps to negotiate. Locals say this is the most photographed courthouse in North Carolina. It's no longer being used as a courthouse. In 2011 Jackson County's main library was moved from its Main Street location to an addition built onto the renovated old courthouse building. Whether you go into the library or not, the building is still a good photo-op.

Should all that climbing steps and walking along Main Street work up your appetite, Sylva has a number of good places to eat. **Lulu's Cafe** (612 W. Main St.; 828-586-8989; lulusonmain.com) has attracted not only local diners but also those from nearby towns with an offbeat menu the owners call "eclectic." They emphasize fresh ingredients and typically offer a seafood dish, a chicken dish, and a vegetarian dish. The restaurant caters to vegans, too. A good example of the eclectic cuisine is Chef McCardle's take on the southern classic fried green tomatoes. His version is topped with crab meat and creole remoulade. The restaurant's offerings include dishes with a variety of ethnic influences—Indian, Asian, Italian, Greek, even down-home Southern. Lulu's maintains an extensive

Waste Not, Want Not

The folks at Lulu's are earnest about supporting local farms and recycling and repurposing whatever goods they can. Chef Devin McCardle emphasizes farm-to-fork ingredients in his offerings. The artwork by his wife, Lindsay, prominently displayed throughout the restaurant, is painted with recycled paints on repurposed skids and pallets. The results are stunning. Centerpieces are made with repurposed Mason jars. Old cooking oil is sent to Jackson County Green Energy Park where it is used to fire pottery kilns.

wine and beer list. The restaurant serves lunch and dinner Mon through Sat, beginning at 11:30 a.m. By the way, there's no Lulu. Never was.

In contrast to the relative sophistication of Lulu's, the **Coffee Shop** (385 W. Main St.; 828-586-2013), almost at the edge of town, is one of those places where working people and retirees eat, day after day. Men meet in small groups early in the morning or at lunch for a little gossip to break up the workday, and old-timers come in knowing a waitress has started getting their regular order ready as soon as she sees them park. The restaurant has been in operation since 1927 and probably doesn't look much different now than it did then, with red booth seating and round stools at the counter, which stands in front of the grill and stove burners. This is a meat-and-three place, specializing in such meals as meat loaf with green beans, mashed potatoes, and slaw. You can also get a sandwich here, a burger that was made by hand, and a slice of homemade pie. The restaurant serves breakfast, lunch, and dinner from 6 a.m. to 8 p.m. Mon through Fri, and until 4 p.m. Sat. Closed Sun.

In addition to a number of standard motels, **Mountain Brook Fireplace Cottages** (208 Mountain Brook Rd.; 828-586-4329; mountainbrook.com) has 13 cottages, each with fully equipped electric kitchen, private bath, and fireplace; some with whirlpool and sauna. The proprietors of Mountain Brook have pulled off an unusual accomplishment. They've taken a group of cottages built

The Usual

"He's coming now," a **Coffee Shop** waitress called to a cook behind the counter. The cook began frying a couple of eggs, sunny-side up, poured a mug of coffee, popped two slices of bread into the toaster, and spooned applesauce into a side dish. By the time an elderly man in a plaid flannel shirt got inside the door, his breakfast was set up for him in front of the end stool at the counter.

in the woods in the 1930s and renovated them without losing the rural feel of the original buildings. No two are alike. They're built variously of log, stone, brick, and frame. The cottages called "Romancers" have a whirlpool-sauna area and a bedroom from which you can see the fireplace in the living room. Guests in all cottages may use the whirlpool spa and cedar sauna in a separate building surrounded by mountain laurel and rhododendron. In another building, the game room includes a pool table, pinball machine, some sports equipment, board games, and a lending library. Other amenities on the property include a picnic area, charcoal grills, nature trails, and a stocked trout pond. You don't need a license to fish here. The Mountain Brook provides bait and tackle, charges a nominal sum for each fish you catch, and expects you to keep the fish, not throw them back. Rates include wood for the fireplace.

Just south of Sylva, on NC 107, Western Carolina University is another significant influence on the area. For visitors, a stop at **Mountain Heritage Center,** on the university's campus, provides a detailed and graphic glimpse of the region's history. A permanent exhibit depicts the migration of the Scottish and English migrants whose descendants came from Northern Ireland to settle in western North Carolina. Other exhibits are built around such themes as early mountain skills and culture, mountain trout, and Appalachian handicrafts. A collection of thousands of western North Carolina artifacts from mountain families illustrates old mountain life. The center also publishes books, tapes, and shorter printed material about mountain culture based on academic research. On the last Saturday in September, some 35,000 visitors congregate in **Cullowhee** for Mountain Heritage Day, a celebration of music, storytelling, food, and crafts. The center is open, free of charge, Mon through Fri 8 a.m. to 5 p.m., except when open to 7 p.m. Thurs from June through Oct. The center operates on the university's holiday schedule, which means the center is closed when the university is not in session. Call (828) 227-7129 for specifics; wcu.edu/mhc.

At Cullowhee, the **River Lodge Bed and Breakfast** (619 Roy Tritt Rd.; 828-293-5431 and toll-free 877-384-4400; riverlodge-bb.com) sits at a bend in the river, with views of the Blue Ridge Mountains on all sides. The lodge was built from 100-year-old hand-hewn logs found in old barns and cabins around the area. In addition to 6 guest rooms, it has a large great room dominated by a stone fireplace and decorated with antiques and Native American artifacts. It's filled with books and art and games such as chess and billiards. Each of the guest rooms is decorated according to a mountain theme, such as mallards in flight and the trout and creel. A hideaway suite with a private entrance has a whirlpool for two and a cathedral ceiling. But the real pleasure of this place comes from the innkeepers, Cathy and Anthony Sgambato, a couple of Italians originally from the Bronx who intended to open an inn in the Adirondacks and

A Mystery Carved in Stone

Lying in a grassy field about 7 miles from Cullowhee, a big gray soapstone boulder known as the **Judaculla Rock** mystifies locals and visitors alike. It is covered with markings that people have variously identified as stick figures, pictographs, and hieroglyphics. The rock is named after a giant Cherokee monster, and one popular legend is that he made the marks when he jumped off a mountain. Others speculate that the rock marks the location of a hidden treasure, that it is a space aliens' map, or that it was an ancient community bulletin board. To find the rock, drive about 4 miles south from Cullowhee on NC 107. Turn left at NC 1737, Caney Fork Road, and follow the signs about 3 miles more, through a farm where the rock is protected by an open shed. A wooden observation deck is in place as well (828-586-2155).

ended up here instead. They love to laugh and tell stories, and their breakfasts go beyond the ubiquitous grits and sausage to include such treats as lox and bagels, sugar waffles, fresh fruits, and ham.

Heading toward Waynesville, you come to the little community of Balsam, which isn't much more than a dot on the map. Here, **Moonshine Creek Campground** (2486 Dark Ridge Rd.; 828-586-6666; moonshinecreekcampground.com) offers RV sites, tent sites, and camping cabins. The RV sites have water, electricity, and sewer. Tent sites have water and electricity. The first thing you notice is how quiet everything is. Moonshine Creek Campground is tucked into a wooded cove off a rural road that winds up and down several hills and around curves from US 441, between Sylva and Waynesville. The facility includes a sparkling clean bathhouse and laundry facilities, as well as a children's playground, camp store, and walking trails. The sites are level and well maintained, with woodland growth providing an unusual degree of privacy between sites. The tent sites are clustered in a grassy creek-side area a bit apart from the RV sites. One RV site, more secluded than the others, sits on a rise next to a waterfall with its stream running down to the creek, so you hear the continuous sound of flowing water. The creek is good for fishing. The camping cabins are simple wood shelters with doors, windows, and beds, but no other facilities inside. The campground also offers a few furnished rentals with bathrooms and kitchens. It is open April 1 to November 1.

From this area it's a drive of approximately 30 miles down NC 107 to **Cashiers,** a community of fewer than 2,000 people at an elevation of nearly 3,500 feet. The drive will seem longer because the road is narrow, steep, and twisting. But it's also beautiful, as is Cashiers itself, with scenic views of even higher mountains, the Blue Ridge Parkway, waterfalls, and multifingered Lake Glenville. This is the home of many waterfalls, including **Whitewater Falls,** which has a total drop of 800 feet. Kevin Adams, author of *North Carolina Waterfalls—Where to Find Them, How to Photograph Them,* calls Whitewater Falls "the most spectacular cascade east of the Rockies." The Whitewater Falls Scenic Area turns off NC 281. This is also home of the smallest US post office, still standing on Whiteside Cove Road. It was in operation from 1903 to 1953.

On NC 107 South, the **Zachary-Tolbert House,** built by Mordecai Zachary in the mid-1800s and virtually unchanged today, is a great opportunity to see a little truth-in-history. Zachary built the house on land that had been Cherokee hunting grounds until the Trail of Tears forced them away. The house had eight rooms, with no electricity, plumbing, central heat, or paint on the inside walls. Mordecai Zachary also built the home's furnishings, using lumber from trees cut on the property for both the house and its furniture. He married Elvira Keener, daughter of a Methodist minister who lived among the Cherokee. They moved into the new home and ultimately had 13 children, who were taught to speak Cherokee. Only three other families ever lived here.

Robert Tolbert bought the house in 1909, and until 1997 Tolbert used the place as a summer home before selling it to people who listed it on the National Register of Historic Places and donated it, along with everything in it, to the Cashiers Historical Society. Much of the original furniture built by Mordecai Zachary remains in the house, along with basic household goods. According to the Cashiers Historical Society, this may be "the world's largest collection of Southern Plain Style furniture made by a single identifiable furniture maker." The historical society has compiled a detailed and fascinating history of the property and its families. They offer guided tours beginning at 11 a.m. Fri and Sat, June through Sept.

sayitthisway

You don't pronounce "Cashiers" the way it looks. Proper pronunciation is *CASHers*. Local wisdom says the difference was the result of an early misspelling by a mapmaker.

Tours take about 45 minutes, and the last one begins at 1 p.m. Call the historical society or check their website for more details (828-743-7710; cashiers historicalsociety.org).

Just north of Cashiers, off NC 107, you'll find a bed-and-breakfast as different from standard motels as it could be, and as unlikely for the area as well. **Innisfree Victorian Inn and Garden House** (write to P.O. Box 469, Glenville 28736; 828-743-2946; innisfreeinn.com) has 5 rooms in the main house and 5 luxury suites in the Garden House, each with private bath, some with Jacuzzi or garden tubs for two, some with a fireplace. The garden house rooms have a wet bar.

This is not a place where you expect to find an old Victorian structure. In fact, although Innisfree is the perfect representation of old Victorian mansions, it is actually a new building. Henry Hoche bought the land in 1981, had the inn built there, and opened it for guests in 1990.

Innisfree is not at all about the comforts of home. Home was never like this. Innisfree is a place of luxury, romance, and exotic furnishings, a special-occasion place. Depending on your room, you have window or veranda views of the mountains and valleys, elaborate bed and window treatments, fine art, and Victorian-period furnishings. In the Garden House you can look out over the green landscape from the showers and tubs. All these rooms carry the names of Victorian writers, and their books are included in each room, so that, for instance, you can lounge in Lord Tennyson's suite and read his work. Breakfast at the inn is served by candlelight, on fine china, accented by antique silver pieces in the room. The inn's common rooms are filled with collections of crystal, silver, and Victorian-esque decor. Innisfree overlooks Lake Glenville, in the Blue Ridge Mountains—the highest lake east of the Rockies. The place seems isolated but is close to the attractions of Cashiers, as well as places for hiking, horseback riding, waterfalls, and boating. The landscape in this area is filled with Christmas tree farms, which have replaced the many fields of cabbage that used to be grown here. This is a good place to visit if you like a party, too, because there's almost always something fun going on—seasonal parties, hospitality hour on the patio with music, and Champagne cruises on Lake Glenville, for instance.

Even though it is away from major highways, in a remote mountain setting, Cashiers has its share of local crafts and specialty shops and tourist attractions. During the peak season, May through October, the area is very, very popular, which means lots of people.

noshadesofgray

Watch for the *Belgian white squirrels* scampering up trees and across roofs around town. This area is noted for these squirrels, which are not albinos—they have normal eyes—and don't seem interested in other kinds of squirrels.

From here you can drive to **Brevard** on US 64. The town's big claims to fame are its proximity to the Pisgah National Forest, the many waterfalls in the area, and the Brevard Music Center. **Brevard Music Center** (349 Andante Ln.; 828-862-2100; brevardmusic.org) holds a festival each summer from late June through mid-August during which almost nightly concerts, from opera to chamber music to jazz, are offered. At the center, which has been operating since 1936, 400 students, ages 14 to post-college, study and play with professional musicians each summer. The main auditorium, Whittington-Pfohl Auditorium, is an open structure that seats 1,800 people, with additional seating on the lawn on both sides of the building. In good weather, audience members are invited to bring a bottle of wine and a picnic basket to enjoy on the lawn. Concerts are also held in several smaller auditoriums on the grounds.

On Main Street, Brevard's center, you'll find a variety of specialty shops, an antiques mall, eating places, and a fine arts co-op. The co-op, *Number 7 Arts,* run by the *Transylvania County Arts Council,* has showrooms at 12 E. Main St. (828-883-2294; number7arts.com). The work of the artisans includes pottery, jewelry, wood, and fabrics, often reflecting a western North Carolina mountain influence. The shop is open Mon through Sat 10 a.m. to 5 p.m.

Brevard Antique Mall (57 E. Main St.; 828-885-2744) has more than 20,000 square feet of shopping space in a former department store. Booths have a great variety of antique furnishings, china, maps, magazines, and vinyl recordings. The mall is open 9:30 a.m. to 5:30 p.m. every day but Sun, when it is open 1 to 5 p.m.

Rocky's Grill and Soda Shop (50 S. Broad St.; 828-877-5375) claims to be Brevard's original lunch counter, dating back to 1942, with little change since then. They serve up soups, sandwiches, shakes, sundaes, and homemade ice cream, but the favorites are the hot dogs and the grilled pimiento-cheese sandwiches. Rocky's is open Mon through Sat 10 a.m. to 6 p.m., Sun 11 a.m. to 6 p.m. The restaurant is next to *D. D. Bullwinkel's General Store* (828-862-4700; ddbullwinkels.com), which bills itself as "reminiscent of an old-fashioned mercantile store," complete with Amish rockers (for sitting and for sale) on the front porch, clothing, footwear, North Carolina jams and jellies, regional crafts, and gift items. Open Mon through Sat 10 a.m. to 6 p.m., Sun 11:30 a.m. to 6 p.m.

You'll have an entirely different kind of experience at *O.P. Taylor's Coolest Toy Store on the Planet* (2 S. Broad St.; 800-500-8697; optaylors.com). John Taylor opened this shop back in the 1980s, and his toys fill 6,000 square feet. John likes fun! His daily costume includes a beanie with a spinning whirligig on top. You know you're going into an unusual place even before you see him, though, because you walk past life-size wooden soldiers to get in. After that, it's everything from card tricks and Erector sets to science kits and model trains. You really don't have to have a kid in tow to go in and play. This isn't the only O.P. Taylor store in North Carolina, but it is the original store and probably the one that most reflects John Taylor's personality. Incidentally, if the store name calls to mind Mayberry of old television fame, it's meant to. The store is open Mon through Sat 10 a.m. to 6 p.m., Sun noon to 5 p.m.

One place in the area that isn't selling anything (although they do take donations) is the *Transylvania Heritage Museum* at 189 W. Main St.

(828-884-2347; www.transylvaniahistory.org.) The museum features some permanent exhibits about area history as well as temporary, changing displays. The exhibits include old photographs and artifacts as well as some unique, seasonal exhibits. The most uncommon of these is the Aluminum Tree & Aesthetically Challenged Seasonal Ornament Museum and Research Center donated by Steven Jackson. In 1991, a friend jokingly gave Steven Jackson, a local home designer, a beat-up aluminum Christmas tree found in a garbage heap. It reminded Jackson of a silver tree in his home when he was a boy. Getting into the spirit of the thing, Jackson had a party and invited guests to bring the "most aesthetically challenged" ornaments they could find. Then a few years later, someone gave Steven a second tree picked up at a yard sale and by 1998, Jackson owned seven. Over the years friends continued finding trees to pass on. Some of them were themed trees like the Marilyn Monroe tree complete with a little fan that blows her skirt up as she plays paddleball. Another was an Elvis tree. After about ten years Jackson decided "it was just too many trees to fit in my house" and donated the collection to the museum. In earlier years, when the collection didn't have a permanent home, Jackson called it the "vagabond museum." The current exhibit features over two dozen trees and Jackson calls himself the "curator emeritus." The trees are on exhibit each year from mid-November to mid-December.

When you are ready to head north to Waynesville, allow enough time to make the drive up US 276. It's winding and slow but also a lot of fun, and what you see going up this route, except for a couple of sites, is authentic, not gentrified, mountain country. The *Sliding Rock Recreation Area* in the Pisgah National Forest is just north of Brevard, about 7.5 miles from the junction of US 64 and US 276. This is nature's version of a commercial waterslide. It is a slippery rock slide of about 60 feet that drops you into a 6-foot-deep pool. Wood steps, places to sit, and a small park office make the spot a little more comfortable, but pictures of injuries that can happen in such a slide and bulletins about how to treat hypothermia make it clear that rock sliding is not without risk. The rushing water in here is beautiful, though, and you don't need to get into it at all to enjoy it.

Continuing north on US 276, you'll come to the entrance to the *Cradle of Forestry in America National Site* (828-877-3130; cradleofforestry.com). The first forestry school in America was founded here in the early 1900s, and the National Historic Site stands today as a commemoration of the importance of forests in the North Carolina mountains. Paved trails take you down to old cabins and a logging train. In the Forest Discovery Center, hands-on exhibits and an 18-minute film explain early forestry in detail. From spring through autumn, the center has a variety of tours, programs, and crafters on-site. Open in season

9 a.m. to 5 p.m. daily. Hours may change. Admission is $5 for adults, free for children ages 15 and younger, and free for everyone on Tuesday.

After this you'll pass an entrance to the Blue Ridge Parkway, the Big East Fork Trailhead into the Pisgah National Forest, and some spots for camping and fishing. Farther north, churches, a trout farm, and some accumulations of junk on private properties dot the roadside. At the community of Cruso, a handmade sign tells you this is "9 MILES OF FRIENDLY PEOPLE, PLUS 1 OLD CRAB."

Following US 23 East from Sylva brings you quickly to **Waynesville,** a town of Scotch-Irish and English founding, at an altitude of 3,000 feet. It is doing an outstanding job of revitalizing its downtown with art galleries and shops selling the work of local crafters, as well as a bookstore, the popular Mast General Store, a high-quality cooking store, a wine shop, and a number of good restaurants and bakeries. In addition, the town holds an ever-increasing number of street fairs, dances, and celebrations, including the **International Folkmoot USA** in July. This international festival of dance and music brings groups from more than 10 countries each year to perform in their national costumes. Call (828) 452-2997 for performance dates; folkmoot.com. Waynesville is also the home of the annual **Ramps Festival.** The ramp is a rank, onion-like, wild plant of no particular virtue, except that every summer the American Legion throws a big party to cook it all the ways they can think of: steamed ramps, braised ramps, ramps a la king, ramps fritters. Presumably, folks eat the results, but that is not as conspicuous as the cooking, which leaves a garlicky odor heavy on the town all day. For some reason it's a popular time and place for politicians to appear. The festival is always held on the first Sunday in May, at the American Legion Park, 171 Legion Dr. A ramp-eating contest is the high point of the day, unless you're one of the contestants, in which case it may be the beginning of a big bellyache for the rest of the day. For more information, call (828) 456-3517; downtownwaynesville.com. Other ramp festivals are held in nearby counties, but an American Legion representative says, "Ours was the first one, and it's the real one. The others aren't like ours."

A popular place to eat in Waynesville is **Maggie's Galley Oyster Bar** (1374 Sulphur Springs Rd.; 828-456-8945). This is a newer location for the restaurant. Its original site was a series of primitive log cabins tacked together. The new building is more contemporary and more upscale. The food at the restaurant includes fresh seafood, steaks, and a good selection of sandwiches as well as seasonal specials such as corned beef on St. Patrick's Day. Sunday brunch includes such atypical offerings as a fried oyster Eggs Benedict and a fried flounder Reuben (in addition to the standard Reuben with sauerkraut and corned beef). The atmosphere is zany, and a meal here, in addition to being good, is a lot of fun. For example, one Easter an employee came to work in a bunny suit. The place is popular with local people. Open 11 a.m. to 9:00 p.m. Mon through Thurs, 11:00 a.m. to 9:30 p.m. Fri and Sat, 11 a.m. to 9 p.m. Sun. Sunday Brunch 11 a.m. to 3 p.m.

An inexpensive but pleasant place to stay is *the Lodge of Waynesville* (909 Russ Ave.; 828-452-0353 or toll-free 888-213-2666). The Lodge is an older 40-unit motel that sits atop a hill just off the highway, looking down on Russ Avenue, which is an area with commercial development—grocery stores, restaurants, and chains—that heads directly into the historic downtown area. But you can't hear any of the noise from this location on an acre of nicely land-scaped grounds, with an outdoor swimming pool, a courtyard including picnic tables and a swing, and nice views of the mountains. Joseph Sutton owns the place; his daughter, Cindy Smith, serves as innkeeper; and the people who work at the desk are mostly family friends. The feeling in the office is quite jovial. Smith says the property was once part of the family home place. The guest rooms are simply furnished with basic motel furniture and bathrooms in good repair. Everything is spotlessly clean. From here it's a drive of 5 minutes or so to everything from a good Chinese restaurant, Maggie's Galley and Oyster Bar, or fast food on Russ Avenue, to the specialty shops and the more trendy restaurants downtown. Because of the swimming pool, courtyard, and picnic area, it's a good place to stay with kids.

One spot in the area has a Waynesville address but is actually out of town and 5,000 feet up, and offers fine food, rustic lodging, hiking trails, and an entry to the Great Smoky Mountains National Park. *The Swag* (2300 Swag Rd.; 828-926-0430 or 800-789-7672; theswag.com) comprises a collection of pioneer buildings that were hauled up the mountain about 30 years ago. Innkeeper Deener Matthews and her husband, Dan, have managed to combine rustic elements such as the rough wood interior walls of the rooms with luxurious amenities, including handmade coverlets on the beds, and coffee grinders, coffeemakers, hair dryers, and terry-cloth robes in the rooms. In the dining room, guests sit around handmade tables to enjoy first-rate food professionally prepared and served. And although the other recreational facilities are tucked unobtrusively into the property, you can find everything from a racquetball court and sauna to a library.

All that is up on the mountain. Down in the valley you'll find some other interesting attractions. *Maggie Valley* is a year-round resort town between Cherokee and Waynesville. On both sides of US 19, or Soco Road, which runs through the valley, you'll see one motel after another, every kind of eating place, and souvenir shops galore—generally not the kind of places an off-the-beaten-path traveler wants to visit at all. But you'll also find a place worth the drive because it began as a labor of love.

Let's Get Lost

Being able to walk through the backyard of the Swag and right into the forest of the Great Smoky Mountains National Park was an opportunity too good to ignore. The hiking trails were all there, well marked and shown on a large map on the grounds. Sorry to say, I forgot to look at it. But figuring that all the trails would loop, I just got onto one and started walking. After walking a couple of hours, I was on a road I had never heard of, with no money in my pocket and no place to spend it anyway.

I asked an old man in a pickup truck where I was. He told me, but I was still disoriented. He gave me a ride to a campground where he introduced me to some friends with a trailer. Within minutes, I was sitting at a picnic table, digging into hot roast beef sandwiches, sliced fresh tomatoes, and mashed potatoes. We were all laughing and chatting so much, it was like a party.

Eventually, the idea of getting back where I belonged came up. Everyone knew right where the Swag was, because a swag is a dip in the mountains. It was about 30 miles away by road, a substantial drive for a stranger to make for another stranger.

The old man not only drove me, but he had fun doing it, telling me all about his family, life in this area, secrets you can learn on back roads, and who lives on them. When we got back to the Swag, he got out of the truck to look around. "Always wanted to see the view from up here," he said. Then we hugged, and he was gone.

That's why I love North Carolina.

The ***Stomping Ground*** is a huge building on US 19 (3316 Soco Rd.) with a massive dance floor and seating for 2,000 people. Kyle Edwards hopes to make it the world center for clogging. The Edwardses are a clogging family, but they've always thought of it as "mountain dancing." Kyle thinks the word *clogging* came into use in 1935, in Chattanooga, Tennessee. His mother and his uncle performed with a Maggie Valley team in the 1920s that performed in the White House for President Franklin D. Roosevelt and the Queen of England. Kyle and his wife, Mary Sue, also danced on teams. Their son, Burton, was a world champion clogger in 1981, when he was 18. (He is running the operation now.) And their daughter, Becky, had won two championships by the time she was 13. It doesn't take a rocket scientist to figure out that if you go to the Stomping Ground, you're either going to clog or watch clogging. Dances and shows are held every night from April through November. A number of large display cases related to clogging give you a lot of information about the history, contests, and fun of the dance. Call (828) 926-1288 for details about times, shows, and admission fees.

If you're in the area sometime between the end of April and the end of November, you might make ***Cataloochee Ranch*** (119 Ranch Dr., Maggie

Valley; 828-926-1401 or toll-free 800-868-1401; cataloocheeranch.com) a desti-nation and spend a few days in its laid-back atmosphere. This is the kind of place to which some families return year after year. You can look down on the town and meadowlands and over at many ranges of the Great Smoky and Blue Ridge Mountains, with meadowland vistas below. The rooms and cabins, which are all different, are set up for everyone from couples looking for a romantic getaway to families with children. Rooms in the lodge and ranch house and cabins, all have private bath, some have a Jacuzzi and fireplace. Rates include breakfast and dinner and activities except horseback riding, all on about 1,000 acres. Some guests who started coming here soon after Tom Alexander and his wife, Judy, opened the place in 1933 (it's still family-owned and family-operated) have brought their children and then their grandchildren here. The mix is lively, and one staff member says part of the pleasure in working at Cataloochee is watching the children grow up. Guests eat family-style in the dining room, where the food is hearty and relies on locally grown produce, homemade breads and jams, and favorites like trout, baked ham, and prime rib. Four nights a week, the resort has a cookout featuring such entrees as steak and chicken. A cookout is a big production, but they've been doing it so long it's down to a smooth-running science. In addition to tennis, swimming, and hiking, the ranch has entertainment a couple of nights a week. This might be storytelling, a magician, bluegrass music, or a hands-on presentation about the timber wolf by a local animal keeper.

Timberwolf Creek, which runs along the valley, apparently got its name from the presence of the animal there in earlier times. **Timberwolf Creek Bed and Breakfast** (391 Johnson Branch Rd.; 828-926-2608 or toll-free 888-525-4218, ext. 2681; timberwolfcreek.com) is snuggled alongside Timberwolf Creek, surrounded by old-growth hardwoods and rhododendron in Maggie Valley. Innkeepers Sandee and Larry run an intensely romantic, small B&B focused on giving guests a special experience with everything from a candlelight breakfast indoors or, when it's nice out, breakfast on a deck over the creek, to Jacuzzi tubs with rose petals for the water. No matter which room you choose in Tim-berwolf's two refurbished buildings, the sound of the creek running briskly fills the air in a way that wouldn't be possible in a recently built facility, because new construction is no longer allowed this close to the water. It's so quiet back here you can hardly remember the busy main road.

The Literary & Crafts Center

It's only 25 miles from Waynesville and the Maggie Valley area to **Asheville,** which is crammed with arts, crafts, antiques, literary and musical people, and a healthy assortment of free spirits deeply involved in the unique Appalachian culture.

After a long period of time during which the downtown area seemed to be going downhill, this part of the city has made a marvelous recovery. The downtown *Asheville Historic District* has an interesting assortment of early twentieth-century architecture, much of it being restored or renovated and filled by specialty shops, galleries, and restaurants. Walking the district, you encounter a rich mix of old and young hippies, artists, entrepreneurs, intellectuals, shopkeepers, businesspeople, tourists, and just folks.

One outstanding example of a renovation that works is right in the heart of the downtown area. The *Haywood Park Hotel* (1 Battery Park Ave.; 828-252-2522 or 800-228-2522; haywoodpark.com) is in a building that once housed Ivey's Department Store. This small independent hotel is luxurious, with fine furnishings, spacious, bright rooms, and such niceties as valet parking and turn-down service. Haywood Park Hotel emphasizes local products, from the handmade soap dishes in the bathrooms and the hand-stitched bedding, to the chocolates on your pillow and the art on the walls.

In the hotel's atrium, independent, local restaurants and shops offer everything from fine dining to flowers to shoes. The chocolates placed on your pillow each night are made fresh daily, with no preservatives, at *the Chocolate Fetish* (36 Haywood St.; 828-258-2353; chocolatefetish.com), a shop where you can watch the candy being made. All the chocolates are handmade in small batches, with top-quality ingredients and no added vegetable oils. Places like candy stores come and go, but this one is a keeper; it has been operating since 1986. The shop is open Mon through Thurs 11 a.m. to 7 p.m., Fri and Sat 11 a.m. to 9 p.m., and Sun noon to 6 p.m.

Also without going farther than the hotel atrium, guests can enjoy fine dining at the *Flying Frog Cafe and Wine Bar* (1 Battery Park Ave.; 828-254-9411; flyingfrogcafe.com), a restaurant run by veteran restaurateurs with a flair for fine dining. The restaurant is open for dinner Wed, Thurs, and Sun 5:30 to 9:30 p.m., Fri and Sat until 11 p.m. Reservations are "strongly recommended."

A more casual atmosphere in the atrium for food and fun is the *Bier Garden* (46 Haywood St.; 828-285-0102; ashevillebiergarden.com) with a choice of more than 200 different beers from all over the world and an appropriately casual menu. They claim to have had the best beer selection in North Carolina since 1994, but given the great surge of new brewers in the area, that would be about as controversial as saying you serve the best barbecue. The pub menu ranges from bruschetta and pizza to a beer-battered cod filet sandwich and a vegetarian grilled shiitake-garden burger. Open daily 11 a.m. to 2 a.m.

From the hotel, a walk in any direction takes you through parts of the historic district, with galleries and arts and crafts shops.

Also downtown in Asheville, at 40 Wall St., *Laughing Seed Cafe* (828-252-3445; laughingseed.com) serves vegetarian and vegan meals in an atmosphere that calls to mind the days of tie-dyed shirts and Volkswagen vans. But don't be fooled by the funky atmosphere. This is a sophisticated restaurant that offers creative entrees and wine and beer to go with them, emphasizing "organic, seasonal, farm to table vegetarian cuisine." But that's not just a come-lately fad here. The restaurant was begun at a smaller location in 1991 and moved into this historic district in 1993. Some of the menu is a global-fusion collection, but it's not a matter of being trendy. You can count on flavor combinations that work. The restaurant is open Wed and Thurs from 11:30 a.m. to 9 p.m. Open Fri and Sat 11:30 a.m. to 10 p.m., and Sun 10 a.m. to 9 p.m. Sunday brunch is served from 10 a.m. to 3 p.m., with the regular menu in place the rest of the day.

One massive undertaking you can't miss in downtown Asheville is the renovated *Grove Arcade* (1 Page Ave.; 828-252-7799; grovearcade.com). This structure, with 269,000 square feet of floor space, is western North Carolina's largest commercial building. It was built in 1929, housing shops on the ground floor and offices above. The arcade was one of the first indoor public markets in the country, and it thrived as the center of Asheville commercial activity until 1942, when the US government took it over to use for activities related to World War II, displacing 74 shops and 127 offices in a single month. Later the building began to fall into disrepair, and the space was too big and expensive for a commercial investor. But local opinion persistently demanded restoring the building to its original appearance and use.

In 2002, with funding and direction from a foundation, the renovation was completed, and the building's cream glaze terra-cotta facing gleams once again. Restaurants and shops sell everything from antiques and art to bread and meat, ice cream and candy. There's a full service barbershop, a store specializing in Mission-style furniture and another selling locally made stringed instruments. Outside the building, bordering on Battery Park Square, vendors in the Portico Market stalls sell everything from musical instruments, jewelry, and original art to farm products. This area is a lot of fun for browsing and interacting with the folks at the stalls as well as with other customers. Open every day, 10 a.m. to 4 p.m., weather permitting.

Also in this part of town, the *Basilica of St. Lawrence,* at 97 Haywood St., has the largest unsupported tile dome in North America. It was designed by Rafael Guastavino in 1909.

At the edge of town stands an attraction so well-known it has become an almost obligatory stop for anyone who wants to say they have seen the area—***Biltmore Estate*** (One Approach Rd.; 800-411-3812 or 828-225-1333; biltmore.com). George Vanderbilt liked Asheville, and he had money. He bought a lot of Asheville, about 125,000 acres, and had a 250-room private home built on the property. (Today only 7,500 acres belong to the estate. The rest is part of the Blue Ridge Parkway or Mount Pisgah National Forest.) The home was famous from the beginning for the beauty of its design and workmanship. The master builders were brought from Europe. The home was also famous for being ahead of its time in its modern conveniences, having early forerunners of washing machines and dryers. Art in the mansion includes originals by Boldini, Ming dynasty china, and antiques that belonged to Napoleon.

It will take you the better part of a day to see the place properly, especially if you go beyond the mansion to explore the gardens and visit the winery. Admission fees to the Biltmore Estate are high. The estate is open daily from 9 a.m. to 5 p.m., with longer hours during peak seasons.

If you're feeling literary, visit the ***Thomas Wolfe Memorial*** (52 Market St.; 828-253-8304; wolfememorial.com). This is the novelist's boyhood home, described in his novel *Look Homeward, Angel* as "Dixieland." In real life it was called "the Old Kentucky Home." Wolfe's mother, Julia, ran a boardinghouse in the rambling Victorian house, and its various rooms and furnishings, along with local people, were all incorporated into Wolfe's novel, mostly in unflattering terms. The people of Asheville didn't like that one bit, which led to Wolfe's second novel, *You Can't Go Home Again*. After Wolfe died, the townspeople relented, as they often do when a troublesome celebrity stops being troublesome and remains merely famous, and bought the house to turn into a memorial for him. It is now a North Carolina State Historic Site. Visiting the house, which has been kept the same as it was when the Wolfes lived in it and has descriptions from Wolfe's writing in appropriate places so you can compare the words with the reality, goes a long way toward explaining the often gloomy tone of his writing. But the Wolfe house was damaged by a fire, apparently set on purpose in 1998. Not only was 30 percent of the house destroyed, but some of the artifact collection also was ruined. Local conjecture suggested that someone was still mad at Thomas. The home was renovated and reopened to visitors in 2004. Guided tours now begin at the modern visitor center behind the old structure. The center exhibits personal items from the Wolfe home, shows an audiovisual presentation about his life and writings, and offers appropriate items in a gift shop. Hours and days of operation fluctuate seasonally. A modest admission is charged for the tour.

One thing you might not expect to find in a mountain city is the ***Botanical Gardens at Asheville,*** 151 W. T. Beaver Blvd., located on a 10-acre site next to the campus of the University of North Carolina at Asheville. The gardens were begun in 1960 by the Asheville Garden Club and designed by Doan Ogden, a landscape architect of repute. The gardens are open all year, and no matter when you visit, you'll find something in bloom, bud, or fruit.

The garden complex has a library and gift shop. You can arrange for garden tours or use a map to explore on your own. Special places on the property include a springhouse, a garden for the blind, a rock garden, an azalea garden, and an herb garden. For more detailed information about the gardens, contact the gardens' office at (828) 252-5190; nctg.co/bwrha. Many appealing places to explore are just a little removed from the downtown area of Asheville, too. For instance, a long-established and reputable place to see and buy regional arts and crafts is the *Folk Art Center,* just east of town at milepost 382 on the Blue Ridge Parkway, about a half mile north of US 70. It has been operated by the Southern Highland Handicraft Guild since 1980 and houses permanent and traveling exhibits and the Allanstand Craft Shop, where you can buy items similar to those in the exhibits. Crafts represented include weaving, pottery, basketry, quilting, jewelry, wood carving, stitchery, and musical instruments. Admission is free; donations are welcome. Open every day except Thanksgiving, Christmas, and New Year's Day from 9 a.m. to 5 p.m., except that it stays open until 6 p.m. Apr through Dec. Closed occasionally for inventory and changing exhibitions (828-298-7928; southernhighlandguild.org). The Guild has an online store that gives you a hint of the amazing work you'll find at the craft shop.

Just about 10 miles outside Asheville, near Weaverville on Reems Creek Road off US 25 North, is another state historic site, the *Zebulon B. Vance Birthplace.* Vance was a Civil War officer, a US senator, and governor of North Carolina. In fascinating contrast to the splendor of the Biltmore Estate, this restored pioneer farmstead has only a five-room log house and some outbuildings. The log house was reconstructed around the original chimneys. The outbuildings, including a loom house, springhouse, toolshed, smokehouse, corncrib, and slave cabin, are furnished as they would have been between 1795 and 1840. Displays instruct you further in the life of the times. Admission by donation. Hours of operation vary because of budget constraints, so call ahead (828-645-6706).

A little west of downtown Asheville, on the campus of the Asheville-Buncum Community College, *the Southern Appalachian Radio Museum* is the kind of attraction that will be a must-see for some people, while others won't give a fig about it. Anyone who has ever been interested in amateur radio, its development and practice, will have a good time here. The museum's exhibits, which continue to increase in number and variety, range from old phonographs like Silverton and Edison to spark gap transmitters and ancient

QSL cards. You may not know what those last two are, but a radio enthusiast will. The museum includes an operating amateur radio station, W4AFM, where visitors may take a turn at the mike. Kids are entirely welcome. Those call letters once belonged to Bill Hayes, who was licensed in 1929 and taught many about radio. One of the most poignant exhibits is the late Bud Keener's "shack" (W4MIQ) donated untouched by his wife. Keener was an active, popular ham radio operator in the area. You'll see everything he used, including a typewriter that didn't have to be plugged in to work. The museum is closed in Nov and Dec, but open every Fri the rest of the year from 1 to 3 p.m. Volunteers manage the place and conduct tours. With a bit of advance notice, you may be able to see the museum another day during the same hours for a fee of $5 per person, children under 13 free (340 Victoria Rd., Elm Building, Rm. 315; 828-298-1847; saradiomuseum.org).

The **North Carolina Arboretum** is outside the city, at milepost 393 (off NC 191). It features southern Appalachian landscape plants on a 426-acre site, as well as hiking and nature trails. The arboretum also has a state-of-the-art greenhouse complex. Call (828) 665-2492; ncarboretum.org.

The Sourwood Inn, also outside Asheville, has been praised by OBP readers as a great place to stay (810 Elk Mountain Scenic Hwy.; 828-255-0690; sourwoodinn.com). People love the inn's location at 3,200 feet, its cedar and stone construction, and its warm, relaxing atmosphere. It's been in operation since late in the 1990s, but it might never have been here at all. Construction was almost complete when a fire destroyed it. Determined to have an inn at this location, the owners started over, and the result is a place that radiates warmth and deep satisfaction with being here, reflected in everything from the food to the attitude of the inn's staff. The inn has several common areas, a lobby with a fireplace, a library, and a game room. Each of the 12 guest rooms has a wonderful view of the Blue Ridge, and the 100 acres on which the inn sits include gardens and hiking trails. A cabin with a fully equipped kitchen and 2 full baths is heated by a Jotul woodstove. Sourwood serves dinner Thurs through Sun, prepared by Chef Kacia Duncan, a graduate of the New England Culinary Institute who has had experience everywhere from France to Oregon. She brings a traveler's flair and an appreciation for fresh, local, organic, seasonal ingredients to the kitchen; hence, such specialties as benne seed–fried trout over lemon-scented orzo with a fresh tomato slice and homemade bread. The inn does not have an ABC license, but guests are welcome to bring their own spirits. Sourwood is open year-round except from the week before Christmas to February; open weekends in Feb, and every day after that.

And just 4 miles north of downtown Asheville, **the Reynolds Mansion Bed and Breakfast** (100 Reynolds Heights; 828-258-1111 or toll-free

888-611-1156; oldreynoldsmansion.com), a bed-and-breakfast in a brick antebellum mansion on a high ridge, may be a testimony to the strength of generations of people who loved the place. It was built in 1847 and passed through generations of the Reynolds family, being variously expanded and renovated. In subsequent years the house served as a boarding house, an osteopathic sanitarium, and a family home. By the time Fred and Helen Faber bought the place in 1977 and moved here from Minnesota in 1981 to restore it, it was in sad shape, and the operative word is "restore," not "cause to be restored." The Fabers did virtually everything, including the gardening and construction work, with their own hands. In 2003, Fred passed away, but Helen and her family continued to run the bed-and-breakfast. Michael Griffith and Billy Sanders bought the mansion from Helen, again did extensive work on the property, and in 2010, opened as the Reynolds Mansion Bed and Breakfast. The rooms and suites are considerably more luxurious than they once were, but the history still tells its own story.

Camping is another popular option around Asheville. At ***Campfire Lodgings*** (116 Appalachian Village Rd.; 800-933-8012; campfirelodgings.com) on a wooded mountaintop, elevation 2,270 feet, you can camp in anything from an RV or simple tent to a luxury cabin or an exotic yurt, just 6 miles north of downtown Asheville and 10 miles from the Blue Ridge Parkway. The facility includes a bathhouse with laundry facilities and private bathrooms with showers—an unusual feature in a campground. Beyond that, it all depends on what you want. Pets are welcome here; a courtesy phone/modem hookup is available; and the 120 acres include hiking trails, a private fishing pond, and meditation spots. Some of the RV sites have phone/modem hookups, and all the RV sites have water, sewer, electric, and cable.

The yurts are large, round, domed tents of insulated canvas set up on a large wooden deck. The screened walls and dome can be opened in good weather or closed against rain. Inside, a bed is made up with luxurious bedding. The yurts have air-conditioning, gas fireplaces, cable TV, and kitchens; 2 have bathrooms, the third has a dressing area and easy access to a bath house. The deck is large enough to put up a tent for families with children. The luxury cabins, which sleep seven, have 2 bathrooms, a gas log fireplace, a fully equipped kitchen, air-conditioning, a washer and dryer, a telephone, cable TV, and linen service. Not exactly roughing it. The views from this campground are stunning, and the wooded sites are large enough to afford considerable privacy. Asheville is a good starting place to visit a number of interesting sites north and south of the city. ***Hendersonville*** is about 22 miles south of Ashville via I-26. This is a community that has gone all out to develop its historic district with museums and shopping.

If you're traveling with kids *Hands On!—A Child's Gallery* (318 N. Main St.; 828-697-8333; info@handsonwnc.org) is going to be fun. The gallery focuses on kids aged 1 to 12, but parents will enjoy it too. For instance the Lego ramp will probably bring back memories of younger years, as will the grocery store for folks who still remember playing store when they were young. The gallery is open Tues through Sat, 10 a.m. to 5 p.m. Donations happily accepted.

Another site on Main Street is the *Mineral and Lapidary Museum of Henderson County* (828-698-1977; mineralmuseum.org). This place is fun for adults and kids alike. Displays include minerals, fossils, geodes, and other artifacts from North Carolina and elsewhere. The display of a dinosaur egg cluster isn't something you see every day. The museum is open Mon through Fri 1 p.m. to 5 p.m., Sat 10 a.m. to 5 p.m. Admission is free; donations gratefully accepted.

Henderson County Heritage Museum (1 Historic Courthouse Square; 828-694-1619; www.hendersoncountymuseum.com) includes a variety of exhibits related to earlier times in the county and in the state. The Shepherd Store is a replica of a turn-of-the century store. A Civil War exhibit of weapons, flags, and uniforms represents both sides of the conflict. North Carolina train history is well noted too. The Apple Valley Model Railroad Club has donated a diorama of the nation's steepest standard-gauge mainline railroad and a model train runs near the ceiling. For kids, two Lego displays contributed by Don and Phoebe Blackwell depict firehouses and vehicles through the ages. The Blackwells remember their children playing with these Legos and have spent time with their grandchildren playing with them too. A gift shop helps raise funds for the museum but in addition a donation box built by the Apple County Crafters sits at the entrance for contributions from visitors.

As the names of various organizations here suggest, apples have played an important role in the development of Henderson County. It's the seventh largest apple producing area in the country. For an interesting look at the

Talking Trees

Here's another place in the area that is fun for kids. In Holmes State Forest, near Hendersonville, seven trees along the Talking Tree Trail have a button that activates a voice when pushed. Each tree tells a little about what its ancestors were historically used for and why. For instance, the white oak says that its ancestors back in the 1700s helped American colonists win the war because the hulls for their ships were made from seasoned oak which is watertight and durable, while the British ships rotted out by the time they got to across the Atlantic.

history of apple development here, check (www.hendersonville.org/apple orchards). Here's a new take on the old saying, "When life gives you lemons make lemonade." How about, "When life gives you apples, make cider"? As of this writing three cideries operate in the area, some producing sweet cider and some hard cider as well. Hard cider has become popular in North Carolina, especially among folks who don't care for beer. For a brochure with the Cheers! Trail map, featuring five breweries, three cideries and two wineries, download it from www.visithendersonvillenc.org/cheers-trail.pdf or call the visitors' information center (800-828-4244) for a printed brochure.

Hendersonville's Main Street sidewalks have been widened to encourage pedestrian traffic and they are lined with a great variety of shops, from antiques to arts and crafts. Eating places there range from a place to get a good hotdog to an Irish pub specializing in such typical Irish foods as corned beef and bangers and mash.

North Carolina's state theater, the *Flat Rock Playhouse* has established a satellite theater at 125 S. Main St. which means you can enjoy dinner and a show all within walking distance (www.flatrockplayhouse.org; 828-693-0731).

The 1898 *Waverly Inn,* a bed-and-breakfast accommodation, at 783 Main Street, is within easy walking distance of the downtown. In its earliest days, the inn, started by the Anderson sisters, was the Anderson Boardinghouse. In all that time since 1898, the place has had only eight different owners. The most recent are Mike and Tracy Burnett, who continue many traditions that have long been in place, including sumptuous breakfasts and a social hour from 5 to 6 p.m. when guests can gather to chat and discover common interests (828-693-9193 or 800-537-8195; www.waverlyinn.com).

One unique, and perhaps odd, attraction, that is most assuredly in Mills River is the *Greenhouse Moto Café* at 4012 Haywood Rd. (www.facebook .com/thegreenhousemotocafe). This place of 7,000 square feet used to be Roses

The Brewery Feud

Sierra Nevada Brewery, at 100 Sierra Nevada Way in Mills River, is in Henderson County, and people in the county insist the brewery is not in Asheville. But Asheville folks consider it part of their wider metropolitan area and use the address Fletcher rather than Mills River, though the rest of the address remains the same. And, as one customer pointed out, their T-shirts say Mills River. Either way, Sierra Nevada originated on the West Coast and opened the North Carolina brewery much later to assure fresh brews in both places. To check hours for tours, food, and brews call 828-681-5300. Check www.sierranevada.com for more information.

Greenhouse. It was standing empty when Jeff Herold, who has been collecting vintage motorcycles for 15 years saw it and decided it would be a great place to keep and display them. He bought the place and turned it into a venue for casual food, craft beers and live music in what you could call a bike museum. As of this writing he has 25 beers on tap and, of course, his huge collection of bikes on display. Herold says he's making it up as he goes along, partly on the basis of customer suggestions as well as using found materials. The stage is "homemade." The place will definitely be a work in process for some time. Maybe the slogan here should be, "If flowers don't get enough likes, try bikes." And this is Henderson County—no escaping apples. Greenhouse Moto Café is across the road from a cider distillery. The café is open Thurs 4 to 8 p.m., Fri and Sat noon to 10 p.m., Sun noon to 5 p.m.

Going north from Asheville, if you take NC 63/New Leicester Highway to Leicester for about 20 miles and make several turns, you'll make your way to the little community of Sandy Mush and the ***Sandy Mush Herb Nursery***, where a huge variety of herbs grows in greenhouses. Other hardy plants grow outside. The nursery has an extensive catalog that you can download on-line free (sandymushherbs.com) but visitors are welcomed on Thursdays, Fridays, and Saturdays from 9 a.m. to 5 p.m. You can also order a print version of the catalog for $5. It's worth the little investment if you're interested in maintaining a library related to plants. In addition to culinary and medicinal herbs, the nursery grows 94 varieties of scented geraniums, as well as perennials, wild flowers and other native plants, trees and shrubs, and bonsai plants. (I once ordered five different kinds of oregano for a booklet I was writing on that herb. When I visited in person, they remembered that order.) This is a place well worth seeing but there is one hitch—it's hard to get there. Some of the way in is steep and narrow. The Sandy Mush Herb folks say, "Some have found our road daunting." They recommend calling ahead for the best directions (828-683-2014).

Another drive northeast from Asheville on US 92, brings you to the little community of ***Burnsville,*** the Yancey County seat. The place comes as a surprise if you're fooled by the population (about 2,000 or less) into expecting a sleepy mountain town where old-timers sit in front of stores and gossip. In popular vernacular, this area is *happening*—not the glitz and population surge of such cities as Charlotte, but a county-wide flowering of arts and crafts. According to the Yancey Chamber of Commerce (106 W. Main St.; 828-682-7413; yanceychamber.com), more craftspeople and artists live and work in the area than in any other area of the United States. You can pretty much run the alphabet, from artists and basket makers to papermakers, sculptors, and weavers. Of course chambers are supposed to brag on their regions, but spending a little time in Burnsville you can see that it's not brag, just fact. The chamber website lists many galleries and shops with everything from jewelry to antiques, all worth a visit.

A defining area feature in recent years has been the **Quilt Trails of Western North Carolina** (quilttrailswnc.org). The trails feature quilt blocks, painted wood squares mounted on barns, businesses, homes, and schools, reminiscent of the classic quilting tradition in America. The concept actually began in Ohio where Donna Sue Groves mounted a block on her barn to honor her mother, who was a quilter. The idea caught on and grew. Today only Kentucky has more of these blocks on display than North Carolina. In North Carolina, six contiguous counties have quilt blocks, with the highest concentration in Yancey and Mitchell Counties.

Some of the quilt blocks on the trail are reproductions of classical patterns. And all the blocks on the trail are supposed to resemble classical patterns. What's interesting is that when you first look at any block that's what you see, something that might've been on Grammy's bed. Then as you learn the story, you perceive the pattern differently; it seems to change as you look at it. Suddenly you see a design made from sneakers found in an old gymnasium, for instance. Even if you don't follow any trails, be sure to stop at the quilt block sundial on the side of the *Yancey Common Times Journal* newspaper building just off the town square in Burnsville. Getting the thing hoisted from the ground and attached to the building was a major project that stopped traffic, including police cars, on the road in front of the building. It's the only quilt block sundial in the world, and it really does tell the time.

Quilts play another role in this area. The town of Burnsville commissioned Barbara Webster to create a 24-foot wide quilt depicting the four seasons in the county, along with scenes from daily life, and historical photographs. It contains 1,310 photographs that Webster had printed on fabric. She designed and pieced the quilt, and Rachel Reese quilted it with a hand-guided quilting machine. This work dominates the entry hall in the **Burnsville Town Center** (6 S. Main St.; 828-682-7209; burnsvilletowncenter.com). If you're interested in quilting (and even if you're really not), this is a must-see. Because the building is used for all kinds of private and public local functions, call ahead to be sure the building will be open.

When it's time to eat, the area has its share of fast food places, but it would be a shame to go there and miss the popular **Garden Deli** on the town square, shaded by a huge willow tree (107 Town Square, Burnsville; 828-682-3946; garden-deli.com). This place is popular with most local people and visitors. It has a casual, bright atmosphere with seating, weather permitting, outdoors as well as indoors. The restaurant has been operated by members of the same family since it was established in 1987 by a native New Yorker, Ed Yuziuk, and his wife, Carolyn. Ed's son, Greg, and his wife, Hiroko, took over the operation in 1996. With this kind of background, the offerings are anything but down-home Southern and way more than standard deli fare. The sandwiches are fat with good meats on good bread. The soups are homemade. And the menu includes a variety of vegetarian meals. Sometimes you have to wait in line for a bit, but if you really can't afford the time, you can call ahead for takeout. Beverages include local beers on tap and a variety of bottled beers and wine. Lunch 11 a.m. to 2 p.m., Mon through Sat; dinner 5 to 8 p.m., Thurs through Sat. Closed Sun. Burnsville has one place that has been around since 1833 and is the one many people associate with the town—the *Nu Wray Inn* (102 Town Square; 828-682-2329; www.NuWrayInn.com). Over the years, everybody from Elvis, Jimmy Carter, and Christopher Reeve stayed here, and in earlier days so did just about everybody who came through town. The building is a three-story clapboard colonial which, for all its fame, went into decline and was closed until Lisa England, a North Carolina native, and her husband, Bob Cohen bought the property and began working on its restoration. They say that it was painted on the outside so that it looked like it deserved pride of place on the square once again, then they tackled the interior, gradually restoring some of the inn's 26 guest rooms. To say that it was a big job puts it mildly. Then in 2014, two couples from the Asheville area, Joey and Jill Farmer and Eric and Christy Wilson bought the place and continue the on-going restoration. As of this writing, 15 rooms are now done and work continues on the remaining 9. But those guests from earlier centuries wouldn't recognize some of the modern additions such as WiFi and high definition satellite TV with complimentary Netflix for instance. What those long ago guests might recognize is the food. The inn has gone back to offering family style lunch and dinner Fri through Sun. (11 a.m. to 8 p.m. Fri and Sat, 11 a.m. to 7 p.m. Sun.) The offerings always include biscuits, three meats and six vegetables. You can pretty much count on fried chicken being one of the meats. Wine and beer are available too.

Another, smaller hostelry, *Terrell House B&B* (109 Robertson St.; 828-682-4505; terrellhousebandb.com) is also a pleasant place to stay at the end of the day. It's within easy walking distance of the downtown businesses and shops. The building, a restored early 1900s colonial, originally served as a dormitory for girls attending a Presbyterian school across the street. Today it's nothing like a dormitory. The B&B has 6 spacious rooms, each with a sitting area, private bath, and air-conditioning. The owners, Laura and Mike Hoskins, are good hosts. Laura, who is British, serves a generous formal breakfast on good china. Mike is an easy conversationalist with a passion for golf. The grounds here are as pleasant as the interior, should you wish to sit outside on a fine day. Some guests use Terrell House as a base for exploring other towns and attractions in the western North Carolina mountains.

Using Asheville once more as a good center from which to explore in different directions, consider spending some time on the Blue Ridge Parkway. There you drive at a leisurely 45 miles per hour through woods and fields with lots of overlooks where you can pull in to enjoy mountain views. Following the parkway takes you to **New River State Park.** Driving northeast from Asheville along the Blue Ridge Parkway takes you higher into the mountains to Blowing Rock and environs. And a scenic ride east along I-40 and NC 226 to Polkville brings you back into the lower elevations of the Piedmont.

If you follow the parkway almost to the Virginia border, getting off to drive north on US 221, you come to the oldest river in North America and the second oldest (the Nile is older) in the world. It's the only major river in the country that runs south to north. Paradoxically called **New River,** it meanders peacefully through more than 100 miles of northwestern North Carolina. The name was the result of surveyors' surprise when they finally chanced upon the river they hadn't known about in this remote part of the state in 1749.

You'll enjoy good access to the river from **New River State Park** (336-982-2587), an area of breathtakingly lovely mountains, valleys, woods, and fields, 8 miles southeast of Jefferson off NC 88 on NC 1588. Compared to other state parks, New River shows up infrequently in travel books and articles, probably because it is in a remote part of the state and because the facilities are primitive. This is the river to find if you like placid canoeing rather than

BETTER-KNOWN ATTRACTIONS
IN THE MOUNTAINS

ASHEVILLE

Biltmore Estate
(828) 274-6333
(888) 804-8258

Blue Ridge Parkway
(828) 298-0398

BLOWING ROCK

The Blowing Rock
(828) 295-7111

CHEROKEE

Cherokee Indian Reservation
(828) 497-9195
(800) 438-1601

Harrah's Cherokee Casino
(828) 497-7777
(800) 427-7247

CHIMNEY ROCK

Chimney Rock Park
(828) 625-9611
(800) 277-9611

wild races through whitewater and want fishing spots not bothered by heavy powerboat traffic. There are canoe landings and campgrounds. The woods are great for hiking and are full of spots that cry out for a simple picnic.

Behind the peaceful scene lies the story of a dramatic struggle that isn't anywhere near being over. It started in the 1960s, when the Appalachian Power Company planned to build a dam there, eliciting tremendous public objection. In protective response Congress designated the area a National Wild and Scenic River in 1976, effectively stopping the power company.

But little funding was ever forthcoming to actually buy and protect the land, and a new force is changing the scene along the river: subdivision and development. New houses, roads, and lots are appearing on what was once farmland or woodland. Although none of it is in the state park, of course, people who like their countryside bucolic and unspoiled are getting nervous, whereas those who value economic development for the area are digging in their heels and sending out the bulldozers.

Given the usual inclination of those who can afford to build in the prettiest places—high on mountain summits, on beaches and islands, and along rivers—it's hard to say what will happen along the New River in the coming decade. The good news is that the state park is, as locals like to call the river, "a national treasure," and should remain a special place to visit for a long time to come. It has four access sites, three for camping and one with a canoe launch for day use.

About 35 minutes north of Asheville, in Madison County, you'll find an interesting cluster of places near the ***French Broad River.*** This river is a step above the Nantahala River in difficulty for whitewater rafting, but the water is warmer, and far fewer users come into the area, so your experience will be considerably more off-the-beaten-path than it is on the Nantahala. The greater part of Madison County is part of Pisgah National Forest, and the Appalachian Trail passes through the county, offering short segments of trail for day hikers. In the little town of ***Hot Springs,*** you can soak in outdoor tubs along the banks of the river. Hot mineral water, flowing constantly from natural springs at a temperature of about 100 degrees, has often been considered therapeutic and is certainly relaxing, the more so if you indulge in a massage while you are there. Spa rates are figured by the hour and vary depending on the time of day. Massage rates are calculated by the half-hour and become proportionately slightly less expensive per half-hour the longer the time you reserve. For information about the hot springs and massages, call (828) 622-7676 or (800) 462-0933; nchotsprings.com. For information about whitewater rafting tours and hiking, contact the Visitors Information Center at (828) 680-9031 or (877) 262-3476; hotspringsnc.org.

Because the town is known for attracting hikers from the Appalachian Trail and bikers, *Mountain Magnolia Inn and Retreat* (204 Lawson St.; 828-622-3543 or 800-914-9306; mountainmagnoliainn.com) comes as a bit of a surprise in Hot Springs. But this inn sits above the town, on a hill, looking directly at the rises of several mountains in the Pisgah National Forest, secluded from the rest of the community by shrubbery, old magnolias, and perennial gardens.

When owners Pete and Karen Nagle bought the house, it had only one floor, though it was built in 1868 with three floors and enough rooms and Victorian furniture to accommodate a family with eight children. In the 1950s the top two floors, a failing roof, and an observation tower were removed to reduce the cost of maintaining the place.

Once the Nagles learned more of the property's history, they engaged an architect and restored the house. The new rooms of the top two stories fit nicely with the first story, which still has the original wood floors and plaster molding. All guest rooms are spacious, with high ceilings and plenty of daylight.

In season, the inn serves dinner every night, and on weekends the rest of the time. (Days and hours may change, so it's a good idea to check what's going on during the time you plan to visit.) The menu changes often, with such entrees as oven-roasted duck breast and seared Asian marinated salmon fillet. The grilled local pork chop is popular, and imaginative vegetarian entrees such as butternut squash lasagna with a roasted red pepper cream sauce are included for diners who love good food but want no taste of anything that once had fur, fins, or feathers. The restaurant also has a nice, moderately priced wine list.

On the drive down I-26, one of the most interesting stops is the *Carl Sandburg Home National Historic Site,* a 240-acre farm called *Connemara,* a bit south of Hendersonville in Flat Rock. Sandburg spent the last 22 years of his life here, mostly writing, while his wife and daughter managed the place as a goat farm. His collection of poems, *Honey and Salt,* was written here when he was 85. The poems contrast with such earlier works as "Chicago," reflecting not only the work of an older man, but also of one living in different surroundings. For instance, in the poem "Cahokia," Sandburg writes about an Indian watching a butterfly rise from a cocoon, flowers sprouting in spring, and the sun moving. The Indian, Sandburg writes, doesn't worship the sun but dances and sings to the "makers and movers of the sun." It takes on added significance when you know that Flat Rock was named for a large granite plateau that had once been a Cherokee sacred ground. Sandburg's life here was influenced not only by the early cycles of nature but also by Cherokee Indian lore. Similarly, looking across the mountains, it's easy to understand how Sandburg might have arrived at his poem, "Shadows Fall Blue on the Mountains."

When you visit Sandburg's study at Connemara, both the man and his poetry seem alive. The study is said to be exactly as he left it, with a shawl tossed over the back of his desk chair, a clunky manual typewriter standing on an upended crate, and stacks of paper and disorderly piles of books everywhere. A fascinating aspect of the entire home is the simplicity of its furnishings. To say the interior is plain puts it mildly. The furniture resembles what you find in a summer camp, functional but not decorative. Also fascinating is the fact that every room is crammed with books, all of which appear to have been well used. Similarly, the rooms where his wife Helga kept records about breeding her goats are functional and were apparently furnished with no thought to decoration. What you find outside seems more carefully designed. You may also walk along trails on the grounds, where you'll see the kinds of plants and wildlife from which Sandburg must have drawn many of his images. Open daily except for Thanksgiving, Christmas and New Year's day from 9 a.m. to 5 p.m. Tours begin at 9:30 a.m., and the last tour departs at 4:30 p.m. Modest admission fee. Inquire about some special seasonal activities (828-693-4178; nps.gov/carl).

The town's **_Historic Flat Rock District_** (historicflatrock.org) is on the National Register of Historic Places. It began about 150 years ago as summer estates for wealthy people from Charleston, South Carolina. Flat Rock has a wonderful place to enjoy a good dinner and spend the night. **_Highland Lake Inn,_** on Highland Lake Drive, is a complex with inn rooms, cabins, and cottages scattered on a wooded property that also has a lake, a swimming pool, and 100 acres of walking trails. The Lindsey family's objective was to create a self-sufficient compound, and although they didn't manage that entirely, they came close. They've sold the property to Jack and Linda Grup, who continue in the same spirit, while providing more luxurious accommodations and emphasizing the country-retreat aspect of the place. The restaurant, **_Seasons,_** serves vegetables and herbs organically grown on the property and provided by local gardeners. The food is simply wonderful. Offerings range from an herb-stuffed free-range chicken breast to some elaborate pasta and seafood dishes, as well as vegetarian dishes. Every bite you take bursts with flavor. Seasons offers a good wine list and full bar service. If you are traveling with children, this is a place where you can take them to see vegetables growing in a garden, look at honeybee hives, and watch a goat being milked. Phone (866) 303-9621; hlinn.com.

From Flat Rock you can head over onto US 176, driving about 12 miles to **_Saluda,_** a little town of less than 1,000 people, with a notable concentration of antiques and artisans. Walking around in the little town itself, you'll find several shops selling local crafts and antiques and a general store that has developed a tourist-oriented slant.

The town is at the crest of the steepest mainline railroad in the country. The business district is on the National Register of Historic Places.

Saluda has a bakery-café that comes as a surprise. ***Wildflour Bakery*** (173 E. Main St.; 828-749-3356; saluda.com/wildflour) concentrates on flavor and nutrition. Debbie Thomas and her daughter Molly created all the recipes using stone-ground flour, ground fresh as needed from untreated wheat and other grains. Ingredients are measured and mixed mostly by hand. For a time, the bakery wholesaled products to local stores, but have since given that up in favor of its café and bakery shop. Wildflour offers a variety of loaves, ranging from the regular oatmeal bread and the nutritious Boogie Bread (seven grains) to gourmet choices such as roasted walnut and English cheddar bread. Molly has told the story of an older customer who came barreling toward the counter with a loaf of dark bread, "clearly on a mission," Molly put it. But the woman wasn't striding up to complain about the price or anything else. Holding the loaf up, she said with a strong German accent, "Now this, *this* is bread!" Open Mon, Wed, Thur, Fri, and Sat 8 a.m. to 3 p.m; Sun 9 a.m. for pastries, 10 a.m. for brunch. Wed and Fri 5 p.m. to 8 p.m. are pizza nights, eat in or take out.

Even if you didn't make it to the bakery cafe, you can still enjoy Wildflour products without leaving Saluda's main street. ***The Purple Onion*** (16 Main St.; 828-749-1179; purpleonionsaluda.com) serves everything from pizza and vegetarian dishes to locally raised trout. Their bread comes from Wildflour, and to the degree that it's possible, meats and produce also are local. The food has been called "Mediterranean fusion," and one couple from California who drove in from a main highway looking for a little place to eat was surprised to find that the food was much the same as they found at home. They'd been expecting a little cafe with down-home Southern cooking. Purple Onion just ain't that! Typically visitors are delighted with this place and its food, and locals are too. The interior of the restaurant is spacious and bright, and in good weather meals on the patio, with views of trees, shrubs, and blooming flowers, could turn even a business lunch festive. The restaurant has a varied list of wines as well as an assortment of good beers, including some from North Carolina. The Purple Onion is also a live-music venue, beginning at 9 p.m., at the end of the dinner hours. The performances range from bluegrass and country to jazz. The Purple Onion is open for meals every day May through Aug; closed Wed and Sun the rest of the year.

A few miles into the country, in a totally different mood, the ***Orchard Inn,*** on US 176, sits atop the Saluda rise on 18 wooded acres at an elevation of 2,500 feet. (828-749-5471 or 800-581-3800; orchardinn.com). The inn comprises 9 rooms in the main house plus 5 cottage suites, each with private bath, some with fireplace and whirlpool tub. The most recent innkeepers are Marc

Nina's Secret

The late jazz/soul singer and classically trained piano player **Nina Simone** was born February 21, 1933, in Tryon. She was one of eight children, four boys and four girls. Simone was playing the piano and singing before she reached the age of 5 and developed her talent in the early years singing in the local church with her sisters. She left home for Philadelphia when she was 17 and later studied at Juilliard in New York. Some of her earliest gigs were in a piano bar in Philadelphia, a job she kept secret from her churchgoing family in North Carolina.

and Marianne Blazar, who bring extensive hospitality experience to the place. The food here has always been good, and the Blazars have expanded the dinner menu to include more choices. The dining room is on a glassed-in porch from which you see views of the woodland in all directions. The inn has a good wine cellar and also serves beer. Jackets are suggested for men at dinner, furthering the sense of escaping the real world. Whenever possible, meals are prepared using local products, and Wildflour Bakery's goods are part of offerings. Dinner is available for guests and the public Thurs through Sat by reservation only. A full gourmet breakfast for guests is included in the price of rooms. Keeping in tune with the times, the Blazars have one pet-friendly cottage, if you arrange for that ahead of time. They charge a one-time fee of $50, mainly to cover the cost of cleaning, and there's one hard-and-fast rule: You can't leave a dog alone in the room.

A stop suggested by several readers of this book is **Pearson's Falls** (2720 Pearson Falls Rd.; 828-749-3031; pearsonsfalls.org). This nature and wildlife preserve is a gift to the public owned and maintained by the Tryon Garden Club since 1929. More than 200 different species of flowering plants, algae, and mosses grow here. The preserve includes the 90-foot falls, which you get to by a short trail of less than a half mile. The area is ideal for a picnic, a photo session, and a little walk. Admission is $5 for adults, $1 for children ages 6 to 12. From March 1 to October 1, the preserve is open Mon through Sat from 10 a.m. to 5 p.m., Sun noon to 5 p.m. November through February the area is open Mon through Sat 10 a.m. to 4:15 p.m., Sun noon to 4:15 p.m. Last admission 45 minutes before closing. Closed Thanksgiving, Christmas, New Year's Day, and the month of January. No pets are allowed in the preserve. To get to the falls from Saluda, head toward Tryon on US 176. Just a couple miles past Orchard Inn, as you head down the mountain, you'll see a giant sign identifying Pearson Falls Road and Pearson's Falls. Turn right. The entrance to the preserve is a mile farther in.

The 10-mile stretch of road from Saluda to **Tryon** is the **Pacolet River Scenic Byway,** which gives you glimpses of the Pacolet River, wonderful vistas, and historic sites as well as more waterfalls. Tryon is known as an equestrian center. The **Foothills Equestrian Nature Center** (3381 Hunting Country Rd.; 828-859-9021; fence.org), is a nature education and recreation center with 5 miles of trails for hiking and riding, horse stables, and family-oriented nature education programs and outdoor concerts. The programs are often seasonal, such as a kite-flying day and a Mother's Day celebration, and most are free. The grounds are open dawn to dusk, 7 days a week; the administrative building, FENCE Center, as it's more commonly known, is open during normal business hours, Mon through Fri. Admission is free.

Not far from the center, **Pine Crest Inn** (85 Pine Crest Ln.; 800-633-3001; pinecrestinn.com) has 35 rooms in a variety of buildings including the main inn, as well as a restaurant and business meeting rooms. The overall theme here is the English Country Hunt, probably due at least in part to the influence of earlier owners who were British. The restaurant serves New American–style cuisine, emphasizing locally available ingredients, and all spirits are available. All rooms have private bath, television, telephone, and VCR players. Some have fireplaces and whirlpool baths.

Downtown Tryon is filled with quaint stores and antiques shops, many of them also reflecting the local interest in horses.

The High Country

The next drive you might make from Asheville continues north on the Blue Ridge Parkway to **Mount Mitchell State Park,** elevation 6,684 feet, the highest point in the eastern United States. You'll leave the parkway at milepost 355.4 to take NC 128 to the 1,500-acre wilderness park. It's a 5-mile drive to the peak, but it will feel a lot longer. The park has hiking trails, picnic areas, a visitor center with maps, camping areas, and a lookout tower from which you can see what must be the most stunning mountain views east of the Mississippi. There are also a restaurant and a refreshment stand. Be careful while you're here. Mount Mitchell is named for Dr. Elisha Mitchell, who fell off the summit and died. Your falling off too probably wouldn't lead to getting the mountain renamed in your honor. Park hours vary depending on the weather and time of year. You can call ahead (828-675-4611).

The next stop you might try along the parkway is at milepost 331, where NC 226 and NC 1100 take you to Emerald Village near Little Switzerland. At Emerald Village, established on the site of the Old McKinney and Bon Ami mines, you can visit the **North Carolina Mining Museum,** which displays

HIGHEST PEAKS IN THE NORTHEAST

1. **Mount Mitchell:** 6,684 feet; Black Mountains, NC

2. **Mount Craig:** 6,647 feet; Black Mountains, NC

3. **Clingmans Dome:** 6,643 feet; Central Great Smoky Mountains, TN

4. **Mount Guyot:** 6,621 feet; Eastern Great Smoky Mountains, NC/TN

5. **Balsam Cone:** 6,611 feet; Black Mountains, TN

6. **Mount LeConte:** 6,593 feet; Eastern Great Smoky Mountains, TN

7. **Cattail Peak:** 6,583 feet; Black Mountains, NC

8. **Mount Gibbes:** 6,571 feet; Black Mountains, NC

9. **Mount Buckley:** 6,568 feet; Central Great Smoky Mountains, NC

10. **Big Tom:** 6,568 feet; Black Mountains, NC

the tools used at the height of gem mining in the area. Outdoor displays and a printed trail guide explain the entire mining process, and you'll have the opportunity to look for your own emeralds, rubies, aquamarines, and the like. If your gem hunting doesn't go well, you can pick up something at the shop or have a rough gem cut, polished, and set into a piece of jewelry. Open daily from 10 a.m. to 4 p.m. April; 9 a.m. to 5 p.m. May, Sept and Oct; 9 a.m. to 6 p.m. Memorial Day weekend through Labor Day weekend. Closed November 1 through March 31. Moderate fee for mining tour (828-765-6463; emeraldvillage.com).

The Orchard at Altapass, close by at milepost 328, provides an experience more at one with nature, rich with history, and just plain fun (888-765-9531; altapassorchard.com). The apple orchard was originally created by the Clinchfield Railroad, beside its tracks, in the early 1900s. Those tracks had been laid following what was probably an old buffalo and elk path. Eventually the railroad ceased to run through the area, and the same route was chosen for the Blue Ridge Parkway. It was bitterly contested in the North Carolina Supreme Court, but ultimately went right through the orchard, dividing it in half. The orchard went into decline. In 1994 Kit Truby bought it, and with her brother, Bill Carson, and his wife, Judy, began working on its restoration and preservation. It's now a family enterprise supported by a nonprofit foundation. It's not just the apple trees you can enjoy here now, but also butterflies, and all kinds of activities celebrating earlier crafts, music, and food. In season, you can pick your own apples, choosing from eight varieties. You can go on hayrides, listen to old-time music, buy fudge, and learn about the history of the area going back to the time of its earliest inhabitants, long before the British came along. If history were taught this way, more people would enjoy studying it. Open Wed through Mon (closed Tue) April 30 through Sept 10, 10 a.m. to 6 p.m.; Sept 11 through Oct 30, 10 a.m. to 6 p.m. daily.

Also nearby, you can take US 221 to get to **Linville Caverns** and **Linville Falls,** just beyond the caverns. If you're back on the parkway, exit at milepost 317.4 and turn left on US 221. Linville Caverns lie under Humpback Mountain and were believed to have been forgotten by the white race until about 100 years ago, when fish that seemed to be swimming out of the mountains caught the attention of explorers. During the Civil War, deserters from troops on both sides hid in the caverns. Today the caverns are lit electrically, showing stalactites and stalagmites and trout that, having always swum in the dark, can't see. Guides lead the tours 2,000 feet underground, pointing out important features and answering questions. Admission is $8 for adults, $7 for senior citizens, $6 for children ages 5 through 12, free for children under 5. Hours and days of operation vary seasonally and are posted on the website. (Call 828-756-4171 or 800-419-0540; linvillecaverns.com.)

Linville Falls comprises two waterfalls at Linville Gorge and a primeval canyon in the sizable wilderness area given to the Blue Ridge Parkway by John D. Rockefeller. The gorge is the deepest cut east of the Grand Canyon. There are hiking trails and picnic spots.

At a convenient spot where the Blue Ridge Parkway and US 221 meet, **Parkview Lodge** (Blue Ridge Parkway and US 221; 800-849-4452; parkview lodge.com) is a most unchainlike place to stay. This is the full-time home of innkeepers Cindy and David Peters. Parkview Lodge consists of a series of knotty-pine-paneled rooms in a long stone building and cabins in the woods, some furnished with locally purchased pieces, old family items, and bed headboards David built by hand. David says that after being there more than two decades renovation is "an ongoing project." The atmosphere fits with the inn's Blue Ridge Parkway mountain location while offering more comfort than a tent or camper. Some of the lodge accommodations are especially designed for private, romantic getaways. Other rooms are more basic, but were renovated in recent years. Rates include a continental breakfast. The lodge's main room, where breakfast is served, also has a wine shop, a cooler with 40 brands of cold beer, and local arts and crafts for sale.

Across the highway and back along a gravel road into the woods, **Linville Falls Trailer Lodge and Campground** (717 Gurney Franklin Rd.; 828-765-2681; linvillefalls.com) has nice sites for RVs of all sizes as well as a section for tent sites. The bathhouses are clean, with plenty of hot water, and laundry facilities are available at the small campground store and office.

In warm months, each campsite is marked with a hanging basket of blooming flowers.

A little jog off US 221 onto NC 194 leads into the little community of **Crossnore,** with a population of just a few hundred friendly people. This is not a place that generally makes it into guidebooks, because it is not tourist-oriented, but it is known for the **Weaving Room and Gallery** (100 D. A. R. Dr.; 828-733-4660; crossnoreschool.org), a hand-weaving center with a gift shop featuring Appalachian crafts as well as woven goods. The operation was founded in 1920 as a way to raise money for the Crossnore School. This school was run by several committed women as a way to educate children in Appalachia, for whom few opportunities existed. The school had a boarding section as well as classrooms. In addition to weaving, the sale of old clothes was a source of revenue for the school. Today sales from the weaving room and a large thrift shop still benefit Crossnore School students. **Crossnore Fine Arts Gallery and Miracle Grounds Coffee and Café** also serve visitors and raise funds for the school. Ben Long has created a fresco at the chapel on the campus, open to the public. The theme is *Suffer the Little Children to Come unto Me.* Many of the models were children who live on campus. (See entry on Ben Long Frescoes, page 49, later in this chapter.) Each of these enterprises has different days and hours of operation, all of which are available on the school's website.

Still moving north along the parkway, you'll come to **Grandfather Mountain,** where, if you've got the nerve for it, you can walk across the **Mile-High Swinging Bridge,** a 218-foot suspension bridge between two peaks that sways in the wind. Should you quite sensibly prefer to put your feet on something more solid, Grandfather Mountain has lots of hiking trails, as well as indoor exhibits and habitats for black bears, otters, cougars, eagles, and deer. You'll need to pick up a moderately priced permit and a trail map at the entrance. Admission is $20 for adults aged 13 to 59, $18 for senior citizens 60 and older, $9 for children ages 4 to 12, children under 4 free (828-733-4337 or 800-468-7325; grandfather.com). Open every day, weather permitting, except Thanksgiving and Christmas, with early closing Christmas Eve.

A few minutes farther brings you to US 321 and **the Blowing Rock,** a cliff 4,090 feet above sea level that overhangs Johns River Gorge, 3,000 feet below, at the town of Blowing Rock. Because of the way the gorge is shaped and overhung, air blows upward, making snow appear to fall upside down and throwing upward light objects tossed over the edge. According to the legend of Blowing Rock, a Cherokee brave leaped to his death here to keep his tribe from making him return to the plains, leaving his Chickasaw wife behind. She prayed to the Great Spirit until the sky turned red and the wind blew her brave back up onto the rock. A wind has blown up from the valley ever since.

Admission is $7 for adults, $6 for senior citizens and military, $2 for children 4 to 11, children 3 and under free. Hours vary with the season and the weather. For details call (828) 295-7111; theblowingrock.com.

Just outside of town, **Cliff Dwellers Inn** (116 Lakeview Ter.; 800-322-7380; cliffdwellers.com) offers some of the best vistas in an area known for great mountain views. The inn is just a mile south of the Blue Ridge Parkway, off US 321. But this place has none of the closed-in feel of many mountain cabins. The inn has 22 rooms, each with private bath, TV, coffeemaker, and refrigerator, plus 3 suites, all with gas log fireplaces. Three suites have whirlpools. The guest rooms are unusually spacious, with large windows to take advantage of the mountain views, and airy, cheerful furnishings that emphasize the light. Balconies with rocking chairs run the length of the building. Look down from the sundeck onto the rock garden; from various other perches see Lake Chetola and the outlet Shoppes on the Parkway, across US 321. One unusual feature that many will welcome is that the building's top-floor rooms face onto a parking area so that you can park outside your door and walk right into your room—no steps.

From here it's a quick drive into Blowing Rock. You are also just 8 miles south of Boone.

Off the main highways outside Blowing Rock, on Shulls Mill Road, **the Inn at Crestwood** (828-963-6646 or toll-free 877-836-5046; crestwoodnc.com) comes as a surprise—a center of luxury secluded in the woods on a winding rural road. This was originally the private summer home of the Moberg family. In 2004 the inn opened with an addition that preserved the old home and increased space for rooms, balconies, and dining. The decor includes framed renderings of many of the senior Moberg's architectural drawings. In its current ideation, the inn comprises a variety of luxurious rooms and suites, **the Table** restaurant, and the **Dawg Star Bar.**

On the same property, new villas accommodate families and larger groups. A spa offers massage, skin treatments, and access to a lap pool, steam bath, Jacuzzi, and fitness center. This is a pricey place to stay, although dinner in the

Running Away from Home

Jan Karon, author of the best-selling *Mitford* series of books, based her novels on her hometown, the village of Blowing Rock. Sometime after she became famous, she moved away from Blowing Rock because, she said, tourists kept wanting to come see her house. Locals sort of forgive her, though. They arrange Mitford festivals in the fall.

Table, open to the public, is in the moderate range. The rooms are luxurious, but their greater charm is views of mountains in all directions. The dining room has walls of windows and spectacular views. The restaurant serves dinner Wed through Sat 5:30 to 9 p.m. The bar opens at 4 p.m. Wed through Sun. You can make reservations online.

For a fun little diversion, stop at 175 Mystery Hill Ln. in Blowing Rock to visit the ***Appalachian Heritage Museum,*** in what used to be the home of the Doughertys, who founded Appalachian State University. It is on US 321/221 North. The home is decorated authentically in turn-of-the-century furnishings and shows how mountain families lived in the early 1900s. Sometimes the museum holds demonstrations of mountain crafts or cooking. There's a separate exhibit of Native American artifacts. The museum is open every day but Christmas year-round, beginning at 9 a.m. It closes at 8 p.m. in summer, and 5 p.m. Sept through May. Museum admission includes ***the Hall of Mystery*** and ***the Mystery Platform and Mystery House,*** where you can experience varied optical illusions and scientific oddities. For information about both places, call (828) 263-0507; mysteryhill-nc.com. Rates are $9 for ages 13 to 59, $8 for seniors, and $7 for children 5 to 12.

Boone is a little college town about 10 miles from Blowing Rock. You will miss it if you just keep on driving along US 321, because the traffic and peripheral development are off-putting. But the town itself, best known as the home of Appalachian State University, typically called "App" by its students, is a lot of fun. King Street, running through the center of town, has a variety of funky stores with some good arts and crafts, books, music, motorcycles, vintage clothing, and antiques. Walking along King and some of the side streets, you'll find small restaurants with the quirky names that seem to go with college towns.

Melanie's Food Fantasy (664 King St.; 828-263-0300; melaniesfood fantasy.com) is popular with college students and their visitors. The people who work here are mostly young and seriously dedicated to providing healthful food that also tastes wonderful. The variety of the menu is substantial, with many imaginative vegetarian and vegan choices as well as some sandwiches and panini with meat. The staff is careful to prepare meat in an area separate from the vegetarian processes. One colossal breakfast illustrates how unimportant meat can be. The Potatoes Madness Breakfast starts with home fries, sautéed onion, green pepper, and mushrooms, and is topped with two eggs and cheese. Then, just in case that's not enough, the dish is served with homemade toast. And the good news is that the restaurant has been operating since 1991. It's not likely to disappear any time soon. The restaurant is open from 8 a.m. to 2 p.m. Mon through Sat for breakfast and lunch, and from 8:30 a.m. to 2 p.m. for Sunday brunch.

Ribbit, Ribbit

I stopped at *the Tomato Shack* on NC 105, just outside Boone, to buy apples and Ashe County cheese curds. This is one of those places that has everything from hot boiled peanuts to sourwood honey and apple butter. I had to put on my glasses to read labels, which led the proprietor and I to joke about going to buy apples then forgetting that you even wanted apples, and about how you can't see to find your glasses without your glasses—that kind of stuff. Then he said, "Where are you from?" Well, gee, I was driving my red muscle Nissan Frontier—a mountain vehicle, surely.

"What?" I said. "You don't think I can pass for local?"

"It's not that," he said. "If you came here often, I'd remember you."

I made a joke as I headed to the door. "Whoooeee—does that mean I'm in trouble?"

Before I could get out the door, he said, "Well, I am getting older, but my daddy always said you don't know from looking at a frog how high it can jump."

A fun and friendly restaurant in an unlikely location, *the Coyote Kitchen* is just past the end of King Street, around the corner in the Wal-Mart Shopping Plaza, off US 321 (200 Southgate Dr.; 828-265-4041; coyotekitchen.com). The owner, Ben Whiteheadcalls Coyote's food "Southwest Caribbean Soul Food," but adds that it's basically Tex-Mex taken a bit upscale. The menu is extensive, the portions large, and the wine and beer choices are pretty good, too. The restaurant is popular with an interesting assortment of people—from rock climbers to businessmen. The atmosphere is quirky. You could well encounter a waiter wearing a straw hat with his Coyote Kitchen T-shirt. Ben says he uses local and organic products to the degree it's possible, and willingly accommodates vegans, vegetarians, and others with special dietary requests, including folks requesting gluten free foods. This restaurant is an area leader in the green movement. They've installed spiral energy-saving bulbs in all the ceiling lights and are using compostable paper products for take-out containers. The Coyote Kitchen is open Sun through Thurs 11 a.m. to 9 p.m., Fri and Sat to 9:30 p.m.

Beech Mountain is close to Boone and Blowing Rock, but in a sense it's far away, or will feel like it as you negotiate the mountain road curves. It's about 23 miles west of Boone, more or less straight up, at a peak elevation of 5,506 feet. The town covers only about 6.5 square miles, with a year-round population of 381, although this occasionally must change a little with a birth or death. The town advertises itself as the highest incorporated town in America. Much of the community's economic base comes from tourist activities—hiking, skiing, fishing, or just relaxing in a vacation condo—"A week at the Beech."

Your first stop probably should be at the ***Beech Mountain Chamber of Commerce,*** 403-A Beech Mountain Pkwy. (828-387-9283; beechmountain.com), to pick up maps, events schedules, and brochures. In that vicinity you'll see a large brick building and a modest building beside it. Contrary to what one might expect, the smaller one is the chamber. "Hiking on Beech" maps trails of varying length and difficulty, along with verbal descriptions and even history. Townspeople are especially proud of a little booklet, "Bike Beech Mountain," which lays out the route of Lance Armstrong and the Tour DuPont. Seems Lance said this is the best place to train in the United States.

The town is now offering an alternative to skiing, too—guided winter hikes. These hikes are scheduled ahead of time, so you can find news about them each season on the website or by calling the chamber. And one of the surprisingly successful winter innovations here is the sledding hill, where kids 12 and under may sled on a safe course for free. If the snow is a little skimpy, a machine blows on some artificial frozen stuff. The children must use plastic sleds, be supervised by adults, and not yield to the temptation to build snowmen on the course. A slope supervisor keeps a watchful eye on the proceedings. As it's turned out, this isn't just a spot for locals; families come from considerable distance, from places where there is little snow, to give their kids a sledding experience. The community continues to expand its activities to appeal to both tourists and local people. The ***Beech Mountain Adventure Trail Park*** officially opened its Emerald Outback section May 1, 2011. The 8-plus miles of ***Emerald Outback Trails*** range in elevation from 4,700 to 5,400 feet, giving the park the distinction of being among the highest such venues on the East Coast. There's a nice combination of single track, double track, and gravel road trails traversing the mountaintop, all accessible from a trailhead in the town of Beech Mountain.

The Emerald Outback is the first phase of the Beech Mountain Adventure Trail Park, which planners say will grow so that it encompasses 25 miles of

All Because of an Old Movie

Folks at Beech Mountain were looking for a way to jazz up a ski weekend in late February. Their solution? Travel back in time. The annual Totally '80s Retro Ski Weekend at Beech Mountain is a collaboration between the town of Beech Mountain and Beech Mountain Resort. Loosely based on the off-beat movie *Hot Tub Time Machine*, the four-day weekend (Thursday-Sunday) encourages participants to dress in 1980s garb on and off the slopes. There is retro skiing daily, live '80s bands at night, and a host of other throw-back activities. It's, like, totally awesome!

Not in Kansas Anymore, Toto

The *Land of Oz Theme Park,* in the Beech Mountain ski area, west of Boone on NC 184, was popular several decades ago but has since fallen out of fashion and closed, except for the first weekend in October, when visitors come into the park to mingle with the Tin Man, Dorothy, and the other Oz characters wandering along the Yellow Brick Road, investigating the old Kansas farmhouse that still has remnants of its 1930s decor, and indulging in quirky nostalgia. For details call (828) 387-9283.

trails. This isn't a pie-in-the sky project. Mountain bikers, hikers, and trail runners designed the project for serious outdoor enthusiasts. The Beech Mountain Parks and Recreation Department was the driving force. Fitness and wellness coordinator Daniel Scagnelli conceived the idea in 2009, and got the trail-building effort going. Most of the labor was volunteer. Workers used hand tools and hand-held power tools. No heavy machinery. They reclaimed some abandoned trails and blended them into a network of trails showcasing unique topography atop Beech Mountain. One trail runs over a former ski slope that is fairly flat with moderate changes in elevation. A system of rough mountain-biking single track will challenge accomplished riders. The Emerald Outback Trails also include unspoiled woods with small waterfalls and creeks rushing, mountain vistas and overlooks. Views extend to one hundred miles or more. The official trail head was marked with signs in the spring of 2011 for the Adventure Trail Park, which is free and open to the public 7 days a week. It's a point of pride in the area that all their development of activities for natives and tourists is locally conceived and accomplished with a lot of volunteer labor. If you're wondering what a real community looks like, this is a place to visit. For trail park information, call (828) 387-3003, or check: www.BeechRecreation .org. The Chamber of Commerce can provide current information.

If you need to buy anything in Beech Mountain, *Fred's General Mercantile Co.* (501 Beech Mountain Pkwy.; 828-387-9331; fredsgeneral.com) is the place to go. Fred Pfohl coined the motto, "If you don't see it, ask for it—if we don't have it, you don't need it," back when he and his wife, Margie, opened in 1979. The store has been open every day since, and it's hard to imagine what you might want that isn't here, from hardware and tools to winter clothing to patent medicines to wine and beer. If you want breakfast, lunch, or dinner, you can get that here, too. *Fred's Backside Deli* invites you to "dine in or carryout." Breakfast eggs are served scrambled and come with toast; the Southern classic biscuit with sausage gravy is on the menu, along with hash browns, grits, country ham . . . all the Southern favorites with a few additions such as bagels thrown in. Lunch and dinner offerings include soup, hot and cold sandwiches, pizza, salads, grilled meats, barbecue, and cookies, pie, and cake. Drinks range from ice tea and milk to wine or imported beer.

Fred and Margie raised their five children in living quarters above the store. Consequently, none of the kids wants anything to do with running it, so Fred and Margie expect to keep on indefinitely. Because they've always been so flexible in accommodating customers at any time of day or night, it's hard to give specific hours of operation, but food is served from 7:30 a.m. to 3 p.m. and the store is open until 10 p.m. Locals have been known to come at 2:30 in the morning "because the baby needs medicine," picking up a six-pack and cigarettes while they're at it. As visitors, it would be courteous to observe normal business hours.

The Brick Oven Pizzeria (402 Beech Mountain Pkwy.; 828-387-4209; beech-mountain.com) is also a family operation. It started as a modest pizza place, and as business took off, the restaurant expanded its menu to include salads, wings, oven-baked pastas, sandwiches, a coffee/cappuccino bar, a candy and dessert counter, and a full bar. Seating includes wooden booths and a front dining room with tables. A family game room has various blinking and winking games, and, since it gets cold in winter, fireplaces where you can warm up. The Brick Oven is open for lunch and operates on into the night as business requires.

Northeast of Boone, it's well worth your time to make a trip to West Jefferson and Glendale Springs, off NC 194 at the juncture with NC 163, to see the *Ben Long Frescoes* in two Episcopal mission churches, St. Mary's Episcopal Church and Holy Trinity. The paintings in St. Mary's include an image of Mary pregnant with Jesus and a depiction of Christ on the cross, with a second view of the transfigured Christ behind it. The paintings in the Holy Trinity church include *The Lord's Supper* by Ben Long, as well as works by his students. The churches, which are only a few minutes apart, are not tended, and visitors may go in any time (336-982-3076; churchofthefrescoes.com).

Ben Long's Frescoes

Ben Long is a native of North Carolina who studied the art of fresco painting in Italy and has worked in several venues around North Carolina. Frescoes are created by mixing sand and lime, applying it to a surface, and then painting on it while it is still wet. Michelangelo's paintings on the ceiling of the Sistine Chapel in Rome, Italy, are frescoes. (See pages xv and xvi for more details about Ben Long's works and where to find them.)

In a completely different mode, West Jefferson is also the home of the **Ashe County Cheese Company** (106 E. Main St., 336-246-2501 or toll-free 800-445-1378; ashecountycheese.com), where visitors can see cheese being made and buy a variety of cheeses, including mild, medium, and sharp cheddars. One of the most popular items here is fresh cheese curds, which are soft, chewy curds before they're pressed and aged into hard cheese. Cheese-making schedules vary, so it's a good idea to call ahead if you want to see the process, but the shop is open (with those divine curds) Mon through Sat, 8:30 a.m. to 5 p.m.

Another drive on US 421, which is an easy highway these days, brings you to Wilkesboro, where you can find connections with topics as diverse as wine and racing and gardens and the jail where Tom Dooley (Dula) was held after being accused of murdering Laura Foster. **Wilkes Heritage Museum** (100 E. Main St.; 336-667-3171; wilkesheritagemuseum.com) includes exhibits in what used to be the courthouse about everything from the relationship between moonshine and stock-car racing to stories of Native Americans and the Civil War. The museum includes the 1860 Wilkes Jail. The museum is open from 10 a.m. to 4 p.m. Mon through Fri. Closed major holidays. Admission is $6 and free for children ages 5 and under.

At **St. Paul's Episcopal Church** (200 W. Cowles St.; 336-667-4231) you'll find two frescoes painted by Ben Long (see sidebar and entry earlier in this chapter on p. 52) about St. Paul the Apostle on the road to Damascus, and in prison writing his epistles to churches. The website for the Cultural Arts Council of Wilkes (cacwilkes.org) offers an especially clear explanation of the fresco process, along with Ben Long's biography. The Wilkesboro Tourism Development Authority is promoting tours for those who'd like to see many more of Ben Long's frescoes (benlongfrescotrail.org). The trail includes 25 counties in western North Carolina. For further information about Ben Long and the fresco process, see pages xv, xvi, 43, 49, and 50.

Wilkes Community College Gardens will be a special treat for people who find something sacred in gardens and for people who love old-time music (1328 S. Collegiate Dr.; 336-838-6100; merlefest.org/gardens.htm). The gardens are incorporated into the landscape of the college's 150-acre campus, with rose, Japanese, and native gardens. But it's the Eddy Merle Watson Garden of the Senses that truly attracts attention and inspires visitors. Eddy Merle Watson (son of legendary blind acoustic musician, Arthel "Doc" Watson) died in 1985, about the time he was fully recognized for his guitar picking in bluegrass country music and the blues. He rolled his farm tractor on a steep hill near his home and was killed instantly. In tribute to him, Wilkes Community College began the Eddy Merle Watson Garden of the Senses, creating a garden that

Hang Down Your Head, Tom Dooley

His real name was Tom Dula, pronounced *Dooley*. The Confederate soldier who was held in the Wilkes Jail before being executed in Statesville for the murder of his fiancée, Laura Foster, claimed his innocence until the moment he was hanged. The popular story is that he rode to the gallows sitting on top of his coffin, playing his banjo, and joking with the executioner that he'd have washed his neck if he'd known the rope would be so nice and clean. Since it was well before the age of TV and live broadcasts, it's hard to know whether this is a true story or the fabrication of a "journalist" looking for something to get attention in a newspaper. Many musicians, including the Kingston Trio, have sung "The Ballad of Tom Dooley."

people who cannot see might enjoy, emphasizing fragrance and texture, with sculptured alphabet walls, and plants labeled with Braille signs. MerleFest was begun as a way to raise money to continue developing the garden, but the festival has taken on a life of its own and is now a huge musical event each year. Much of the money it raises still goes to the gardens, while the influx of music lovers swells the local economy. The event is alcohol-free, suitable for families, and has been praised in recent years for the efficiency of crowd and traffic management that keeps jam-ups of people and vehicles from spoiling the musical experience.

Valle Crucis is close to the Blowing Rock–Boone area, but totally unlike it in nature. Although the little town sees hundreds and hundreds of visitors, it manages to continue operating and looking like a small town except for the visiting hordes. It's a good off-season stop. The town's history dates back to 1780, when Samuel Hix, the first known white settler in Valle Crucis, staked a claim to 1,000 acres. Later he traded the land for a gun, a dog, and a sheepskin. Eventually it became an Episcopal mission, named Valle Crucis because three creeks came together in the shape of a cross. Today the mission serves as a retreat for many church denominations.

People stop most often at the *Mast General Store,* on NC 112/194, listed on the National Register of Historic Places as one of the best remaining examples of an authentic, old country store. Here you can still buy penny candy, seeds, leather boots, Woolrich sweaters, flannel shirts, long johns, and just about anything else you can think of, mostly stacked, not too neatly, along wooden shelves, as well as the inevitable designed-for-tourists soaps, candles, and gewgaws. The Mast General Store has a couple of other locations now, but this is the original 1883 landmark (866-367-6278; mastgeneral store.com).

A quick jaunt east from Asheville for about 50 miles on I-40 brings you to three places that may still be some of the area's best kept secrets: ***Morganton, Glen Alpine, and Valdese.*** Morganton, with a population of fewer than 20,000, between Glen Alpine and Valdese, is a lively, growing little city full of surprises. *Reader's Digest* has listed Morganton as one of the top 10 places to raise a family. It's also a fun place to visit with one. A good starting place is **the History Museum of Burke County** (201 W. Meeting St.; 828-437-1777; thehistorymuseumofburke.org). The displays, consisting mainly of artifacts donated to the museum, are arranged in rooms by category and there's nothing stuffy about them. Kids will probably respond to the doctor's and dentist's offices, which contain enough old equipment to make you grateful for modern treatments. One young docent calls the dentist's office "the torture room." And if you've got a little age on you, you might look at the old beauty parlor with a machine for using heat to create permanent waves and remember seeing your mother all wired up to one. You might also look at the school room with its attached desks that had holes on top for inkwells and recall having sat in something similar back in the day, struggling through penmanship with a stick pen and a bottle of ink. Another room is filled with 1,200 model airplanes, all built by one man. The girl's bedroom from the 1950s could invite nostalgia, too, while a woman's vanity crafted from a goat feed barrel attests to the ingenuity of earlier times. The museum is open 10 a.m. to 4 p.m. Tues through Fri; 10 a.m. to 2 p.m. Sat; closed Sun and Mon.

Train buffs will get a kick out of the ***Morganton Railroad Depot and Museum*** (624 S. Green St.; 828-438-5272), part of the history museum. The depot was built in 1886, when rail transportation became vital to people in the western part of the state. The depot has been restored to its 1916 condition and displays a large collection of 19th and 20th century railroad memorabilia, including a large collection of dining car tableware. Call for hours.

Creating a Fresco

A fresco requires many steps, beginning with the artist's sketching his conceptualization on paper. Next the artist makes full-size drawings (called cartoons) of his figures. The drawing is attached to the wet plaster of a wall or ceiling so that the figures are transferred to the plaster. Then the artist must apply color before the plaster can dry. As the plaster hardens it seals in the colors. For a more detailed description of the process, including photos of stages in the work, see benlong frescotrail.org/process.html.

Another impressive site to visit in Morganton is the ***City of Morganton Municipal Auditorium*** (401 College St.; 800-939-7469; commaonline.org). The thousand-seat auditorium has great acoustics and show schedules, but for a more casual visit the attraction is the ceiling fresco, *Sacred Dance & the Muses,* by Benjamin F. Long IV. More often referred to simply as Ben Long, he has been creating frescoes in North Carolina since about 1974. The *Sacred Dance & the Muses* is his most recent and ambitious. For one thing, it's on the ceiling of the building's gallery. And it's huge—about 24 by 33 feet. This fresco shows seductive women from Erato, goddess of romantic poetry, to Thalia and Terpichore, goddesses of comedy and dance, all loosely clothed in flowing fabrics. They're mingled with a diverse gathering of people and animals. The people resemble members of Long's family, his friends, his teacher, and even his family pets. Long put himself into the scene, too, sitting on a ladder clutching a handful of paint brushes, looking exhausted, which he probably was. He worked with a team of artists and apprentices from mid-January 2004 to mid-April. Ironically, now viewers can observe the scene in comfort, reclining in chairs mounted on a revolving platform that moves slowly beneath the fresco. The gallery is open from 9 a.m. to 5 p.m., Mon through Fri, as well as during public performances in the auditorium.

If you work up an appetite wandering around town, try ***Mountain Burrito,*** an unusual eatery you can visit at its home location (408 Fleming Dr.; 828-438-5088; facebook.com/morganton.mountainburrito). The place is notable in several ways. First, the owners deliberately put in common seating rather than small tables or booths so that you may end up chatting with folks you've only just met. Nobody waits on these tables. You walk through a service area with people on the other side to prepare your burrito to order, cafeteria-style. The offerings are limited to burritos, tacos, nachos, soup, salad, and chips. These come with your choice of chicken, fish sometimes, steak, pork, or veggies, plus whatever additions you choose from a long list that includes beans, sautéed peppers, onions, and cheese plus a choice of as many of seven salsas you wish. Beverages include sweet and unsweet tea, Coke products, some decent bottled beers, and bottled water. Soups are homemade fresh daily. Some people order the tacos, which are soft, not crisp, just because the burrito is so huge. Then you find a place at the big table and dig in. The overall effect is of a lively extended family party, with kids, business people, workmen, all talking and eating and generally having a fine time of it. Perhaps this atmosphere works so well because the food is wonderful—fresh, prepared on the scene with a notable absence of canned anything. The restaurant is open Mon through Sat from 11 a.m. to 9 p.m.

Another fun place to stop is **Catawba Valley Brewing Company** (212 S. Green St.; 828-430-6883; catawbavalleybrewingcompany.com). This is just 2 miles from I-40 off exit 105. Using equipment scavenged from defunct old breweries, the company opened in 1999 in the basement of an old two-story brick building that had once been a textile mill in nearby Glen Alpine. By 2007 things were going well enough to warrant a move to the larger Morganton location on South Green Street. This is a big clattering building that now includes a tasting room and has lots of space for musicians who perform, some pool tables, and places you can sit with friends to eat food you've brought in or had delivered. It's casual. Very casual. But the beers are top-quality microbrews, some available year-round, others seasonal, and they may well be served to you, complete with a description, by the person who created the recipe. Hours are 5 to 9 p.m. Mon and Tue; 5 to 10:30 p.m. Wed, Thurs, and Fri; Sat 1 to 10 p.m.; Sun noon to 7 p.m. Check the website for special events and their days and times. Since the move to South Green Street, the company has opened breweries in Asheville and Biltmore Village.

Morganton has another feature that you may or may not get to experience: **the Brown Mountain Lights.** People have been reporting these mysterious, unexplained lights low on Brown Mountain for many generations, variously describing them as balls of fire, white bobbing blips, and hovering reddish lights. Depending on the reports, the lights hover or bounce or dart away, or don't appear at all. Stories go back to the 1800s, with the lights attributed to everything from spirits of dead Cherokee hunters to automobile lights. Nancy Roberts, the late writer of many mysterious doings in the Southeast, conjectured that maybe the lights were actually UFOs as they land and take off, checking to see what our planet is like. Just 21 miles north of Morganton on NC 181, a well-tended overlook provides a place to park and watch for the lights. In some areas where people used to report seeing lights, trees have grown up so much you can't see anything but treetops; but this area has been kept pruned down, specifically for "sightings." It wouldn't hurt to take a camera.

Just a short drive east of Morganton, via US 70, the community of **Valdese** has both fascinating history and places to visit. Valdese was established in 1893 by 11 families, Waldenses, a religious group who left Italy hoping to be able to earn enough in this area to support their families. But they had a lot of history before they even got here. For centuries they had been persecuted in Italy by the Roman Catholic Church, which said only priests could read the Bible. Waldenses believed everyone should be able to gather and study the Bible. After being exiled to the Swiss Alps, some of the Waldenses eventually were able to go back to their valleys in Italy safely, but as their numbers grew and the available farmland did not, the Waldenses decided to establish a colony in the foothills near Morganton. They called their settlement Valdese and in time joined the Presbyterian Church. *The Trail of Faith* (401 Church St.; 800-635-4778 or 828-0874-1893; waldensiantrailoffaith.org) is a series of 14 building replicas depicting the early struggles of generations of Waldenses in the practice of their faith. Visitors can follow the exhibits tracing a religious heritage many believe goes back to the Apostles, through the years of persecution and exile, to settling Valdese. Exhibits include a replica of a cave in Italy where believers hid to worship in secret, a small stone seminary where the Bible was translated into French, and an outdoor community bread oven built in Valdese. Open Mon through Fri 9 a.m. to 5 p.m., April through Oct. Closed Sat and Sun, Thanksgiving, Christmas Eve and Day, New Year's Day. Self-guided tours are $7 for adults, $6 for seniors, $4 for teachers and students.

Waldensian Heritage Museum (208 Rodoret St. South; 828-874-1111; waldensianheritagemuseum.org) fills out the story with displays of everything from baptismal gowns and wooden tools to photos of early one-room homes. A dollhouse from 1919 suggests children did have some fun. But perhaps the most telling of displays is a pulpit, some pews, a podium and table, and a communion chalice from the Presbyterian church as it was in 1899. Museum hours vary so call ahead. *Waldensian Heritage Wines* (4940 Villar Ln. NE; 828-879-3202; waldensianwinery.com) illuminates another aspect of the Waldenses lives. They liked *good* wine. They still do. They are, after all, Italian. The winery's motto is "Life is too short to drink bad wine." In the early days of their settlement, the Waldenses made wine in their homes. Today they produce a variety of wines, using many of the old techniques plus some modern equipment and innovations in a 4,000-square-foot facility. Much of their process is still manual. The people who work there are unpaid volunteers. The various wines offered today range from Heritage Burgundy Valdese, a dry red as it was made by first generation Waldenses in Valdese, to Waldensian White Sweet, a nod to the southern sweet tooth. The winery is open Thurs through Sun from 1 to 6 p.m., except for holidays. Free guided tours with opportunities for tasting and purchasing wines are available then. Much more information about the community is available at the Valdese Department of Tourism in the Old Rock School at 400 Main St. West (828-879-2126; visitvaldese.com). The school contains two art galleries and other attractions, as well as the tourism office. The galleries are open 9 a.m. to 5 p.m. Mon through Fri, but check for hours of operation, which are not always predictable.

At Glen Alpine you can visit a winery that is another of those quirky North Carolina business combinations: *Lake James Cellars and the Old Mill Antiques* (204 E. Main St., NC 70; 828-584-4551; lakejamescellars.com). Here you can sample wines, shop for antiques, and sip a glass of wine on the porch, all at the same place. The big 1915 building was once a textile mill. The space now houses a rambling antiques mall with some top-quality offerings, a wine tasting and sales area, and a space devoted to producing and bottling the wines, which are made from locally grown grapes. A tasting, which costs $5, includes 6 different wines of your choice and the wine glass to keep as a souvenir. You choose from two separate wine lists, one for dry wines, the other for sweet. Each wine is described in detail to help you decide what to try. After your tasting, you might wander among the antiques sipping a glass of something you liked. There's an easy, casual air about the place, with family members, and sometimes their pets, coming and going, as well as antiques vendors bringing in merchandise for their booths and stopping to chat. Open Tues through Sat, 10 a.m. to 6 p.m., Sun 1 to 5 p.m.

You might spend the night in *the Inn at Glen Alpine* (105 Davis St.; 828-584-9264; innatglenalpine.com). This bed-and-breakfast home has 4 guest rooms in a 1913 country manor that has been beautifully restored, with pocket doors and (nonworking) fireplaces. The first floor has 12-foot ceilings, and the floors in the living room, dining room, and library are parquet designs of yellow pine inlaid with walnut. Antique furnishings are carefully arranged so as not to overwhelm the spaces, and the overall effect is one of light and comfort. The 4 guest rooms are spacious, two of them suites. In 2014 Teresa and Craig Sellman bought the inn and spent several months in renovation before reopening it. They called the renovation "putting lipstick on the pretty lady" because it was already such a splendid building. The addition of a commercial kitchen expands the possibilities for breakfast, accommodating special dietary needs, and providing food to take with you as you explore the area.

The Foothills

When you want to begin heading for lower elevations, a drive of about 40 minutes on US 74, heading southeast from Asheville, takes you to the little vacation community of *Lake Lure.* Everything centers on the 1,500-acre lake, which has 27 miles of shoreline. The area is surrounded by the Blue Ridge Mountains. It's in the heart of the thermal belt, where the climate is almost always a bit milder than the extremes of heat and cold found in the rest of North Carolina. The temperate climate makes Lake Lure excellent for boating, fishing, hiking, and horseback riding year-round. Lake Lure, Chimney Rock, and Bat Cave, three tourist towns, run together one after another along the narrow mountain road.

For hiking you have your choice of hundreds of trails. Organized hikes leave from *Chimney Rock at Chimney Rock State Park* (828-625-9611 or 800-277-9611; chimneyrockpark.com), located on US 64/74 in Chimney Rock.

There are hiking trails of varying difficulty, easier paths, and even an elevator to the top. (However, as of this writing, the park is undergoing capital improvements and the elevator is not in service.) From the top you can look down and see Lake Lure and mountains in all directions. Hickory Nut Falls, one of the highest waterfalls in the East, is on the grounds. Hours and days the park is open vary seasonally, as do rates. Call ahead for current information. In bad weather the park closes. For simpler hiking you can ask almost any local person to recommend a favorite trail. These personal favorites are loosely kept secrets because no one wants them to become overrun with "lookey-loos" and littered with aluminum cans, but locals gladly share the information with anyone who cares enough to ask personally. The town marina, on the lake and right next to US 64/74A, has boats for rent, and *Lake Lure Tours* runs hourly tours and twilight and dinner cruises (877-386-4255 or 828-625-1373; lakeluretours.com).

From here it's an easy drive up either US 74A or NC 9 to I-40, where you'll come to *Black Mountain,* an interesting village that was once a Cherokee Indian center and now is a thriving community specializing in all kinds of top-quality arts and crafts. The town has taken to calling itself "the front porch of western North Carolina," a name that seems to suit the peaceful but interesting atmosphere of the community.

In May and October, Black Mountain sponsors the Mountain Music Festival, during which musicians play the old mountain music on dulcimers, fiddles, bagpipes, and mandolins. In August the Sourwood Festival features more music and dancing and a large arts and crafts show. These events are fun; they're also well attended, so if you have any notion of being in Black Mountain when they occur, you will need to arrange for lodging well ahead of time. (For details call 800-207-8759 or check the website: exploreblackmountain.com.)

The Black Mountain Inn (1186 W. Old Hwy. 70; 800-735-6128 or 828-669-6528; blackmountaininn.com), has 7 guest rooms. The building has an interesting history. In the 1800s It was a stagecoach stop. At the beginning of the 20th century it was a TB sanatorium, In the 1940s it was a studio and retreat where artists and writers such as Norman Rockwell and John Steinbeck spent time. The decor is casual country. The inn's website offers both photos and detailed descriptions of each room. Breakfasts include a main course such as eggs Benedict or French toast, plus fruits and home-baked breads.

The Red Rocker Inn (136 N. Dougherty St.; 828-669-5991; redrockerinn .com) is a long-established, 17-room inn long known for its food, served in portions that leave guests needing a walk after dinner. The kitchen staff prepares dinner each day according to the number of guests registered that night at the inn, but if you make a reservation you can still enjoy the food, even if you're not an overnight guest. But it's a pleasant place to stay, with a nice mix of old-time feel and contemporary comfort. The rooms all have private baths. In cool weather, gas fireplaces add warmth to the public rooms and some of the guest rooms. The proprietors take special pride in the long row of red rocking chairs on the porch and go so far as repainting them regularly to keep them looking bright and shiny. In 2014 the proprietors undertook major renovations to keep the place in good condition. They took up the carpet in the guest rooms and found oak and pine floors, which they refinished, replacing the carpet with area rugs. Another, fun, change was the addition of a fire pit outside to enjoy evenings.

Visiting the **Song of the Wood,** at 203 W. State St. (828-669-7675; song ofthewood.com), a workshop and salesroom devoted to dulcimers and unusual string instruments and their music, leaves you feeling exhilarated and refreshed. Jerry Read Smith makes hammered dulcimers and the even more unusual bowed psaltery, a small triangular instrument played with a violin-type bow, similar to a medieval bowed harp. JoAnn, Jerry's sister, manages the showroom. Everything about the shop is devoted to keeping the old music alive, producing fine-quality handmade instruments, and surrounding you with music.

You'll first be attracted by the music coming through outside speakers. When you get inside, they'll play lots more music for you. You may hear the music from their independent record albums, *The Strayaway Child, Homecoming, One Wintry Night,* and *Heartdance.* The shop sells a highly personal selection of other tapes and albums, mainly hammered dulcimer music, piano music, and Celtic music. The shop is light and airy, with instruments on the walls, a fuel-efficient wood-burning stove, and a mountain rocker. But it's the handcrafted instruments that steal the show: mountain and hammered dulcimers, Celtic harps, strum sticks, and more, all beautifully displayed. You're invited to sit down and try any of the instruments or listen to the recorded music. If you're interested and ask, you can almost always manage to be shown through the design studio and workshop in a building about twenty minutes away and have the whole process explained to you. Also, the Song of the Wood website is unusually interesting and definitely worth a look. Open from 10 a.m. to 5 p.m. Mon through Sat.

As for other shopping, the streets are lined with crafts shops, antiques shops and antiques malls, a craft co-op, a chocolate shop, and a coffee roasting shop.

In the old Black Mountain Fire Department building, the **Swannanoa Valley Museum** (223 W. State St.; 828-669-9566; swannanoavalleymuseum .org), focuses intensely on local history from the Stone Age to the present. For instance, exhibits depict the lives of Native Americans, early settlers, the coming of the railroad, and Billy Graham and other famous valley personalities. One of the museum's most popular programs is a series of hikes to points of historical interest in the valley. To participate in a hike, call for details. The museum isn't open in winter because it's too costly to heat the big building. It is open Apr through Oct, Tues through Fri 10 a.m. to 5 p.m.; Sat noon to 4 p.m.; closed Sun and Mon. Sometimes, if you call, it is possible to make an appointment to see the museum during other hours. Admission is free but donations are gratefully accepted.

Immediately after Black Mountain, you come to *Old Fort,* an area that was still considered Cherokee Indian land for some time after white pioneers began pushing in during the mid-1770s. At the beginning of the American Revolution, General Griffith Rutherford assembled 2,500 troops to attack the Cherokees, who seemed to be siding with the British. Afterward the Indians conceded a huge portion of land, a pattern that was repeated often up to the time of the Trail of Tears in 1838. In subsequent years the Western North Carolina Railroad became important here. The *Mountain Gateway Museum,* in the 100 block of Water Street, tells the story, as do the Stepp and Morgan cabins that were moved here later. The site is a branch of the North Carolina Museum of History. It's not a big, splashy place and deserves your attention for that very reason. Admission is free. Open Tues through Sat 9 a.m. to 5 p.m.; Sun 2 p.m. to 5 p.m. Closed state holidays (828-688-9259; mountaingatewaymuseum.org).

Places to Stay in the Mountains

ASHEVILLE

Campfire Lodgings
Appalachian Village Road
(800) 933-8012
campfirelodgings.com
Campsites are comfortable; yurts are luxurious.
Inexpensive to moderate

Cedar Crest Inn
674 Biltmore Ave.
(828) 333-5459
(800) 252-0310
cedarcrestinn.com
This structure was built by many of the craftspeople who worked on the Biltmore Estate, putting all that grandeur on a more human scale.
Expensive

The Sourwood Inn
810 Elk Mountain Scenic Hwy.
(828) 255-0690
sourwoodinn.com
This is a secluded place full of light with wonderful mountain views.
Moderate

BLACK MOUNTAIN

The Black Mountain Inn
1186 W. Old Hwy. 70
(828) 669-6528
blackmountaininn.com
A peaceful location with a sense of history.
Moderate

The Red Rocker Inn
136 N. Dougherty St.
(828) 669-5991
redrockerinn.com
An inn long famous for its food.
Moderate

BLOWING ROCK

River Lodge Bed and Breakfast
619 Roy Tritt Rd.
(828) 293-5431
(877) 384-4400
riverlodge-bb.com
A fun place with great innkeepers, good food, and nice rooms.
Moderate to expensive

DILLSBORO

The Chalet Inn
285 Lone Oak Dr.
(828) 586-0251
(800) 789-8014
thechaletinn.com
Here's a quiet place with an Alpine atmosphere.
Moderate to expensive

The Dillsboro Inn
146 North River Rd.
(828) 586-3898
(866) 586-3898
dillsboroinn.com
The Tuckasegee River provides relaxing music.
Moderate to expensive

The Jarrett House
100 Haywood St.
(825) 586-0265
(800) 972-5623
jarretthouse.com
People come to eat and stay to sleep.
Inexpensive

HENDERSONVILLE

1898 Waverly Inn
783 Main St.
(828) 693-9193
(800) 537-8195
waverlyinn.com
A comfortable B&B within easy walking distance of downtown attractions.
Moderate

HOT SPRINGS

Mountain Magnolia Inn and Retreat
204 Lawson St.
(800) 914-9306
mountainmagnoliainn.com
Glorious views.
Moderate

LINVILLE FALLS

Parkview Lodge
US 221 and Blue Ridge Parkway
(828) 765-4787
(800) 849-4552
parkviewlodge.com
The accommodations are simple and close to many attractions.
Inexpensive

MAGGIE VALLEY

Cataloochee Ranch
119 Ranch Dr.
(828) 926-1401
(800) 868-1401
cataloocheeranch.com
Rates here include breakfast and dinner.
Moderate

SALUDA

Orchard Inn
NC 176
(828) 749-5471
(800) 581-3800
orchardinn.com
Back in the 1980s, a reviewer described this hilltop location and dining experience as "quite magical." Still true.
Moderate to expensive

SYLVA

Mountain Brook Fireplace Cottages
208 Mountain Brook Rd.
(828) 586-4329
mountainbrook.com
A family-run operation where the rates remain the same all year.
Inexpensive

TRYON

Pine Crest Inn
85 Pine Crest Ln.
(828) 859-9135
(800) 633-3001
pinecrestinn.com
Pine Crest is popular for special events and business gatherings.
Moderate to expensive

THE MOUNTAINS WEBSITES

Cherokee History
cherokee-nc.com

Great Smoky Mountains
visitsmokies.org

List of Movies Shot in North Carolina Mountains
ncfilm.com

Official North Carolina Website
visitnc.com

Transylvania Waterfalls
visitwaterfalls.com/travel

WAYNESVILLE

The Swag
2300 Swag Rd.
(828) 926-0430
(800) 789-7672
theswag.com
So high above mountain tops one guest said it is "close to God."
Expensive

Places to Eat in the Mountains

ASHEVILLE

Bier Garden
46 Haywood St.
(828) 285-0102
ashevillebiergarden.com
Casual atmosphere, huge beer selection, lots of food choices.
Moderate

Flying Frog Cafe and Wine Bar
1 Battery Park Ave.
(828) 254-941
flyingfrogcafe.com
Run by veteran restaurateurs with a flare for fine dining.

Laughing Seed Cafe
40 Wall St.
(828) 252-3445
laughingseed.com
One of Asheville's oldest, most popular vegetarian/fusion restaurants.
Moderate

Tupelo Honey Cafe
12 College St.
(828) 255-4863
tupelohoneycafe.com
A farm-to-fork restaurant putting a contemporary spin on Southern cooking.
Moderate to expensive

BREVARD

Dugan's Irish Pub
29 W. French Broad St.
(828) 862-6527
http://duganspub.com
Top o' the morning to you! Brews, food, and all things Irish.
Moderate

Rocky's Grill and Soda Shop
50 S. Broad St.
(828) 877-5375
Rockysnc.com
Some people say they have the best hot dogs and ice cream around.
Inexpensive

DILLSBORO

The Jarrett House
100 Haywood St.
(800) 972-5623
jarrethouse.com
People go here especially for fried chicken, country ham, and light biscuits.
Moderate

FLAT ROCK

Seasons at Highland Lake Inn
180 Highland Lake Rd.
(866) 303-9621
hlinn.com
Lavish Sunday buffets are a family favorite.
Moderate

HOT SPRINGS

Mountain Magnolia Inn
204 Lawson St.
(800) 914-9306
mountainmagnoliainn.com
Everything is made from scratch on the premises with an emphasis on locally grown ingredients.
Moderate to expensive

SALUDA

The Purple Onion
16 Main St.
(828) 749-1179
purpleonionsaluda.com
Fusion cuisine—a surprise if you're expecting down-home Southern cooking.
Inexpensive to moderate

TRYON

Pine Crest Inn Dining Room
85 Pine Crest Ln.
(828) 859-9135
(800) 633-3001
pinecrestinn.com
A fine-dining menu changes daily.
Expensive

WAYNESVILLE

Maggie's Galley Oyster Bar
1374 Sulphur Spring Rd.
(828) 456-8945
maggiesgalley.com
Try a fish sandwich for lunch.
Inexpensive to moderate

The Upper Piedmont & Sandhills

Sir Walter's Country

Raleigh, the state capital named for Sir Walter Raleigh, offers a variety of historical sites, museums, and fine old architecture in addition to the government buildings downtown.

Plan on stopping at **Historic Oakwood,** at North Person Street between Jones and Boundary, if you're interested in Victorian homes. This historic district of more than 400 homes, many restored, is considered one of the best examples of an unspoiled Victorian neighborhood in the country.

Several museums deserve your attention. **The North Carolina Museum of History** (919-807-7900; 5 E. Edenton St.; ncmuseumofhistory.org) concentrates on exhibits, artifacts, and dioramas related to state history, transportation, and, of course, the Revolutionary and Civil Wars. It also has good exhibits about women in North Carolina. The museum is open Mon through Sat from 9 a.m. to 5 p.m. and Sun from noon to 5 p.m. Closed major holidays. Admission is free.

At the **North Carolina Museum of Natural Sciences** (11 W. Jones St.; 877-462-8724; naturalsciences.org), you divide your attention between stuffed and skeletal remains of what

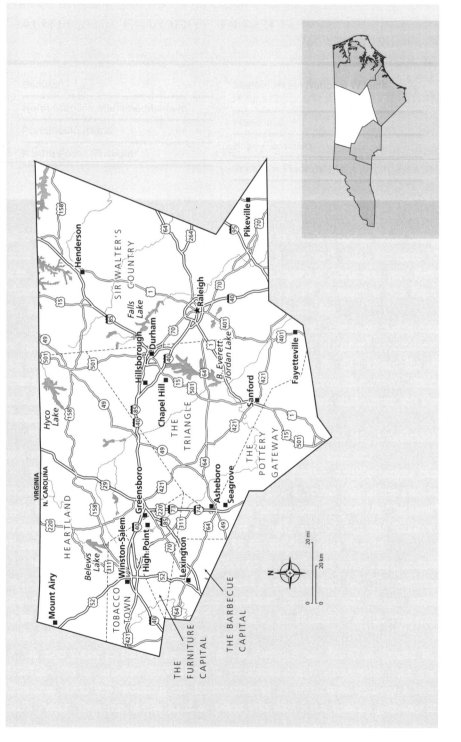

once was, and living specimens of what still is, from across the state. In the whale hall a 50-foot whale skeleton hanging from the ceiling dominates the exhibits. Another highlight is "Willo," the first dinosaur discovered with a fossilized heart. The living conservatory here is filled with live monarch butterflies and ruby-throated hummingbirds, in a re-creation of a dry tropical forest that also has cacti, heliconias, and orchids. Museum hours are the same as those at the museum of history. Admission is free.

Black history is beginning to receive organized, formal recognition in this area. The *African-American Cultural Complex* (119 Sunnybrook Rd.; 919-250-9336; aaccmuseum.org) displays a large collection of items created by African Americans in three houses along a nature trail. They include innovations in science, art, business, medicine, politics, and sports. Hours by appointment.

The *Martin Luther King Jr. Memorial Gardens* (1500 Martin Luther King Jr. Blvd.; 919-834-6264; king-raleigh.org) features a life-size statue of Dr. King and a 12-ton granite water monument honoring 25 pioneers in civil rights and education in a setting of more than 8,000 flowers. The park is open 24 hours a day. Admission is free.

For insight into life in Raleigh's early days for both plantation owners and their slaves, visit *Mordecai Historic Park* (1 Mimosa St.; 919-996-4364; raleighnc.gov/mordecai), at the juncture of Wake Forest Road and Mimosa Street, just a mile from the state Capitol and downtown Raleigh. With several thousand acres, this was one of the largest plantations in Wake County before the Civil War, growing corn, wheat, cotton, and food for the people on the plantation. To give you an idea of its size, the area now known as Historic Oakwood stands on what used to be Mordecai property. Five generations of

ANNUAL EVENTS IN THE UPPER PIEDMONT

MOUNT AIRY

Budbreak Wine Festival
(last Saturday in April)
(336) 719-2345
budbreakfestival.com

OLD SALEM

Reenactment of original Fourth of July held in 1783
July 4
(336) 721-7300
oldsalem.org

WINSTON-SALEM

Annual Piedmont Crafts Fair
(mid-November)
(336) 725-1516
piedmontcraftsmen.org

the same family lived in **Mordecai House,** and their 18th- and 19th-century furnishings, art, and books still fill the place.

Slaves did all the labor on the plantation. Records show that some of them grew their own rice and practiced traditional African farming, crafts, cooking, and music there. The park includes a re-created kitchen garden of vegetables, herbs, fruits, and flowers typical of the mid-19th century. An 1842 kitchen from Anson County has been set up next to the garden where the original kitchen probably stood.

Open Tues through Sat 9 a.m. to 4 p.m., Sun 1 to 4 p.m. Tours begin on the hour. Admission is $5 for adults, $3 for seniors and children ages 7 to 17, free for children 6 and under. When school tours are in process, the public is not admitted, so call ahead to be sure a public tour will be available when you visit. Also allow time for the **North Carolina Museum of Art** at 2110 Blue Ridge Ave. (take the Wade Avenue exit off I-40). The building, designed by the architect Edward Durrell Stone, who designed the John F. Kennedy Center in Washington, DC, and the original Museum of Modern Art in New York, is important; so are the eight major collections. Arranged in chronological order, they cover 5,000 years of art, displaying work by artists from Botticelli to Monet to Andrew Wyeth. You'll also find exhibits of Jewish ceremonial art along with Greek and Roman sculpture. Tours are available at 1:30 p.m. A cafe and gift shop operate during museum hours. The museum (919-839-6262, extension 2154; ncartmuseum.org) is open Tues through Sat from 9 a.m. to 5 p.m. (until 9 p.m. Fri) and Sun from 10 a.m. to 5 p.m. Closed Mon and major holidays. Admission is free, except for some special exhibits.

Another approach to art is **Artspace** (201 E. Davie St.; 919-821-2787; artspacenc.org), a nonprofit visual arts center in downtown Raleigh where you can watch artists at work and also visit shows in Galleries One and Two and the Upfront Gallery and lobby. Artists sell work out of their studios as well as from the galleries and in the gift shop. Artspace is open from 10 a.m. to 7 p.m. Tues, 10 a.m. to 6 p.m Wed through Sat. The first Friday of every month, Artspace is open until 10 p.m. Admission is free.

The **Raleigh City Museum** (220 Fayetteville St.; 919-996-2220; raleighcity museum.org) gives you an intensely local, idiosyncratic look at the people and history of the town. This is one of those places that came into being because of the determination of people who live here. Beth Crabtree, a local historian, determined that the city needed a special home to honor its history and collect its artifacts before they became scattered, and in the early 1990s she began working to make it happen. After her death, another local woman, Mary Cates, picked up the torch and marshaled even more support. The resulting museum, with both changing exhibits and displays of artifacts, is housed in the ground and first floors of the old Briggs Hardware Store, a building dating from about 1890–1900. The private, nonprofit museum collects artifacts through the effective device of asking for them: "Share your artifact and its historical story." The results range from 18th-century tools and portraits to photographs and household items, and the collection continues to grow. The museum is open Sun 1 p.m. to 10 p.m., closed Mon, 9 a.m. to 4 p.m. Sat., Tues through Fri 10 a.m. to 4 p.m., First Fridays open 6 to 9 p.m., Sat 1 to 4 p.m. Admission is free. Fayetteville Street is between Salisbury and Wilmington Streets, a block from the Capitol.

An unusual restaurant for a Southern town is the ***Irregardless Cafe,*** at 901 W. Morgan St. (irregardless.com). When they describe it, people tend to call it the "vegetarian restaurant," but it does serve chicken, steaks, and duck as well as the vegetarian entrees. Don't be fooled by the sprouts in the salads. These aren't old hippies or young health-food nuts; they're folks who've figured out how to get the best flavor out of fresh ingredients with the least amount of doctoring. Their slogan now is "We were 'green' before it was the thing to be." The menu changes daily to take advantage of fresh vegetables and meats. To dispel the notion that you're doing something that's good for you, you can order anything you like from the full bar. The homemade desserts will keep you on the sinful side, too. Open for lunch Tues through Fri from 11:30 a.m. to 2:30 p.m.; dinner Tues through Thurs from 5:30 to 9:30 p.m., Fri and Sat to 10 p.m. Dancing until midnight Saturday. Sunday brunch 10 a.m. to 2 p.m. Call (919) 833-8898 to make dinner reservations. Reservations are not necessary for lunch or brunch unless you have a large group.

If you like gardens, here are three worth a stop: The J. C. Raulston Arboretum, Joel Lane House Gardens, and the Raleigh Municipal Rose Garden.

The arboretum at North Carolina State University at 4301 Beryl Rd. (take the Hillsborough Street exit off the beltline; 919-515-3132; ncsu.edu/jcraulston arboretum), grows thousands of plants from around the world. In addition to special interest areas, such as the silver-and-white garden and a Japanese garden, a long perennial garden shows what it's possible to grow outside in North Carolina every month. Open daily from 8 a.m. to dusk. Admission is free.

Joel Lane House Gardens, at the corner of St. Mary's and West Hargett Streets (160 S. Saint Mary's St.; 919-833-3431; joellane.org), and the ***Raleigh Municipal Rose Garden,*** at 301 Pogue St., in a residential neighborhood near North Carolina State University. The Joel Lane House Gardens are authentic colonial revival style, with espaliered fruit trees, pomegranate trees, a grape arbor, and, in the herb garden, medicinal and culinary herbs. The gardens are open daily from sunrise to sunset, with tours available March to December 1, Tues through Fri from 10 a.m. to 2 p.m., and 1 to 4 p.m. Sat. Admission is

AUTHOR'S FAVORITE PLACES
IN THE UPPER PIEDMONT

North Carolina State University Arboretum	Seagrove
Cedar Creek Gallery	Old Salem
Hillsborough	Selma
	Ava Gardner Museum

free. The **Raleigh Municipal Rose Garden,** which has an amphitheater for concerts and stage productions, contains 60 different varieties of roses, about 1,200 plants, with something in bloom from late May until fall. Seasonal flowers, trees, and shrubs are included in the garden. Open daily, sunrise to sunset. Admission is free (919-821-4579; raleigh-nc.org/parks&rec/).

For a nice break from the city, head north, either on US 1 or on US 401 and NC 39, to Henderson, not far from the Virginia border. The **Kerr Lake State Recreational Area** (269 Glasshouse Rd.; 252-438-7791; kerrlake-nc .com) is a 50,000-acre lake that stretches from North Carolina into Virginia, with 800 miles of shoreline. You'll find everything from picnic areas to camping facilities and hiking trails. The area has 700 campsites, 21 boat ramps, 14 picnic shelters, and 3 community buildings. Admission to the park is free, but there is a fee for camping. Fees vary depending on whether you want a tent or RV site and what services you require. The Vance County Tourism organization sponsors July 4 fireworks and a Labor Day Parade of Lights flotilla.

While you're in the area, treat yourself to the **Cedar Creek Gallery** (1150 Fleming Rd.; 919-528-1041; cedarcreekgallery.com), a workplace and sales outlet for top-quality craftspeople. Their brochure says, "Expect to be overwhelmed," and that's not hype. The gallery displays are spread through many rooms. Much of the work is pottery, but you'll also find fine glass, handmade stereopticons, stringed instruments, jewelry, and toys that are too splendid to put into the hands of kids. The quality is so outstanding that people tend to walk along talking in hushed tones, though that's not at all the demeanor of the artisans themselves. In the rear of the gallery, the **Museum of American Pottery** displays the entire range of local pottery, from the old folk pottery of places such as Cole and Jugtown to the works of contemporary studio potters. The exhibits include information about basic potting procedures and such things as salt glazes, too. From Henderson go south on I-85, take the second Butner exit (186), turn left on US 15 North, turn right at the first crossroads, and left on Fleming Road to the gallery. Open daily from 10 a.m. to 6 p.m. Closed Christmas and Thanksgiving.

From Raleigh, driving southeast on US 70 toward Goldsboro takes you to **Selma and Smithfield,** two small towns that you can easily visit on the same day. But if you are an antiques lover, you may decide to devote a full day to the town of Selma. As you head in this direction, the landscape gradually flattens out.

Signs from US 70 (as well as from I-95 and I-40) will direct you to Selma, a town that has pulled itself from the doldrums of empty old buildings to become an antiques mecca. The story begins in 1997, when Bruce Radford, town manager, was trying to figure out a way to restore the town to its earlier vibrancy. The town needed a theme, he thought. And it came to him during a golf game. He swung at the ball and got an inspiration, more or less at the same time. The golf ball went into the woods, but his idea was so good it flourishes even now that he has moved on. Using some financial incentives, promise of advertising support, and a lot of local enthusiasm, the town of Selma has seen its downtown buildings restored as antiques malls and shops, many with living quarters upstairs, artisans' studios, and shops for such antiques-related activities as upholstering.

itstartedwith akiss

According to local lore, Tom Banks would speed past Ava on his bicycle and yell, "Hey, girlfriend!" One day, she ran after him, pulled him off the bike, and kissed his cheek. Banks was smitten permanently.

When you're through here, hop back on US 70 and follow the signs a few miles to Smithfield and the **Ava Gardner Museum.** Ava Gardner was born in this area, lived here when she was young, and is buried here. The museum was started by Tom Banks, who met Ava while she waited for rides near the campus of Atlantic Christian College, which he was attending, in the little town of Wilson.

Later he became a publicist on one of her movies, *My Forbidden Past.* No matter what else he did in a career that took him from New York to Florida, he kept up with what was happening to Ava, making scrapbooks of newspaper clippings about her. He also collected photographs, posters, audio- and videocassettes from her movies, and anything else he could find. In the 1970s he visited her in London and told her he was going to donate everything to start a museum in her honor.

In 1981 he bought the teacherage in Smithfield where she had lived when her mother taught school. He moved his collection there and opened the museum in 1982.

Since then the museum's had a few different locations, and the collection has continued to grow with donations of costumes, Ava's good china from her years in London, even her collection of Frank Sinatra records. The museum now has more than 100,000 items, and is finally housed in a permanent location at 325 E. Market St., in what used to be a Belk's Department Store.

The museum is open Mon through Sat 9 a.m. to 5 p.m., Sun 2 to 5 p.m., closed Dec. 24 and 25, Easter, and Thanksgiving. Admission is $10 for adults, $9 for senior citizens 65 and older, military and teens 13 to 17, $6 for children ages 6 to 12. Children under 6 admitted free (919-934-5830; avagardner.org).

The Triangle

In a sense, **Durham** is closer to Raleigh than it used to be. With both communities expanding laterally, it's not hard as you drive between the two places to imagine that they'll soon run together. And when people speak of "the Triangle," they're typically including Raleigh. But the increasing development has brought more traffic, which slows driving between Raleigh and Durham, so Chapel Hill and Durham more often package themselves as a tourist unit not necessarily including Raleigh. Durham is a tobacco town; Duke University was endowed by and named for the Duke family, which made Durham a tobacco center.

Although tobacco is not as important in the area as it once was, and smoking is no longer allowed in any North Carolina restaurant, criticizing smokers is not a good way to make friends here. The Duke family pioneered in marketing cigarettes in America. You can understand something of the mystique and importance of tobacco by visiting the **Duke Homestead State Historic Site and Tobacco Museum,** established on the Duke family farm. Take the Guess Road exit off I-85 to 2828 Duke Homestead Rd. Depending on when you're here, you'll see tobacco being planted, cultivated, harvested, or prepared for market and have the opportunity to participate in part of the processing.

On the property, the old family house, two tobacco factories, a curing barn, and a packhouse show you how it used to be. In the visitor center, tobacco-related exhibits include advertising, signs, machinery, and an old cigar store Indian. Open Tues through Sat 9 a.m. to 5 p.m. Hours change, so it's a good idea to call ahead (919-477-5498; nchistoricsites.org/duke).

Duke money also created a dominant institution in this area, **Duke University.** In 1924 a $6 million gift from the family made it possible to expand what was then Trinity College. A large endowment and subsequent grants followed. The result is Duke University's two large campuses spread west and east of Durham, with great stone buildings and acres of grass and woods seeming to be enough for a huge student population. In fact, everything is large except the student body. Enrollment is in the neighborhood of 10,000 students, most of whom have to walk a lot to cover the large distances. The campuses are called, appropriately enough, East Campus and West Campus. You get to East Campus by following the signs from US 15/501 Bypass to NC 751 onto Duke University Road. The Georgian buildings of the original college are here.

To get to West Campus, take the Hillsborough Road exit from I-85 and go east on Main Street. On the West Campus the massive Gothic *Duke University Chapel* dominates (919-684-2572; chapel.duke.edu). James Duke, founder of the university, planned it that way. In March 1925, when he was walking the woods that have become West Campus, he designated the highest ground as the chapel site, saying that he wanted the central building of the campus to be "a great towering church" so dominating that it would have a spiritual influence on the young students who studied there. This edifice is worth a visit.

Horace Trumbauer of Philadelphia, who designed Duke's mansion on Fifth Avenue in New York, was the chapel's architect. The chief designer was Julian Able, the first black architect graduated from the department of architecture at the University of Pennsylvania.

Duke chose to have the church built of gray stone from a quarry in nearby Hillsborough. The result is a Gothic church patterned after the original Canterbury Cathedral. A 210-foot tower soars skyward, housing a 50-bell carillon. A 5,000-pipe organ was built into the rear of the nave several decades after the chapel's construction.

The organ, designed by Dirk Andries Flentrop of Holland, is based on an 18th-century organ of classical design, constructed of solid wood and using no electricity except to power the blower. It was built in Holland, where it was played to ensure its quality. It was then totally dismantled, with each pipe wrapped separately, and shipped to Duke University. After the organ's first official use at Christmas 1976, one critic wrote that the organ "breathes music." In daylight the red, green, and gold trim on its mahogany seems to combine with the glow of its 5,000 long, slender pipes.

Sunlight streams through 77 stained-glass windows. These and the ornamental lead and gold symbols in the doors of the building were designed and created by G. Owen and Bonawit, Inc., of New York.

Instead of kings and saints at the portals, the chapel memorializes Protestant heroes such as Luther and John Wesley, and historic figures Thomas Jefferson and Robert E. Lee.

James Duke, his brother Benjamin, and their father Washington are entombed in a small memorial chapel. Statues, showing all three men lying comfortably pillowed and gracefully draped, are carved in marble atop their tombs beneath the windows. The chapel is open daily from 8 a.m. to 10 p.m. during the academic year, and until 8 p.m. in summer. Don't plan on Saturday or Sunday afternoon visits without calling ahead, because these times are popular for weddings, funerals, and special events when visitors are not welcome. Interdenominational worship services are at 11 a.m. on Sun.

Also on the West Campus, the **Sarah P. Duke Memorial Gardens** (426 Anderson St.; 919-684-3698; gardens.duke.edu) have lots of open grass for kids to romp on and paths through wooded areas, as well as all kinds of seasonal flowers, a gazebo, and a lily pond. The 55 acres feature more than 2,000 kinds of plants, including the Blomquist Garden of Native Plants and the Asiatic Arboretum. Admission is free.

Another stop to feed your fascination with natural science is the **Museum of Life and Science & Magic Wings Butterfly House** (433 Murray Ave.; 919-220-5429; ncmls.org). Spread over 84 acres, the museum has a variety of science and nature displays, including a mock-up of the *Apollo 15* and a nature center with native animals. A train ride through the outdoor park gives you a chance to see everything from bears and wolves to farm animals. And the tropical butterfly house, the largest museum butterfly house east of the Mississippi, features species from Asia, Africa, and Central and South America. Open from 10 a.m. to 5 p.m. Mon through Sat, noon to 5 p.m. Sun March 14 to Sept 12; mid Sept to March, Tues through Sat, 10 a.m. to 5 p.m., Sun noon to 5 p.m. Closed New Year's Day, Thanksgiving, and Christmas. Admission is $16 for adults, $14.00 for senior citizens, and $11.00 for children ages 3 to 12, 2 and under free. Miniature train ride is $2.75 extra.

Two attractions in Durham pay homage to the role of African Americans in the region. **Hayti Heritage Center** (804 Old Fayetteville St.; 919-683-1709; hayti .org) features works and artifacts of African Americans, visual arts galleries, and dance and community meeting spaces. Both contemporary and traditional art, by local, regional, and national African-American artists, is on display. Hayti was once a focal African-American marketplace with thriving neighborhoods. The center is downtown, easy to find by taking Expressway 147 to exit 12. Hours of operation vary so call ahead before your visit. **St. Joseph's AME Church,** at 804 Old Fayetteville St., was one of the first autonomous African-American churches in America. The church was originally the sanctuary for St. Joseph's AME Church, which was begun in 1869. Phone and website are the same as Hayti Heritage Center.

Historic Stagville (5825 Old Oxford Hwy.; 919-620-0120; stagville.org) is a center for African-American studies and a place to learn about African-American

BETTER-KNOWN ATTRACTIONS
IN THE UPPER PIEDMONT

RALEIGH

North Carolina State Capitol

(919) 733-4994

WINSTON-SALEM

Old Salem

(336) 721-7300

(888) 653-7253

plantation life, culture, and society before the Civil War. Historic Stagville has an 18th-century plantation house, part of which contains offices, with the rest open to the public. Four slave houses and an 1860 barn are on the property as well. Displays and research here emphasize the various cultures from which the slaves came, forming a new African-American culture in which self-reliance flourished. The barn, for instance, was built by master-craftsmen carpenters: slaves. Research here also demonstrates that there was more to the lives of the slaves than working all day for the master, although they certainly did that. But in their own community and homes, they also cultivated vegetable gardens, participated in athletic events, and took part in community affairs. Artifacts found on the property suggest that slaves brought from various parts of Africa kept some of their traditions and secret religious practices, which they used to create a new African-American culture. Some paranormal investigators have visited here to look into various reports of ghostly sightings. Historic Stagville is open from 10 a.m. to 5 p.m. Tues through Sat. Admission is free.

While you're in the Triangle, take a picnic to the ***B. Everett Jordan Lake,*** a 47,000-acre lake created by the US Army Corps of Engineers for flood control. All water recreation is available at some part of the lake—boating, swimming, and fishing—as well as hiking and camping. As you drive around in the area, you'll probably notice several different roads, all marked with signs, leading into access areas. One is US 64 at NC 51, which leads to several recreation areas. Another is off US 64 going north on US 15/501, a point southwest of Durham, which takes you from Pittsboro, through Bynum and into Chapel Hill, home of the ***University of North Carolina at Chapel Hill.*** Chapel Hill and Durham are so close together that residents frequently live in one community and work in the other. The area south of Chapel Hill is still fairly rural and is a popular living area for university people with an itch to rusticate.

About 8 miles south of Chapel Hill, on US 15/501, just outside the community of Pittsboro, you'll find one of the most unusual examples of gentrified rural living imaginable. ***Fearrington Village,*** built around what used to be a barn, silo, farmhouse, and a few outbuildings, now comprises an inn with 33 rooms, a restaurant, several smaller eating places featuring everything from beer and wine tastings to wood fired pizza, a series of shops, a residential area with town houses and freestanding homes, and such services as a pharmacy, bank, and beauty shop. It really is a village—an upscale one—in the middle of perennial gardens and fields dotted with cows. Not just any cows, of course: Scottish Belted Galloway cows, black at both ends and white in the middle, like walking Oreo cookies. Nobody milks these cows or eats them. They're pets. Or stage setting.

More than 25 years ago, R. B. and Jenny Fitch bought the Fearrington family dairy farm and started work on a planned community here. They didn't tear down existing buildings, and they built new ones to fit in unobtrusively. For instance, the granary became the market, deli, and cafe. The old milking barn houses a home-and-garden shop. The Potting Shed, in the old corncrib, sells plants propagated from the Fearrington gardens.

Living here isn't for anybody with shaky finances, and neither is staying at **Fearrington House Inn,** with rates running to several hundred dollars a night. The prices at the **Fearrington House Restaurant** and the smaller eateries, however, are comparable to those in restaurants anywhere.

Activities such as touring the gardens, which are wonderful, are free. And you can browse in McIntire's, a good independent bookstore, shop for wine and gourmet treats, pick up handmade pottery and jewelry, and perhaps attend a reading by a well-known author in the renovated barn.

For more information about food, lodging, and activities in Fearrington Village, call (800) 316-3829; fearrington.com.

The town of **Pittsboro** is worth wandering through, too. It has lots of antiques shops and the kinds of stores that cater to people fixing up old houses, as well as a natural foods store and several restaurants. This is the kind of place where "real" farmers still mix on the sidewalks with men in Bermuda shorts and Birkenstocks.

The earliest settlers of this area were families who moved from the plantations on the coast to get away from the humid summer heat and the illnesses that came with it. The town of Pittsboro was formed in 1787. The early buildings were modest frame structures, but the new courthouse in 1843 was the first brick building. For a small town, Pittsboro had a lot of activity. Crowds gathered to see a Confederate statue unveiled, a murderer hanged, and President Theodore Roosevelt coming through. When electricity came in 1922, people danced in the street. This and a good bit more about the town's history is detailed in an outstanding little brochure, "Pittsboro Historic District," which includes a map of local structures and short paragraphs about their history. Most of the stores and restaurants in town have copies.

Another brochure, "Chatham County," also free in the stores, suggests a self-guided walking tour that begins at the present courthouse. The courthouse is at the center of a highway circle typical of many small Southern towns, with shops and restaurants lining the circle as well as streets radiating out from the curve.

A brochure called "Historic Pittsboro Antiques Walk" maps antiques, collectibles, and memorabilia shops within easy walking distance.

A potter, Lyn Morrow, has a shop and studio just 5 miles north of Pittsboro on US 15/501 that is a "must stop" if you enjoy places that are offbeat but still deal in quality. ***Lyn Morrow Pottery*** is located inside a house she's painted in cobalt blues and turquoise. Assorted metal sculptures stand around the front yard. Lyn says people sometimes wonder why she painted her house in such psychedelic colors, but when you see her pottery, you understand. It's not remotely psychedelic, but blue and turquoise are her predominant colors, and in that way her pottery stands out from that of other potters whose work she sells. She's been a potter for more than 34 years and not only knows her craft but also knows all the potters in a wide region as well. Lyn Morrow Pottery is open Tues through Sat 10 a.m. to 5 p.m., Sun 12:30 to 5 p.m. (919-545-9078; lynmorrowpottery.com).The attractions and people of this Pittsboro area reflect its proximity to Chapel Hill and the influence it has on the area.

Chapel Hill, almost the geographical center of North Carolina, is recognizably a college town, the kind in which the campus and the town meet at a wall running along the campus green, where students sit on the wall to see and be seen, and where the businesses across the street are mostly campus-oriented. Visitors actually tour the campus, less because of its history than because it is so Norman Rockwellish, sort of an artist's conceptualization of a campus, with trees and grass and historic buildings—even some ivy here and there.

Franklin Street, running along the edge of the university campus and bordering the town, is where town and gown come together. Local people pride themselves on having prevented the street from turning into nothing more than a row of souvenir shops, as has happened in many college towns. Lindsay Chappell, writing for *Images Magazine,* said, "If you could stand at one end of Franklin Street and see all the way to the other, you'd pretty much be glimpsing the soul of Chapel Hill." Along this street you find art galleries, coffeehouses, restaurants, beer spots, and shops. ***Crook's Corner*** (610 W. Franklin St.; 919-929-7643; crookscorner.com) seems to serve townspeople, students, and visitors in about equal numbers. The restaurant's signature dish is shrimp and grits. The restaurant offers a huge variety of beers. Crook's Corner is such an institution in town that people plan to go there for celebrations of all kinds, from family reunions to graduations to winning prizes in contests.

The chef, for more than a decade, has been Bill Smith, who looks as though he enjoys food but does not appear particularly cheflike, even in costume, so perhaps it was inevitable that he publish *Seasoned in the South: Recipes from Crook's Corner and from Home*. It's a compilation of his recollections about people in Chapel Hill, famous people who've visited the restaurant, advice on cooking, and recipes. This is the kind of book one can enjoy reading, whether intending to cook or not. And if you eat at Crook's, it's good to know that the spectacular banana pudding gets some of its glory from a large amount of butter. Open for dinner beginning at 5:30 p.m. Tues through Sun, brunch Sun 10:30 a.m. to 2 p.m.

A couple of blocks away, **Carolina Brewery** (460 W. Franklin St.; 919-942-1800; carolinabrewery.com) claims the title of Chapel Hill's first microbrewery and serves contemporary American fare, including many dishes made with beer. Carolina Brewery was named "best brewpub in the Southeast" one year. Carolina Brewery is open Wed through Thurs 11 a.m. to midnight, Fri and Sat to 1 a.m., Sun 11 a.m. to 11 p.m. Chapel Hill is known for the quantity and quality of its arts and crafts, not just in the retail arena but also in its programs at the University of North Carolina and in the university's **Ackland Art Museum** (101 S. Columbia St.) at the corner of Columbia and Franklin Streets. The museum claims its collection of Asian art is the most significant in North Carolina. Other exhibits in the museum show collections of Indian and Western

The Only True, Authentic, Genuine Corn Bread

This is wisdom from true, authentic, genuine Southerners: If it's sweet, it isn't corn bread. If it's fluffy, it isn't corn bread. If it wasn't baked in an iron skillet, it isn't corn bread. And if it's made with yellow, rather than white, cornmeal, it probably isn't corn bread.

Recipes for Southern corn bread vary little. They call for cornmeal (preferably white), egg, buttermilk or sour milk, and baking powder and baking soda mixed together; this is poured into a hot skillet where a generous portion of fat has melted, and it is baked in a hot oven. Lard used to be the fat of choice; these days it's butter. This produces a round of corn bread that is crisp on the outside and moist inside. One of the best ways to eat it is with a bowl of pinto beans, a slice of raw sweet onion, and a glass of sweet tea.

As for that soft stuff that has flour and sugar mixed in with the other ingredients, Scott Lewis, one of the authors of *The Gift of Southern Cooking,* says, "That's a Yankee thing."

They Won't Eat People

Several of North Carolina's botanical gardens grow a variety of carnivorous plants. The more you see of them, the more fascinating they become in their shapes and colors and growth patterns. The common Venus fly trap you find mixed in with houseplants in retail stores doesn't begin to suggest the differences of these exotic plants. If you get interested in them as you tour gardens, North Carolina horticulturists sometimes suggest the book *The Savage Garden* by Peter D'Amato. It is packed with pictures and information about the different species, where to get them, how to grow them, and (if you really get hooked) how to propagate them.

art, as well as pottery and wood carvings, two areas especially intrinsic to the state. The entire collection totals more than 17,000 pieces, including a broad representation of the history of European painting and sculpture, with works by Rubens, Delacroix, Degas, and Pissarro. African and Asian art are also well represented. The museum is open Wed through Sat 10 a.m. to 5 p.m., Sun 1 to 5 p.m. Admission is free (919-966-5736; ackland.org).

Right next door to the Ackland, students, faculty, and visiting artists in the university's art program exhibit their work in **Hanes Art Center.** Admission is free. Call (919) 962-2015 for hours.

The **North Carolina Botanical Garden** (100 Old Mason Farm Rd. off US 15/501 Bypass) is one of the largest natural botanical gardens in the Southeast, with 600 acres of land that includes nature trails, aquatic plants, herbs, and a surreal-looking collection of carnivorous plants, some of which make the Venus fly trap look mundane. Collections of regional plants are arranged in settings to simulate their natural habitat. The gardens are open weekdays from 8 a.m. to 5 p.m., Sat 9 a.m. to 5 p.m., Sun 1 to 5 p.m. During daylight savings time months, the gardens are open an hour later. Admission is free. Call 919-962-0522; ncbg.unc.edu.

Make a quick 12-mile side trip north on NC 86 to **Hillsborough,** where a lot of history is condensed in a small area. Hillsborough was a capital of colonial and revolutionary North Carolina and a center of politics. During the Revolution Cornwallis's troops grouped for deployment here. The state convention to ratify the federal Constitution met here in 1788; in 1865 the Confederate general who signed the surrender in the Civil War headquartered here. Colonial, antebellum, and Victorian architecture mingle comfortably along the streets. The Hillsborough Historical Society likes to say that the town is a living, not a reconstructed, community.

Everybody Celebrates

The first Sunday in December, the community celebrates the *Christmas Candlelight Tour,* which begins at the Alexander Dickson House. People of all ages help get ready for it. A volunteer inside the Dickson House jokes about being almost as old as the building. Outside, volunteers have lined the walkway with luminaria, and a little boy who can't be more than a year or two old is carefully inserting a candle into each holder, while his parents and their friends watch and help.

As you drive toward the town, no matter which way you take, your first reaction is going to be that this guidebook has made some kind of mistake, because you'll be driving past all the standard convenience stores, fast-food restaurants, and grocery chains that ring most communities these days. But keep going, because moving on into town is kind of like discovering Brigadoon.

The town has become more aggressive about advertising to attract tourists in the past few years. One of the town's ads says it is "an easy day trip from just about anywhere." This is true, but Hillsborough is also rather removed from other attractions in the area, sitting, as it does, almost at the Virginia border.

To pick up a map for a walking tour, stop at the *Orange County Visitor Center,* 150 E. King St. You can also get information about shops, museums, and restaurants in the area.

The visitor center is in the *Alexander Dickson House,* an 18th-century farmhouse with marvelous woodwork. The small rooms remind you that people lived in this area without grandiose mansions. One room has a fireplace of brick and slate, the floors are pine, and the walls are painted in subdued blue and cream shades. Because you're in the South, you're inevitably going to get a bit of Confederate lore here. The Dickson House was the last headquarters of the commander of the largest Confederate armies to surrender to the Union. The house does not stand in its original location, which was at the southwest intersection of what are now I-85 and NC 86. The Hillsborough Preservation Fund bought the house and the outbuilding General Wade Hampton had used as an office and moved them a mile and a quarter to the center of town.

Part of the charm of the house and the town is that the preservation and activities seem to be family affairs, with people of all ages involved in taking care of the area, planning tours and special events, and greeting tourists. In Hillsborough, historic preservation doesn't feel like a stuffy look back so much as an ongoing community activity.

A good example of this is the garden and courtyard outside the Dickson House, maintained by volunteers. *Helen's Garden* was dedicated in 1990 in the name of Helen Blake Watkins and her late husband, who moved to Hillsborough in 1956 and contributed to local landscaping and preservation projects. After her husband died, Helen donated land she owned as the new site for the Dickson House. A Chapel Hill landscaper designed the garden to show plants that were typically used for food and medicine, with something growing almost all year long. Even in December a few blue flowers bloom, Carolina jessamine climbs across the roof of the outbuilding, and rosemary grows as high as a tall man. Crows circle lazily overhead as though they are watching over the garden. The garden is free and open to the public every day. Visitor center hours are Mon through Sat 10 a.m. to 4 p.m., Sun noon to 4 p.m. Admission is free (919-732-7741; historichillsborough.org).

Montrose Gardens (320 St. Mary's Rd.; 919-732-7787; visitnc.com/listing -montrose-gardens) is a nationally known complex of gardens that Governor William Alexander Graham and his wife, Susan Washington Graham, began in the mid-19th century. In addition to gardens for sun-loving plants, you'll find a rock garden and a woodland garden.

Another interesting site in Hillsborough is the *Burwell School Historic Site* (319 North Churton St.; 919-732-7451; burwellschool.org). The house and outbuildings were built about 1821 and served as a school for women—they called it a "female school" back then. The house includes furnishings from the days when the Reverend and Mrs. Burwell lived in and ran the school there. The property has a nice formal garden as well. Admission is free.

The Hillsborough Garden Club founded the *Orange County Historical Museum* (201 N. Churchton St.), at the corner of Churchton and Tryon Streets, in the Confederate Memorial Building, to show how people lived in Orange County from the days of the Indians to the end of 1865. Mostly the museum contains local pieces, including a display of old dental instruments, a 160-year-old working loom, and an old hand-pumped organ from the local Presbyterian Church. The museum is open Tues through Sat 11 a.m. to 4 p.m., Sun 1 p.m. to 4 p.m. Admission is free. Call (919) 732-2201; historichillsborough.org.

Find more history at *Occaneechi Indian Village* (at the foot of Camerson Street, by the Eno River), a reconstructed village with huts, a cooking area, and a sweat lodge that appear as they would have from the late 1600s up to about 1710.

The reconstruction is a cooperative effort by the Occaneechi Band of the Saponi Nation, the town of Hillsborough, Orange County, and the University of North Carolina. Although the village attracts tourists, it is also a tool the tribe uses to teach the history and customs of the Occaneechi people. They lived in North Carolina in the early 1700s but moved with other small tribes to Virginia by 1710. By the 1780s, the Indian people began moving back to the Piedmont area, settling near Hillsborough to farm, hunt, and fish. The tribe reorganized in 1984 and has been working to educate its own people and their neighbors about their practices. This includes holding powwows and festivals and making presentations in schools. For more information about their activities, call (919) 732-7741 or check the website, obsn.org.

After your Hillsborough side trip, you can follow US 64 west from Pittsboro to Asheboro. This little community of something more than 16,000 is home to the ***American Classic Motorcycle Company and Museum*** (336-629-9564; heartofamerica.com), a meeting spot for Harley-Davidson enthusiasts at 1170 US 64. Proprietor Ed Rich distinguishes between enthusiasts and bikers. "The bikers, they're more the party types. The enthusiasts are into history and restoration."

Rich started collecting old Harley-Davidsons in 1971 and has been building the collection ever since, opening the museum in 1980. His is one of the largest privately owned collections in the country. The collection of more than 30 bikes fills the second floor of his store. One of his treasures is a red 1936 model El61 knucklehead, one of only two known to exist in original condition. It has the original paint and 17,000 miles on the odometer.

You don't have to know anything about Harleys to enjoy this place. It's enough to see the enthusiasm of others. Rich is like a missionary when it comes to teaching people about the world of Harleys. "A lot of heritage and history go with it," Rich says. His enthusiasm is so great that for a long time he taught a course in motorcycle restoration at the local community college. The shop and museum are open 6 a.m. to 2 p.m. Mon, 11 a.m. to 4 p.m., Tues through Sat, 1 p.m. to 4 p.m. Sun.

A larger museum to check out is the ***North Carolina Aviation Museum and Hall of Fame*** next to the Asheboro Regional Airport (2222-6 Pilotsview Rd.; 336-625-0170; ncairmuseum.org). This place probably should include something about the military in its name, because in addition to such artifacts as the 1941 Flitfire Piper flown by Orville Wright, a variety of wartime experimental and unmanned planes are included. Two hangers display all kind of weapons, vehicles, equipment, and uniforms from World Wars I and II, Korea, and Vietnam. Total museum space covers 20,000 square feet. Perhaps the most appealing aspect of the operation is that so much is always going on here, from fly-ins to visiting exhibit planes and new acquisitions. Many local people devote time and energy to the museum, which is well into its second decade. The museum is open Apr through Oct, Mon through Sat 10 a.m. to 5 p.m., and Sun 1 to 5 p.m.; fewer days and shorter hours during winter months. Admission is $10 for adults, $8 for students and veterans, $5 for students under 18, children 5 and younger free.

Time was you couldn't find much else to say about Asheboro and environs, but that's changed a lot. The once-sleepy little community is developing a lively downtown with shops for local crafts, an antiques mall, a renovated movie house from the 1930s used for local productions, and frequent installations by local artists. Much of the activity in the community is based on enthusiastic volunteers, which creates a sense of vibrancy. One amusing place is the popular restaurant **the Flying Pig** (208 Sunset Ave.; 336-610-3737; the flyingpigasheboro.com). That name derives from the fact that until 2008, Asheboro and Randolph County remained one of the few communities in the state still forbidding alcohol sales. The prohibitionists declared, "We will have alcohol in Asheboro when pigs fly." Must've happened. The Flying Pig offers all spirits, including a choice of good beers, prominently displayed against a brick wall. The varied menu here includes appetizers, pizza, sandwiches, and desserts. A limited menu offers meals for kids under 10 for $3.99. (Kids are welcome here and one said it was fun "because they really like kids.") One adult reviewer grumped that Southerners would eat hubcaps if they were fried. Indeed, lots of fried offerings are on the menu, but then so are such items as grilled chicken breast and a variety of salads. That said, two of the restaurant's signature items are Angry Okra and "pig wings." Angry okra is actually slices of jalapeño pepper deep fried and served with ranch dressing. Pig wings are pork shanks basted with a sweet barbecue sauce. One zany item that will appeal to folks who collect T-shirts in their travels—a T-shirt with, you guessed it, a picture of a pig with wings, The Flying Pig is open Mon and Thurs, 5 p.m. to 11 p.m., Fri 5 p.m. to 1 a.m., Sat noon to 1 a.m., Sun noon to 11 p.m.

The Isom family offers an opportunity to visit their family farm at **Millstone Creek Orchards** (506 Parks Crossroads Church Rd., Ramseur; 336-824-5263; www.millstonecreekorchards.com). Their crops start with berries in early June and continue with peaches and apples into autumn. You can participate in activities here as much or as little as you wish. You can pick you own fruit or buy it from the Apple Barn farm store. You can simply walk along the nature paths on the acreage and enjoy being away from traffic and noise. In any case, we're not talking about a single kind of apples or berries or peaches. Each is produced in several varieties as their season progresses. Even if you pick your own, the store is worth a visit too. Here you can find everything from fresh, unpasturized apple cider made without preservatives and eat-on-the-spot apple slushies made from the cider to a fabulous apple cake made with pecans and coconut and finished with a buttermilk glaze. Special events at the farm are scheduled each year after the season opens. During the peak season, Sept and Oct, admission of $8.00 is charged. Kids under two free. The farm is closed

Monday and Tuesday. open Wed through Sat 9 a.m. to 5 p.m., Sun 1 p.m. to 5 p.m.

The Pottery Gateway

For an experience with all kinds of native and exotic animals go to the south side of Asheboro on US 220, where signs and arrows direct you to the ***North Carolina Zoological Park.*** The zoo (800-488-0444; nczoo.org) is big, set on more than 1,000 acres, though not all are being used yet. It's famous, and it's certainly not far off the beaten path. Go anyway. It got to be big and famous because they're doing such a good job with the concept of keeping the animals in natural environments without bars. Sometimes a natural gulf separates the people from the animals, sometimes a clear barrier. For instance, the aviary, under a glass dome, houses hundreds of exotic birds along with thousands of tropical plants. In other sections you can watch elephants, herds of antelope, and even crocodiles, all apparently blissfully unaware of an audience or confinement. In 2010, the zoo had more than 1,000 animals and 60,000 plants in exhibits ranging from tropical to native.

If you are traveling with an eye to understanding the state of North Carolina, the North Carolina Streamside exhibit is special. It depicts the wildlife and habitat from the mountains to the coast in a series of displays with everything from fish and snakes to otters splashing in a pool. Seeing everything involves walking a couple of miles or more, but for a modest fee you can ride in a tram that follows the same route as the footpaths. Admission to the park itself is $15 for adults; $13 for senior citizens; $11 for children 2 to 12. Open daily from 9 a.m. to 5 p.m. Apr through Oct. Closed an hour earlier in winter. Closed on Christmas Day.

East of the zoo, 5 miles from Asheboro at 2728 Fairview Farm Rd., the ***Richland Creek Zipline Canopy Tour*** offers a view of the area from an entirely different perspective—zipping along suspended from a mile of cable line along Richland Creek above the forest at the base of Purgatory Mountain. Okay, there's no path, so it isn't beaten, but the adventure is becoming more popular. The operation emphasizes safety and provides guides, but it's definitely not for everyone. If you're scared of heights, don't even think about it. You have to be in good health without joint problems, not pregnant, and weigh between 45 and 270 pounds. You can't wear open-toe sandals or very short shorts. Everyone must wear helmets, which are provided, though you are welcome to bring your own. This experience isn't cheap, either: $40 for adults and $30 for children under 12, though some group rates are available. Payment by check or cash, no credit cards. Phone (336) 629-9440 for reservations. For a more detailed sense of the activity visit richlandcreekzipline.com. Open 7 days a week, 9 a.m. to 6 p.m., weather permitting.

Pisgah Covered Bridge, one of only two left in North Carolina, spans a branch of the Little River. Located on US 220 in the little community of Pisgah, the area also has hiking trails, picnic tables, and parking. It's an ideal setting for taking pictures, too. The fifty-four-foot-long bridge was built in 1911 in an era when horse and wagon transportation was common for the massive sum of $40. The bridge was damaged in 2003 but has been renovated. It is open daily from dawn to dusk (800-626-2672; pisgahcoveredbridge.com).

You could spend all day at the zoo. The amount of time you spend at the aviation museum or the Zipline canopy tour depends on your level of enthusiasm—part of a day, perhaps. But the next attraction, ***Seagrove*** and the potteries, could take a week.

The Asheboro area has at least half a dozen motels from which you could make an easy jog to Seagrove. Or you could stay right in the Seagrove community.

The ***Duck Smith House Bed and Breakfast*** (465 N. Broad St.; 336-873-7099 or 888-869-9018; ducksmithhouse.com) is a fully restored 1914 farmhouse with a fireplace and it is furnished with antiques and original artwork. It's owned and run by two sisters, Barbara and Suzanne Murphy. It has 4 guest rooms, each with private bath, and serves a luxurious breakfast as part of the rate. Although the setting is semirural, the house is just about a half mile, walking distance, from the center of town, so you can visit several potteries without driving anywhere.

Another place to stay combines a pottery with a bed and breakfast. ***Seagrove Stoneware Inn and Pottery*** at 136 W. Main St. (336-707-9124; seagrovestoneware.com) has 3 guest rooms as well as a guest kitchen (a rare convenience). Rates include a full breakfast. The B&B is decorated with pottery from around the country and showcases the work of proprietors Alexa Modderno and David Fernandez. The two work in different pottery styles, one or the other bound to be a want maker for folks who love hand turned pottery. The gallery offers opportunities for you to try your hand with the clay yourself. It's a whole lot harder to do than the professionals make it look. Gallery hours are 10 a.m. to 5 p.m. Mon through Sat, 11 a.m. to 4 p.m. Sun. You may be able to visit at other times by calling for an appointment.

The ***North Carolina Pottery Center*** (233 E. Ave., at the junction of US 220 and NC 705) has exhibits that trace the history and development of North Carolina pottery from the prehistoric Native Americans to the contemporary turners, with more than 200 items. One large display showing the current work of more than 90 potters in the area will give you a sense of what each produces so you can search for those that appeal to you and skip those not to your personal taste. The center is open 10 a.m. to 4 p.m. Tues through Sat. If the weather is bad enough to close county schools, the center is closed, too. Also closed major holidays. Admission is $2 for adults, $1 for students in grades 9 to 12, free for students from kindergarten to grade 8. This is a good place to pick up maps and brochures showing pottery locations. Call (336) 873-8430 for information or visit ncpotterycenter.org.

Also on US 220 in Seagrove, **_Seagrove Family Restaurant_** (8702 US 220 South; 336-873-7789) serves breakfast, sandwiches, salads, and such dinner items as hamburger steak with cheese and grilled onions, baked ham, and fried chicken. If a local friend wanted to buy you lunch, this is where you'd probably end up, and if you wanted the most popular item on the menu, when it's available, you'd order the fried chicken. Or you could have liver and onions, a rare offering in restaurants. Open Mon, Wed, and Sat 5:30 a.m. to 2 p.m., Thurs and Fri 5:30 a.m. to 8 p.m.

Before you start, accept the fact that it's physically impossible to stop at every pottery in one day. It was impossible a few years ago when they numbered less than 40; now that there are approximately 100, your only alternatives are to choose your stops selectively or to plan several trips. New places open regularly, so don't limit your stops to those mentioned here.

The people whose job it is to promote tourism in the area have all but thrown up their hands in despair over keeping up with the growing number of potteries or with trying to tell you when they are open. As a representative for Randolph County Tourism puts it, "If somebody decides to go to the beach for a week, they just close down and go."

This is not true of all the potteries; many run thoroughly professional businesses with enough staff to keep things going even during vacations. But as Dan Triece of DirtWorks Pottery explains, potters in the area these days fall into roughly three groups: those open 7 days a week, those open 5 days a week (usually Tues through Sat), and those who operate on weekends. The weekend potters generally have other jobs and throw pots as a hobby.

Up Close

The North Carolina mystery writer **Margaret Maron** wrote _Uncommon Clay,_ a mystery novel set in Seagrove that gives you a good idea of how the people of the community relate to each other and their work. She spent a lot of time here to learn about the potting world, and although her story is fiction, the kinds of rivalries and friendships she describes really do exist.

Seagrove's best-known annual event is the ***Seagrove Pottery Festival,*** sponsored as a fund-raiser by the Museum of North Carolina Traditional Pottery. Each year on a Saturday and Sunday in mid-November, the festival includes an auction of signed and dated limited-edition pottery by local potteries, as well as booths by local potters and other traditional crafters, who demonstrate, display, and sell their wares. In true Tar Heel tradition, the festival provides lots of pork barbecue and chicken, too. For exact dates, phone (336) 873-7887.

A second big event is the annual ***Seagrove Winterfest,*** in mid-February. This is when most pottery shops have taken a rest after the Christmas rush and have their shelves restocked. Then potteries often introduce their new shapes, glazes, and colors. For more information, call (336) 873-7887.

Originally this part of the country attracted production potters who made the storage jugs, pitchers, crocks, and bean pots farmers used every day, because both the heavy red clay for potting and the timber stands for fueling the kilns were right here. No doubt local moonshine was one of the products that got stored in the jugs. A rich culture developed around potting, complete with family traditions in design and glazing. As other materials came along for making utensils to cook and store food, the potters turned more to producing items for tourists. But the actual potting stayed basically the same. Over three and four generations, feuds and disagreements came up, and sometimes a member of a famous potting family would splinter off to start an independent pottery.

The old families continue making the same kinds of pottery today. Tourists and gift shop owners buy it up faster than the wheels can turn.

Newcomers fill out the scene with more artistic studio pottery, which is usually more elaborately shaped, decorated, and glazed. These pieces take longer to make.

Some of the new potters are local young people who have studied in the well-respected program at Troy Technical College nearby. Others, transplants from elsewhere, have been attracted by the concentration of potters that draws customers and ensures support. It would be wrong to say that all new potters make studio pottery and all old-timers practice production pottery, however. You'll find a good bit of crossover. The best thing to do is simply look at the work, talk to the potters, and make your choices.

Many of the materials these days are shipped in from elsewhere rather than dug from local ground, and some kilns are fired by oil, gas, or electricity rather than wood. But the atmosphere is still that of a unique culture engrossed in a hands-on kind of work.

Wherever you stop, talk to the people. They're used to it, they like it, and it's an integral part of the experience. As you do, you can't help noticing the arthritic hands of some of the old potters. As a younger artisan explained it, "My pots will never be quite as good as theirs, because you need to keep wetting the clay with cold water for the very best results, and I use warm water. I've seen what 20 and 30 years of cold water and clay does to your hands. I'm afraid I'm not quite that dedicated."

A good way to understand the possibilities in the potting community before you begin is by visiting the **North Carolina Pottery Center,** at the junction of US 220 and NC 705 (see complete listing on p. 83). Brochures and maps are available here as well as displays of more than 200 items.

The largest concentration of potteries begins on NC 705, off US 220. The state road numbers are clearly marked, so it is easy to follow the map through the countryside, traveling from one pottery to another. No two are alike, nor are their wares. Part of the fun is in the discovery and surprise; you don't need full information ahead of time about each place, but the following are a few guaranteed to be special. They are all marked on the free maps, which are available at every pottery as well as the Pottery Center. The following listing is far from complete but gives you an idea of the various kinds of work done by some of the established potters. To see more information about any pottery that does not have a website listed here, go to discoverseagrove.com/nc-potters.

Phil Morgan Pottery (966 NC 705; 336-873-7304; seagrovepotteries.com) features Phil's elegant crystalline glazes on porcelain and his wife's more traditional earthenware, much of it in pleasing muted rose and blue tones and decorated with flowers.

Potts Pottery (630 E. Main St.; 336-873-9660) is a newer endeavor by Jeff and Linda Potts. Linda's grandmother was a Cole—the Potts say they represent the ninth generation of Coles, famous traditional folk potters. They use local clay and produce traditional earthenware tableware and serving pieces. Some of the glazes, especially the blue, resemble those of the old Cole pottery, but you will see differences in sheen.

Ben Owen Pottery (2233 S NC 705; 336-879-2262 or 910-464-2261; ben-owenpottery.com) displays the work of Ben Owen III, who was recognized as a boy for having superior talent, on a par with that of his grandfather. Young Ben works as an artist, producing shapes and designs inspired by Egyptian and Japanese work. His pots are on display in museums around the country. The Owen family has been famous for its bright red glazes.

At **Westmoore Pottery** (4622 Busbee Rd.; 910-464-3700; westmoorepot tery.com), open since 1977, Mary and David Farrell make reproductions of the earthenware and salt-glazed stoneware typical of the 18th and early 19th centuries. They also make stunning reproductions of Moravian pottery as well as create new designs in the old traditions. The couple and the pottery have received national attention in more than one country-oriented magazine for their work. It is especially popular with people involved in authentic historic restoration and representation.

The people at *Cady Clay Works* (3883 Busbee Rd.; 910-464-5661; cady clayworks.com), John Mellage and his wife, Beth Gore, produce wood-fired pieces with vibrant colors and contemporary designs. They usually have some spectacular, extra-large bowls that are surprisingly lightweight for their size.

DirtWorks Pottery (1226 NC 705; 336-873-8979; www.giftedpottery.com/ pottery-by-artist/dirtworks-pottery) is the permanent showroom of Dan Triece. Triece has won awards in the Southeast, especially for his copper luster raku. The shop carries woodcrafts, basketry, jewelry, and other North Carolina crafts as well as work by other regional potters.

Turn and Burn (124 East Ave.; 336-873-7381; turnandburnpottery.com) produces a variety of pots, including horsehair and shino, a glaze from Japan notable for having a high feldspar content and being unpredictable in the kiln. David Garner, who says he grew up so surrounded by the craft he can't remember the first time he saw a pot made, has been potting for more than 20 years.

Milly McCanless and her husband, Al, started *Dover Pottery* (321 Dover Pottery Dr.; 910-464-3586; doverpots.com) early in the 1980s. She is a first-generation potter who got into it because she had a dollhouse and wanted to make dishes for her miniature dining table. Then she discovered she was good at throwing big pots, too, and realized there was a much better market for them than for miniatures.

The Poole family owns and operates *Rockhouse Pottery* (1792 NC 705 South; 336-879-2053; www.visitnc.com/listing/rockhouse-pottery) specializing in hand-carved pottery, Tar Heel (North Carolina) themes, stoneware, saltware, and large and small planters.

At *Whynot Pottery* (1013 Fork Creek Mill Rd.; 336-873-9276; whynotpottery .com) you'll find stoneware in a variety of contemporary shapes and glazes, pieces that are especially well balanced.

Jugtown (330 Jugtown Rd.; 910-464-3266; jugtownware.com) operates somewhat more commercially than the other potteries, including handwoven rugs and placemats, handmade toys, and other North Carolina folk crafts in its retail stock. Jugtown has been operating since 1920. The Jugtown stoneware is uniform enough in appearance to look nice beside the more regular, mass-produced commercial dinnerware and seems practically indestructible. There is a bathroom here, too. That may seem like a small thing, in the abstract, but after you've spent some time driving these country roads where you don't find pit stops every few miles, it's something to appreciate.

Bruce and Janice Latham, at *Latham's Pottery* (2 miles north of Seagrove on Alternate 220; 336-873-7303; www.latham'spottery.com) produce traditional functional pottery, including canister sets, bowls, and pitchers, much of it in the popular bright blue glaze sometimes referred to locally as "market blue."

Tom Gray Pottery (1480 Fork Creek Mill Rd.; 336-873-8270; clay.com/tgp) specializes in what Tom calls "pots for rituals—the most important of which is putting our feet under the table with family and friends." In other words, he makes items for preparing, serving, and eating food.

Although some early glazes contained lead, today's are lead-free and safe for table use. If you have any concerns about lead, ask in the pottery.

The hours of the various potters may vary by a half-hour or so in opening and closing, but most are open from 8:30 a.m. to 4:30 p.m. Tues through Sat. Many are closed all day Sun, though some open Sun afternoon. The best time to go is Friday afternoon, after most of the kilns are opened on Thursday to bring out the new pots. Saturday morning is a good time, too, but by afternoon the wares will already be thinning out.

For a broad overview of potteries in the area, check visitrandolphcounty.com.

Heartland

Another possible trip from Asheboro is the short hop up US 220 to *Greensboro,* a pleasant city with a historic downtown and lots of surprises. There's some Revolutionary War history here, in a strange sort of way. Cornwallis won a battle against General Nathanael Greene's American troops, but in the process he lost so many men that he ultimately had to surrender at Yorktown. The *Guilford Courthouse National Military Park,* 6 miles north of Greensboro on US 220, commemorates the loss and the win with exhibits on the battlefield and displays and films in the visitor center (336-288-1776; nps.gov/guco). Hours vary seasonally. Admission is free.

Drawing on more recent events, Greensboro holds special significance for blacks. In 1960 black students from *North Carolina A & T State University* (originally the Agricultural and Mechanical College for the Colored Race) began the first sit-ins at Woolworth's segregated lunch counter. A & T is Jesse Jackson's alma mater. On the campus of North Carolina A & T State University, the *Mattye Reed African Heritage Center* displays African masks, paintings, black history books, and art objects. Open Mon through Fri 10 a.m. to 5 p.m. Closed on University holidays (336-334-7108; www.ncat.edu/cahss/departments/vpa/visual-arts/university%20galleries.html). Admission is free.

Less than 10 miles east of Greensboro, the *Charlotte Hawkins Brown Memorial State Historic Site* (336-449-4846; ah.dcr.state.nc.us) honors Dr.

Brown's 50 years as head of another school for blacks, Palmer Memorial Institute. The buildings are gradually being restored, and plans are to make the memorial a center for contributions of North Carolina blacks, including a research center with collection and computer facilities devoted to North Carolina black history. The complex includes cottages and dormitories, outdoor exhibits and trails, a visitor center in the old teacher's cottage, and a picnic area. Dr. Brown's house has been restored, and some of her original furniture reupholstered. Open Tues through Sat from 9 a.m. to 5 p.m. Closed for major holidays. Admission is free.

Local history from the time of the early Indians to date shapes the displays at the *Greensboro Historical Museum* (130 Summit Ave., Greensboro; 336-373-2043; greensborohistory.org) in what used to be the First Presbyterian Church. In a re-creation of 19th-century Greensboro, the museum displays a general store, the drugstore where William Sydney Porter (O. Henry) once worked, a post office, a law office, a firehouse, a cobbler's, and a blacksmith's.

Other exhibits include room settings from historical homes, an exhibit of household items and clothing of Dolley Madison (a Greensboro native before she became First Lady), and a collection of antique automobiles. Open Tues through Sat from 10 a.m. to 5 p.m. and Sun from 2 to 5 p.m. Closed holidays. Admission is free.

If you're traveling with kids (or even if you're not, come to think of it), don't miss the *Natural Science Center* (4301 Lawndale Dr.; 336-288-3769; natsci.org), where you can easily spend a day immersing yourself in the sights and sounds of everything from dinosaurs to star systems. This is a "participation museum," where you don't have to tell the kids "look, don't touch." For instance, you can put your hand into a real dinosaur footprint, pet and feed animals in the zoo, observe sunspots in the live solar observatory, and turn your imagination loose in the planetarium. The transparent anatomical mannequin, which you might want to save until after lunch, lets you study what goes on inside the skin of the human body. The museum is open Mon through Sun from 9 a.m. to 5 p.m. The zoo is open Mon through Sun from 9 a.m. to 4 p.m. Admission is $12.50 for adults, $11.50 for senior citizens and children 3 to 13.

When you've had enough of indoor attractions, Greensboro has four gardens worth some attention, collectively known as the *Greensboro Gardens.* The *Greensboro Arboretum, Bog Garden,* and The Tanger Family *Bicentennial Garden* feature most of the plants native to the Piedmont region. *Gateway Gardens* at 2924 East City Gate Blvd. is still a work in progress but will eventually cover eleven acres. The arboretum is on West Market Street at Lindley Park. It has nine labeled collections of indigenous species. The Bog Garden is at the corner of Hobbs Road and Starmount Farms Drive and features a variety of plants that thrive in wet areas. You don't have to worry about getting wet, though, because you follow a raised walkway through the wetlands. The Bicentennial Garden is at the corner of Cornwallis Drive and Hobbs Road. It emphasizes mass plantings of bulbs, annuals, and perennials, along with flowering trees and shrubs. Gateway Gardens, so called because of its location on East City Gate Boulevard, is also just a half mile from Business I-40 and I-85. So far one of the most popular features here is the children's garden, which includes the Heritage Garden and statues of giant carrots, frogs, and a giraffe. Admission to the gardens is free. Call (336) 373-2199 or (800) 344-2282 for more information; greensborobeautiful.org.

In a more formal setting on the campus of University of North Carolina at Greensboro, the **Weatherspoon Art Museum** is located at Spring Garden and Tate Streets (336-334-5770; weatherspoon.uncg.edu). The museum, which has six galleries and a sculpture courtyard, is nationally known for its collections of modern and contemporary art, 6,000 objects mostly created after World War II. The permanent collection includes Matisse prints and bronzes, the Dillard Collection of Art on Paper, with 500 items, and 600 Japanese woodblock prints from the 18th through the 20th centuries. The museum is open Tues, Wed, and Fri from 10 a.m. to 5 p.m., Thurs 10 a.m. to 9 p.m., Sat and Sun 1 to 5 p.m. Admission is free. The museum's website offers an excellent overview of museum holdings and samplings of work from various collections. It also details changing exhibits.

Tobacco Town

From Greensboro you're looking at a drive of only about 20 miles west on I-40 to **Winston-Salem,** the tobacco town. It would be hard to overstate the influence of the R. J. Reynolds Tobacco Company. While Richard Joshua Reynolds was directing a rapidly growing business and hiring increasing thousands of people in the tobacco factories, his wife, Katharine, set about a long series of community improvement activities for the benefit of those same families. With Reynolds money and Moravian artistic influence, the area developed into a cultural center that still ranks high in the country today.

Perhaps the most audacious Reynolds act in later years was the lock-stock-and-barrel move of Wake Forest University from Wake County to Winston-Salem in 1950. President Truman came to wield the shovel in the groundbreaking ceremony. The **Museum of Anthropology,** on the campus, is billed as the only museum devoted to the study of world cultures, covering Africa, Asia, Oceania, and the Americas. Open Tues through Sat 10 a.m. to 4:30 p.m. Closed major holidays as well as during winter break, about mid Dec to early Jan (336-758-5282; moa.wfu.edu). Admission is free, but donations are welcome.

After studying the impact of Reynolds and tobacco, turn your attention to the Moravians. Moravians came from Pennsylvania to settle the area in 1753. They built Salem as a totally planned, church-governed community in 1766. Winston wasn't founded until 1849. In Salem, arts and crafts flourished; in Winston, it was tobacco and textiles. By the early 1900s the two towns had grown together and consolidated. It would be hard to say whether tobacco or the Moravians left the greater mark on the area, nor is it really pertinent; in the early days tobacco wasn't a dirty word, and nobody saw anything wrong with a strong relationship between church and chew.

If you see only one attraction here, it certainly should be **Old Salem,** a Moravian town restored so carefully that when you walk the streets and go into the buildings, you feel as though you've entered a time warp. To give you an idea of the pains staff people take with getting it right, people responsible for demonstrations of cooking and household activities take turns preparing research papers and consulting old diaries, journals, and letters to discover exactly how the households might have run. Unlike traditional historians who mainly study battles, politics, and industrial development, these re-creators also try, as well, to piece together the elements of day-to-day life. This isn't the only historic site where such activities are going on, but it's hard to imagine one where they're being treated any more earnestly or where the subject matter is any more fascinating. This attention to detail extends even to the food cooked from old Moravian recipes. The original gingerbread recipe used fresh gingerroot, but recipes in later years have shifted to powdered ginger because it's easier to find and keep. The Old Salem recipe still specifies fresh, grated ginger. At the **Winkler Bakery,** costumed bakers make cookies and bread in a wood-fired brick oven. The baked goods are for sale.

Costumed guides in the old kitchen cook in the huge fireplace and iron with flatirons heated there, all the while sweating genuine sweat—a fascinating reminder in this age of air-conditioning that just getting from one day to the next once took a lot of energy. Among the demonstrations offered in Old Salem are music from an organ built in 1797, potting, baking, and spinning.

Not all the buildings in the historic district are restored as tour buildings. Some are private homes. The presence of automobiles and real people living real lives doesn't seem to detract from the atmosphere; indeed it simply makes it feel more alive. Whatever tours you take, start at the visitor center (336-721-7300 or 888-653-7253; oldsalem.org). Moderate to high admission fees, depending on how many features you wish to tour. Get tickets for all Old Salem tour attractions at the visitor center, open Tues through Sat 9 a.m. to 5 p.m., Sun

12:30 to 5 p.m. All hours for attractions at Old Salem may vary. Call the visitor center or check the website for specifics.

Old Salem Gardens are reputed to be the best-documented restored community garden in America. Their authenticity is possible because the Moravians kept meticulous records. Many of the gardens have been re-created on their original sites and produce the same varieties of vegetables, flowers, and herbs described in old records. The attention to horticultural detail goes beyond the garden squares to include old cultivars of fruit trees in orchards, flowering vines on fences, and native trees in the landscape.

Having toured Old Salem, you'll need to eat at the *Old Salem Tavern Dining Rooms* (736 S. Main St. in the district; 336-722-1227; thetaverninoldsalem .ws). Continuing the sense of reenactment, costumed staff serves Moravian-style cooking as well as contemporary fare. Specialties include chicken pie and gingerbread from the old recipes. All spirits are served. The restaurant is open for lunch 11 a.m. to 3:30 p.m. and dinner 5 p.m. to 9 p.m. Tues through Sat, 11 a.m. to 3 p.m. Sun. Closed Thanksgiving, Christmas Eve supper, and Christmas Day.

Also in Old Salem, the *Museum of Early Southern Decorative Arts* (336-721-7360 or 888-258-1205; mesda.org/mesda.html) gives you a close look at the results of extensive research into the regional decorative arts of the early South. The exhibits include furniture, paintings, textiles, ceramics, silver, and other metalware. You can't just wander in here. Guides take you through the building in small groups. You may buy tickets at the Old Salem Visitor Center.

You might end a day in this historic manufacturing and artistic town at *Brookstown Inn,* a restored 1837 textile mill at 200 Brookstown Ave. (336-725-1120; brookstowninn.com). The history of the inn matches that of the city for interest. Moravians opened the Salem Cotton Manufacturing Company and later sold it, and the buildings were subsequently used as a flour mill and then as a moving-company storage house. The conversion to an inn created large

The Giant Coffeepot

A tin coffeepot is incorporated into the Old Salem logo. The actual pot stands high on a pole at Main Street and Brookstown Avenue. It's more than 7 feet tall and is supposed to be big enough to hold 740 gallons of coffee. The story is that it was used in the early days for large gatherings at Moravian Love Feasts. But who could possibly have lifted it? Moreover, the thing has no bottom. Never did. It was made by a tinsmith in the 1800s as a sign to identify his shop as the original tin shop, so people wouldn't go wandering into his competitor's place.

guest rooms with odd nooks and crannies and high ceilings. An upstairs wall is covered with the graffiti (protected by an acrylic plastic sheet) of the young factory girls who boarded there. The decor is early American, with many hand-made quilts and country accents. Rates include wine and cheese in the parlor, homemade cookies and milk, and continental breakfast in the dining room.

While you are in the Winston-Salem area, take a few minutes to drive to the old **Shell gas station** at the corner of Sprague and Peachtree Streets. You'll know you're there when you come to a huge orange and red structure shaped like a seashell, with two old gas pumps standing in front. This old gas station sold Quality Oil products in the 1930s and then fell into disuse and disrepair. It had a big crack sealed with a strip of black tar, and vandals had broken windows and fixtures and littered the ground.

Sarah Woodard, who wasn't even born when the station was in its glory days, oversaw the renovation, which was completed in 1997. Almost any time you stop in, some old-timers who remember when the station was operating are apt to be standing around reminiscing about earlier times. One of them says he always thought the Shell was the prettiest thing in town—and he still does.

US 52 runs through Winston-Salem. After exploring this area, you might head north on 52 to take in **Mount Airy,** Andy Griffith's hometown. Although it is located almost at the Virginia border, and technically it is in the mountains, the drive over the Blue Ridge Mountains is slow and sometimes treacherous, so it doesn't work well to include it as a mountain attraction close to others. Knowing how to classify Mount Airy's location can be a little confusing. The National Park Service considers it part of the mountains, but the North Carolina tourism people call it part of the Piedmont. At any rate, it's only about 90 miles from Winston-Salem to Mount Airy via US 52 North. An 11-mile stretch of the route has been named **the Andy Griffith Parkway,** and about 5.5 miles of it passes through the town of Mount Airy, the place many fans of *The Andy Griffith Show* believe was the model for the fictional Mayberry. Griffith always insisted that Mayberry was not really based on Mount Airy, but it's hard to tell that to the hordes of visiting tourists, and it seems local people are starting to live the fiction, or at least to sell it. The **Andy Griffith Museum** (218 Rockford St.; 336-786-7998; andygriffithmuseum.com) opened in 2010 in a 2,500-square-foot museum that cost more than half a million dollars to build. It houses a mind-boggling number of items, from old photos and pictures to the off-white suits Griffith wore in the show *Matlock.* The keys to the jail and items from Sheriff Andy Taylor's desk sit on a replica of that desk. The chair Don Knotts used as Deputy Barney Fife in Mayberry, bronzed and autographed by cast members when Fife left the show, sits in a place of honor. While many of the artifacts have been contributed by Emmett Forrest, a schoolmate and close friend of Andy's, other items have come from the actress Betty Lynn, who played Thelma Lou on the show (and actually moved to Mount Airy in 2007) and the widow of actor Don Knotts. The museum is open Mon through Fri 9 a.m. to 5 p.m., Sat 11 a.m. to 4 p.m., Sun 1:30 to 4:30 p.m. Tickets are $3 per person.

The museum sits next to the **Andy Griffith Playhouse** at the same address and telephone number (surryarts.com), which stages a mind-boggling number and variety of life performances, from *The Taming of the Shrew* to *Hairspray*. On the lower level of the playhouse, an area is devoted to the Siamese Twins exhibit, all material about Eng and Chang Bunker, the conjoined twins who lived from 1811 until 1874. Their lives fascinate many people. They were born in Siam, now Thailand, and their fame led to the "Siamese" appellation being applied to other conjoined twins. After a career as touring celebrities in America, they settled in White Plains, just west of Mount Airy, and some local people are descendents. The **Old Time Music Heritage Hall** is also located here. It is devoted to preserving and promoting the area's old-time music, with jam sessions, dances, concerts, and free lessons for children. Close by the playhouse, **Blackmon Amphitheatre** (231 Spring St.) another Surry Arts project, has all kinds of lively activity—children's theater, bands, Christian praise, old-time music, and shag events for instance. A full schedule is available at surryarts.org or call the Surry Arts Council at (336) 786-7998 for more information.

One way to take in the town's Mayberry highlights as well as some other local history is with a squad car tour. The vehicles are Ford Galaxies, vintage replicas of Barney's patrol car. Several tour guides drive passengers around the town, narrating as they drive and pulling over at some significant locations. Each guide has developed his own patter, and they've all found details to include that you don't find in most of the material about the Mayberry–Mount Airy connection. All tours begin at **Wally's Service Station** (625 S. Main St.;

Old Time Radio Today

Tune to **740 AM, WPAQ,** a local radio station that plays bluegrass and old-time string music. Ralph Epperson first signed the station on air on Groundhog Day, 1948. His goal was to play the kinds of mountain music people in the listening area liked and played, not the stuff the other stations were cranking out, all sounding the same. It was a time when announcers talked about local activities and read the obituaries on-air. Mr. Epperson has died, but the station continues in his model (336-786-6111; wpaq740.com).

Braggin' Rights

A clerk in the Rockford General Store was trading one-liners with a customer about how small the town of Old Rockford Village is. The customer won with, "This town is so small that the person who left the porch light on last December won a prize for best Christmas decorations."

336-789-6743; tourmayberry.com), and you need to book ahead of time. The price is $30 "for a carload."

As for the town-wide **Mayberry Days,** it's hard to give a full description because the occasion keeps growing, but it's the last weekend in September. They celebrated the 21st year of the event in 2010. Or perhaps "events" would be a more accurate term, since so much goes on, including a golf tournament, parades, barbecue, gospel singing, a silent auction, celebrity appearances, and lots of music. If you don't like crowds, give it a miss, but if you're a true Mayberry fan, you'll probably enjoy it (mayberrydays.org).

But there's more to Mount Airy than fandom. **The Old Time Heritage Hall** (301 N. Main St.; 336-786-4478; oldtimeheritagehall.com) features displays related to the area's history and culture. Of course the Andy Griffith heritage is represented, but there's a lot more. Some exhibits represent life as it was before transportation made it easy for people to get in and out of the region completely surrounded by mountains. Others trace developments into more modern times. Displays arranged on three floors show home-life, children's activities, transportation, medicine, war, clothing, even broadcasting. Adults $5, senior citizens and students $3, Tues through Sat 10 a.m. to 5 p.m.

People who prefer not to think of Mount Airy as Mayberry, sometimes call their town **"the Granite City."** As you drive or walk about the community you'll notice many buildings, old and new, made of granite. Mount Airy is home to the largest open-faced quarry in the world, covering about 90 acres. It's been in full operation as a quarry since 1889, and geologists say the deposit is so deep it could continue to be worked for another 500 years. Currently it is operated by the North Carolina Granite Corporation (336-785-5141; ncgranite .com) and is producing 2,000,000 feet of granite per year. There's an observation area from which you can watch the whole quarrying process daily from 8 a.m. to 5 p.m., but something this big is visible from other spots too. To get to the observation area, take NC 103 East and go about 2 miles from downtown Mount Airy. The entrance is on the left. If you're a photography buff, the quarry is both a great opportunity and a challenge.

Now, for a taste of this area's rural life, get out your North Carolina transportation map and look at the blue highways just off US 601, south of Mount Airy. Go south on the blue highway that crosses NC 268 at Level Cross, which takes you into rural Surry County. Comparatively speaking, you might consider Mount Airy the "urban" part. Head for the little town of Dobson and **Old Rockford Village.** This is what country folk used to call a "poke and plumb" spot: Poke your head out the window as you drive, and you're plumb out of town.

The focal point here is **Rockford General Store** (5174 Rockford Rd.; 336-374-5317; rockfordgeneralstore.com). It's a hard place to define—partly touristy, partly a local source for everything from lye soap to pickled eggs and homemade fried apple pies, as well as more than 100 kinds of old-fashioned candy. The store meanders in several directions, with wooden-floored rooms filled with reminders of earlier times. Outside the store on the porch, a red wooden bench invites you to sit, and a checkerboard is set up with rocks as playing pieces, ready for anybody who wants a game. Annie Barnett, who owned the store and spent most of her time there, died in 2003. New owners have taken it over, and it remains an important part of the community. Open Wed through Sat 10 a.m. to 5 p.m., Sun noon to 5 p.m. Closed Mon and Tues.

Whether you actually go into the store or not, driving these back roads gives you a glimpse of rural North Carolina as it really is, not as parts of it have been gussied up for tourists. Driving along these two-lane macadam roads with the car windows down, you can hear a "bobwhite, bobwhite, bobwhite" bird call. The warm air in summer smells of recently cut hay, although the fields are planted mostly in corn. New orange Allis Chalmers tractors, sometimes standing right beside old ones, dot the landscape. This stretch has as many trailers as conventionally built homes, and cable TV probably doesn't come out this far, because TV satellite dishes stand in lots of yards. Here and there an old log building has been restored. Others are crumbling to the ground. Driving these miles slows you down and reminds you that not everyone lives strapped with cell phones and pagers.

You could continue rusticating for a while with a stay at **Pilot Knob Inn Bed & Breakfast** (336-325-2502; pilotknobinn.com). It's on 100 wooded acres at the base of nearby Pilot Mountain. Seven tobacco cabins, each at least 100 years old, are now luxurious guest accommodations with a whirlpool tub, fireplace, central heat and air, and kitchen area with a refrigerator, coffeemaker, and microwave oven. The main lodge has luxury suites with private entrances. A full breakfast, pretty much whatever you want, is included in the rates for cabins and suites. It's prepared in a spacious, modern kitchen and served in an equally spacious breakfast room. In warm weather you can take a dip in the swimming pool out back or walk along the private lake on the property.

The Barbecue Capital

On US 52, about 20 miles south of Winston-Salem, the town of *Lexington* is a must-stop for barbecue freaks. More than a dozen restaurants in this little town serve pork barbecue (if it's made with anything but pork it isn't really barbecue!) "Lexington style." The town has at least 20 barbecue restaurants, mostly—maybe even entirely—run by people whose families have been involved with barbecue for several generations. The first barbecue restaurant was in a tent in the middle of town, opened by Sid Weaver in 1919. Lexington barbecue is generally called "western style," though you need to be careful about what you say, because a slip of the tongue regarding barbecue in North Carolina is grounds for deportation to another country—preferably vegetarian. Authentic Lexington barbecue is made by cooking pork shoulders slowly over hickory wood fires until the meat is falling-apart tender, basting it with a "dip" of vinegar, ketchup, water, salt, and pepper. Some barbecuers may add a few other ingredients such as red pepper. As the drippings from the meat fall into the hot coals, the smoke rises to flavor the meat. Then the pork is chopped by hand to be served in sandwiches or on plates accompanied by red slaw and hush puppies. Bits of tomato make the slaw red.

Each year in the fall, the *Lexington Barbecue Festival* attracts in the neighborhood of 100,000 visitors. It's held in eight roped-off blocks of uptown Lexington and goes on with a variety of events besides eating. Check barbecue festival.com for all kinds of details about Lexington barbecue, including current dates.

Eastern barbecue, typical on the coast and for some distance inland, uses the whole hog. After roasting, not necessarily over a wood fire, the meat is pulled from the bones by hand and chopped. The baste contains no tomato, and the barbecue comes with white or yellow slaw.

Talking the Talk

When you order barbecue at any of the 20 or so barbecue restaurants in Lexington, you'll be asked if you want it chopped or sliced. The sliced barbecue, obviously, comes in bigger pieces; the chopped usually has more of the crispy crust that formed on the outside of the shoulder as it roasted. Then you must choose whether you want a sandwich, plate, or tray. A sandwich comes on a soft, white roll, with barbecue and slaw. A plate includes barbecue, slaw, french fries, and rolls or hush puppies. A tray is a small container with barbecue and slaw. All barbecue is served with "dip" on the side as additional seasoning for the meat.

Complications arise in the disagreement about which is where and which is better because, inevitably, some places began blending techniques, and it's possible to come across eastern barbecue in the western part of the state and vice versa. "Real" North Carolinians can get testy on the subject. You can plunge into huge discussions on the subject, as well as participants' recommendations for their favorite barbecue spots, simply by typing "eastern nc barbecue" and "western nc barbecue" into a Web browser.

The Furniture Capital

High Point used to be mostly about manufacturing and selling furniture. The town, already active in the lumber business, first got into furniture building in the early 1880s, when a local lumber salesman noticed the big difference between the price of wood as it left the sawmill and the price it brought once it had been shipped away and turned into furniture. Sensibly, he and two local merchants risked all they had to start a furniture company close to the source of the wood. It was the right idea in the right place at the right time. Sales took off, and the future was set. At one time, High Point had 125 furniture manufacturing companies. Most of them are gone now, as companies sent their work off shore.

A valuable museum in the High Point area is the **Springfield Museum of Old Domestic Life,** established in 1935 in the third Quaker meetinghouse of the Springfield Meeting (555 E. Springfield Rd.; 336-882-3054). Museums, like history books, tend to focus on extraordinary events, wars, and politics and not on the commonplaces of day-to-day life. This museum is an exception. Here you can inspect the artifacts of daily life that have been used in the neighborhood for 200 years or more—spinning equipment, utensils, farm items, clothing, pictures from homes, toys, and a slew of fascinating odds and ends. The curator says, "Most of what we have has been donated by local Quakers."

She likes to emphasize the items that were commonplace in their day, objects crudely made to fill an immediate need. If you didn't know the way in which many of them had been used, you probably never could figure out what they were for. Such artifacts simply cannot be replaced.

One example is the log lifter. It looks like a crutch for a giant. Log lifters were devices created to get logs from the ground to high points in the walls when building log cabins. One man stood at each end of the log with a lifter and heaved.

Another example is a homemade Noah's Ark, with all the animals, two by two. This was a Sunday toy, made during the time when children in the community weren't allowed to play on Sundays with their regular toys, or do

How the Experts Rate
North Carolina Barbecue

Blind Taste Judging

Judge No._____
Code No. _____

	Poor	Fair	Good	Very Good	Excellent
Appearance	2 4 6 8	10 12 14 16	18 20 22 24	26 28 30 32	34 36 38 40
Tenderness	2 4 6 8	10 12 14 16	18 20 22 24	26 28 30 32	34 36 38 40
Taste	4 8 12 16	20 24 28 32	36 40 44 48	52 56 60 64	68 72 76 80

Total Score:_____

Key:
Appearance: Texture, color, fat to lean ratio, burnt meat.
Tenderness: Moist and tender vs. dry and tough.
Taste: Sauce too hot, too mild, or excessive vs. a pleasing blend of sauce and meat.

much else. It was carved about 100 years ago by Yardley Warner for his twins, probably because he sympathized with the children's restlessness and wanted to make them a religious toy to keep them occupied on Sundays.

Another uncommon exhibit is the 4-foot-long tin horn the coachman blew at each stop of the stagecoach along the Old Plank Road. The number of blasts blown told people at upcoming stops, such as Nathan Hunt Tavern, what passengers would be wanting when they got there. Old Plank Road was built between Fayetteville and Winston-Salem by laying down boards next to one another to form a firm-surfaced highway. Part of the old road is now Main Street. A plank from the road and a notched mile marker are also in the display. A traveler in the dark could stop at the marker and feel the number of notches on it to know how far it was to Nathan Hunt Tavern. A model shows a stage-coach on a plank road with markers to give you an idea how it all worked.

Visiting here is more like going into an attic than a museum. "There's so much stuff, and you can handle it. You don't get the feeling of things resting on velvet that you can't touch," the curator says. The museum is open by appointment. Admission is free.

The *High Point Historical Museum* (1859 E. Lexington Ave.; 336-885-1859; highpointmuseum.org) exhibits more traditional kinds of material related to the town's history, including military displays. The numbers "1859" in the phone number and the address stand for the year the town of High Point was founded.

You have to admire a museum that can pull off something like that. A display of old telephones takes you back to before Ma Bell; a collection of furniture made in High Point; as well as woodworking tools take you back to the first manufacturing in town. Also on the property are the restored 1786 John Haley House, a weaving house, and a blacksmith shop. Demonstrations are offered in these buildings on weekends. The 1754 Hoggatt House, which was damaged by fire in 2004, has been restored. The museum has also acquired the piano on which saxophonist John Coltrane composed many of his jazz pieces, including "Blue Train" and "Moment's Notice." Coltrane's mother played this piano, and later his children did. Some of the keys have words written in Coltrane's hand—"sticking," and "out of tune." Open Wed through Sat 10 a.m. to 4:30 p.m. Admission is free. An 8-foot tall bronze statue of John Coltrane with his saxophone stands at the intersection of Commerce Avenue and Hamilton Street.

Another way to glimpse earlier times in High Point is by staying at *J. H. Adams Inn* (1108 N. Main St.; 336-882-3267; jhadamsinn.com). This 31-room inn is quite grand. It's a 1918 Italianate Renaissance mansion, built by the Hampton Adams family as a home and place for entertaining. It was extensively renovated in 2000, preserving such historical touches as the grand staircase and marble fireplace, while also providing all modern luxuries and amenities. The rooms are furnished with collections from the region's fine furniture makers. Each room has a private bath, telephone, TV, high-speed Internet access, and refrigerator; some have a microwave, some have a whirlpool bath. The inn has a restaurant, Hampton's, serving dinner in a dining room overlooking a courtyard, but it may be closed for private parties from time to time. Inquire about specific dates when you make your reservation.

At 101 W. Green Dr., the *Doll & Miniature Museum of High Point* (336-885-3655; dollandminiaturemuseum.org) contains more than 2,700 dolls collected by Angela Peterson from around the world, as well as some impressive miniature displays created by a local craftsman. She picked up everything— crèche dolls, a Shirley Temple collection of 120 dolls, and Bob Timberlake dolls, as well as enough dollhouses and furnishings to create a miniature village. Before the collection was housed here, it was in several rooms of the retirement home where Peterson lived. In fact, she said she chose that particular place to live after "auditioning" a number of possibilities because this place expressed an active interest in her doll collection. The home may have ended up being more interested than she was. Somewhere along the way, when she was in her late eighties or early nineties, she began referring to the collection as "the damned dolls," because it took so much work to keep their costumes clean and properly pressed. The dolls were moved into the building on West Green Drive after her death and were known as the Angela Peterson

Doll and Miniature Museum. Then people interested in dolls or miniatures, or both, began to donate items, and the name of the museum was changed to reflect its growth, which now includes loaned exhibits. For instance, one woman made and donated a Barack Obama doll, an addition to a growing collection of African-American personality dolls. Among the miniatures, the bedroom displays made by Starling T. Efird in about 1940 stand out. They represent furniture styles produced by the furniture manufacturers of that era. The work is comparable to the Thorne Rooms at the Art Institute of Chicago depicting typical European room interiors, that were built at about the same time. The museum is open 10 a.m. to 4 p.m. Mon through Fri, Sat 9 a.m. to 4 p.m., Sun. 1.p.m. to 4 p.m. Closed November and March. Admission is $5 for adults, $2.50 for seniors and students. A remarkably unsouthern place to eat in High Point is the ***Penny Path Café and Crepe Shop*** at 104 E. Martin Luther King Jr. Drive (336-821-2925; www.facebook.com/thepennypath). It also goes by the name "Lucky Penny Crepes" but it's the same place. The Buzov family opened the creperie in 2003 and the café has become a popular place for local people. Among the offerings, the cheesecake gets rave reviews, but it's the crepes that star here. A favorite is the Kitchen Sink, going back to the old line that a recipe includes everything but the kitchen sink. When you order crepes you can watch them being made right in front of you. One customer said they were better than any he'd had in France. The menu includes a variety of chai and coffee lattes as well as such unusual beverages as European iced coffee. Incidentally, there really are pennies in the path going into the place. The café is open 10:30 a.m. to 8:30 p.m. Tues, Wed and Thur, 10:30 a.m. to 9:30 p.m. Fri and Sat, and 10:30 a.m. to 4:30 p.m. Sun.

Places to Stay in the Upper Piedmont

ASHEBORO

Hampton Inn-Asheboro
1137 E. Dixie Dr.
(336) 625-9000
hamptoninn.com
Moderate

DURHAM

Comfort Inn University
3508 Mt. Moriah Rd.
(919) 490-4949
comfortduramnhotel.com
Inexpensive

Morehead Manor Bed & Breakfast
914 Vickers Ave.
(888) 437-6333
(919) 687-4366
moreheadmanor.com
A small, elegant place to stay, walking distance to downtown.
Moderate to expensive

GREENSBORO

Battleground Inn
1517 Westover Ter.
(336) 272-4737
battlegroundinnnc.com
Close to the University of
North Carolina campus, the
airport, and the Coliseum.
Inexpensive

Courtyard by Marriott
4400 W. Wendover Ave.
(336) 294-3800
mariott.com/gsown
Inexpensive to moderate

HIGH POINT

Biltmore Suites Hotel
4400 Regency
(336) 812-8188
(888) 412-8188
biltmoresuiteshotel.com
This is an all-suites hotel.
Inexpensive to moderate

MOUNT AIRY

Hampton Inn
2029 Rockford St.
(336) 789-5999
(800) 565-5249
hamptoninn.com
You can book
accommodation in the
modest house that was the
Andy Griffith home through
the Hampton.
Moderate

Mayberry Motor Inn
501 Andy Griffith Pkwy.
North (US 52)
(336) 786-4109
http://mayberrymotorinn
.com
A simple motel on nice
grounds, all Mayberry
themed.
Inexpensive

RALEIGH

**Holiday Inn Brownstone
Hotel**
1707 Hillsborough St.
(919) 828-0811
(800) 331-7919
brownstonehotel.com
An eight-floor hotel in
downtown Raleigh.
Moderate to expensive

WINSTON-SALEM

**The Augustus T. Zevely
Inn**
803 S. Main St.
(800) 928-9299
http://winston-salem-inn
.com
The only place to stay right
in Historic Old Salem.
Moderate to expensive

Brookstown Inn
200 Brookstown Ave.
(336) 752-1120
brookstowninn.com
You can walk to Old Salem
from here.
Moderate

THE UPPER PIEDMONT WEBSITES

Durham
visitdurham.info

Greensboro
visitgreensboro.com

High Point
highpoint.org

Lexington
visitlexingtonnc.com

Raleigh
visitraleigh.com

Winston-Salem
visitwinstonsalem.com

Courtyard by Marriott
3111 University Pkwy.
(336) 727-1277
marriott.com/intcy
Moderate

Places to Eat in the Upper Piedmont

ASHEBORO

Bamboo Garden Oriental Restaurant
801 W. Dixie Dr.
(336) 629-0203
Your choice of buffet or menu service here.
Inexpensive

CHAPEL HILL

Crook's Corner
610 W. Franklin St.
(919) 929-7643
crookscorner.com
A long-time favorite in town, specializing in upscale Southern cooking.
Moderate to expensive

HIGHPOINT

Lucky Penny Café & Crepe Shop
104 E. Martin Luther King Jr. Dr.
(336) 821-2925
www.facebook.com/thepennypath
As the name implies, crepes are the specialty here, but lots of other choices are available too.
Inexpensive

LEXINGTON

Jimmy's Barbecue
1703 Cotton Grove Rd.
(336) 357-2311
Some say this is the best barbecue around.
Inexpensive

Lexington Barbecue
100 Smokehouse Ln.
(336) 249-9814
lexbbq.com
Others insist *this* is the best barbecue in town.
Inexpensive

MOUNT AIRY

Goober's 52
458 N. Andy Griffith Pkwy.
(336) 786-1845
goobers52.com
Notable for a kid's menu ranging from grilled cheese to spaghetti; easy for families.
Inexpensive

SEAGROVE

Seagrove Family Restaurant
8702 US 220 South
(336) 873-7789
A favorite with locals. Peach cobbler is popular.
Inexpensive to moderate

The Lower Piedmont

Statesville

With Winston-Salem as a starting point for this drive, in less than an hour, you can head west on I-40 to **Statesville,** a community of fewer than 25,000 people. This area was the site of Fort Dobbs, built during the French and Indian War to protect settlers. The fort is commemorated at the **Fort Dobbs State Historic Site** (438 Dobbs Rd.; 704-463-5882; fortdobbs .org) with a variety of archaeological sites, artifact displays, and nature trails. The site is open 9 a.m. to 5 p.m. Tues through Sat. Closed for major holidays. A variety of commemorative and interpretative programs are ongoing.

I-40 and I-77 meet here, and this has led to a lot of development on the periphery—hotels, chain restaurants, and service stations, along with automobile dealerships, grocery stores, and other businesses that are standard around North Carolina cities these days. Statesville doesn't advertise itself heavily as a tourist center, so you could easily drive on by and miss several appealing attractions. The downtown historic area has more than 100 restored buildings, some dating from as early as 1860. The **Statesville Convention and Visitors**

THE LOWER PIEDMONT

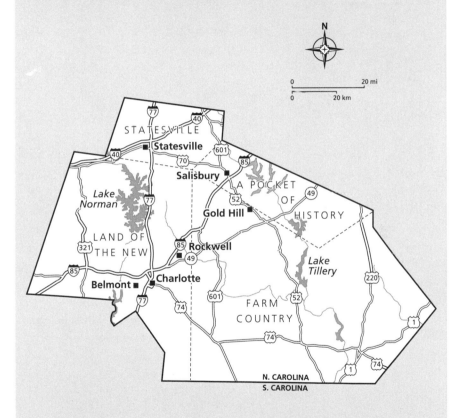

ANNUAL EVENTS IN THE LOWER PIEDMONT

BADIN

Best of Badin Festival
Third weekend in September
(704) 422-3713

Badin Volunteer Fire Department
Barbecues
Second Saturday in October;
fourth Saturday in January
(704) 422-3614

CHARLOTTE

Southern Ideal Home Show
(mid-October)
(800) 849-0248

GOLD HILL

Gold Hill Founder's Day
(late September)
(704) 279-5674

Autumn Jubilee
(early October)
(704) 636-2089

STATESVILLE

Carolina BalloonFest
(mid-September)
(704) 818-3307

Bureau (111 Depot Ln.; 704-878-3480 or 877-531-1819; downtownstatesvillenc .org) is located in a train depot built in 1911. It's a good place to pick up brochures and local maps during normal business hours.

Statesville is especially known for its annual hot air balloon festival, a tradition that has occurred for more than 30 years. The ***Carolina BalloonFest*** is held every fall at the Statesville Regional Airport (704-818-3307; carolina balloonfest.com). To get to the airport, take I-40 west to exit 146 or 148 to US 70. The airport is at Aviation Drive. This has grown into a big party, with about 50 hot air balloons, mass ascensions (weather permitting), live entertainment, rides in hot air balloons, North Carolina wine tasting, lots of food, and arts and crafts.

A Pocket of History

It takes about half an hour to drive from Statesville via US 70 to Salisbury. Two kinds of people live in ***Historic Salisbury***—those whose families have been in place for generations and those who have moved in recently, mostly from up north. Both share an almost smug conviction that theirs is one of the most congenial, historically interesting communities in North Carolina. I say *almost* smug because they're right. With a population of fewer than 30,000 people, the community supports a symphony orchestra, two respected colleges, and an independent bookstore. Although this is one of the oldest towns in the area, and the entire 23-block downtown community of commercial and residential buildings dating from 1820 to 1920 is on the National Register of Historic Places, it receives relatively little attention from outside. The Historic Salisbury Foundation and an active group of supporters are trying to change that (historicsalisbury.org).

They point to the 1898 *Grimes Mill,* a roller mill with all its original machinery in five floors; the *Civil War Salisbury Confederate Prison Site and National Cemetery,* where the largest number of unknown Civil War soldiers are buried; and the restored *Railroad Depot.* All of them are open to the public.

Then there's the Historic Salisbury walking tour, which includes the homes in the National Register Historic District. Some of these homes are open to the public. The *Dr. Josephus Hall House* (226 S. Jackson St.; 704-636-0103; historicsalisbury.org), for instance, is a large, 1820 antebellum house that sits among old oaks and boxwoods that have been in place nearly as long as the house. Dr. Hall was chief surgeon at the Salisbury Confederate Prison during the Civil War. After the war the Union commander used the house as headquarters. Somehow the grounds and the interior escaped the destruction typically associated with Yankee occupation in the South, and the Hall House contains nearly all its original furnishings. Open Sat and Sun from 1 to 4 p.m. Modest admission fee.

Just about a block away, the *Utzman Chambers House* museum (116 S. Jackson St.; 704-633-5946; rowanmuseum.org) is a notable example of architecture from the Federal period. It shows the life of a prominent local family during the early 1800s. An early 19th-century garden features four formal beds of flowers and herbs native to the Piedmont in 1815. Open Apr through Nov, Sat only from 1 to 4 p.m. Modest admission fee.

The *Rowan Museum* has exhibits related to Rowan County history in the old courthouse, 202 N. Main St. (704-633-5946; rowanmuseum.org). The old courthouse building was built in 1857, for the princely sum of $15,000, and was

BETTER KNOWN ATTRACTIONS
IN THE LOWER PIEDMONT

CHARLOTTE

Discovery Place
(704) 372-6261
discoveryplace.org

NASCAR Hall of Fame
(704) 654-4400
nascarhall.com

AUTHOR'S FAVORITE PLACES
IN THE LOWER PIEDMONT

Waterworks Visual Arts Center

Reed Gold Mine

Kluttz Piano Factory

used as a court building until 1914, when it became the community building. Since then, at one time or another, it has served as almost everything for which the town needed a building: public library, American Red Cross headquarters, chamber of commerce, and adult night school. When the flu epidemic hit the town in 1918, the community building became an emergency hospital and kitchen. This site is often reported to be haunted. Open Fri through Sun, 1 p.m. to 4 p.m. No admission fee but donations gratefully accepted.

The Rowan Museum includes another house a few miles outside of town that gives you a glimpse of early country life in the county. The **Old Stone House,** built by Michael Braun between 1758 and 1766, reflects the traditions of the German Rhinelanders who settled in the county in the early 1700s. Braun came to the area from Philadelphia, Pennsylvania, and the stone house will look familiar to anyone who has traveled the country roads in Pennsylvania and seen houses built on the Quaker plan. The house has been beautifully restored, and the museum is working to continue developing the property. The house is furnished with a collection of North Carolina and Pennsylvania pieces and looks much as it probably would have when Braun lived in it. One piece, a weaving loom in an upstairs room, has been in the house as long as anyone can remember.

To get to the Old Stone House from Rowan Museum, turn right on Innes Street, and go 4.2 miles (Innes Street becomes US 52 South) into Granite Quarry, and turn left on East Lyerly Street, which is also called Old Stone House Road. The house sits on the right, beside the road, about 0.6 mile farther on. Modest admission fee. The house is open from 1 to 4 p.m. Sat and Sun, Apr through Nov. The hours may change, and sometimes you can arrange to see the house at another time. Call the museum at (704) 633-5946 for more information, or check the website.

Moving from the historic to the contemporary, the **Waterworks Visual Arts Center** (123 E. Liberty St.; 704-638-1882; waterworks.org) features changing exhibits of contemporary art. The outdoor sculpture garden is especially pleasant on clear, sunny days. The gallery used to be in a building that was first used as the Salisbury Waterworks and then as the city police station. Now it is in a renovated and expanded building that used to be a car dealership. Its large open spaces are especially suited to displaying art. Open Mon, through Fri 10 a.m. to 5 p.m.; Sat 10 a.m. to 2 p.m. No admission fee, but donations are accepted gratefully.

In downtown Salisbury, a thriving business area that you really must see for its remarkable old factory, old train station (where Amtrak now stops), and business buildings, you can break the fast-food habit by having a bite of lunch at *Spanky's,* an old-fashioned ice-cream parlor that serves not only home-made ice-cream concoctions but also good soups, salads, deli sandwiches, and cheesecake (corner of Main and Innes Streets; 704-638-0780; www.facebook .com/spankysicecream.). Spanky's actually makes 75 different flavors of ice cream, but the original owner, who learned his craft as a student in dairy science at Penn State, explained, almost apologetically, that they keep only 25 flavors on hand at a time! When a new owner took over, the ice cream recipes were part of the deal and are as good as ever. You can't beat chocolate chip mint in a waffle cone. But ice cream alone is hardly a balanced diet. The Ruben sandwiches and potato soup are big favorites. The restaurant is in an old build-ing that in 1859 was the tallest in North Carolina. Open Tues through Sat from 9 a.m. to 8 p.m., Sun noon to 4 p.m.

Just a couple of blocks away, *the Sidewalk Deli* (120 S. Main St.; 704-637-3354; www.facebook.com/SidewalkDeli)) has been a local favorite since it was first opened in 1996 by Scott McCombs and Rick Anderson McCombs. During the week this is a lunch favorite for Salisbury locals, especially those who work in the downtown area, and on Saturday it is packed by folks whose Saturday routine usually includes lunch at the Deli—older citizens, families with young children, teenagers, groups of women, and downtown shoppers. Visitors tend to find the place by chance, just wandering the downtown busi-ness district. When Scott McCombs died in his early fifties in 2010, custom-ers mourned. But family and staff continued in Scott's good-humored mode, without breaking stride, continue serving everything from sandwiches, soup, salads, and homemade cakes, as well as the pimiento cheese for which the McCombs family have become famous in the area. In addition to the standard beverages, especially sweet tea, the Deli also has a nice selection of good beers. The Deli has some tables set up on the sidewalk, but inside, murals, a central fountain, old window frames, and a metal balcony mounted on the walls call to mind an oasis in an urban area—hence the name. Open 11 a.m. to 3 p.m. Mon through Sat.

One eating establishment in Salisbury has become an institution that brings together people of every class in the community. *Hap's Grill* (116½ N. Main

St.; 704-633-5872; visitnc.com/listing/hap-s-grill) sells nothing but hot dogs and hamburgers, and Coke or Cheerwine (see sidebar on p. 111) in glass bottles. The original proprietor was Hap Alexander. He opened the grill in an 8.5-foot-wide space (formerly an alley) the day after Thanksgiving in 1986. Greg Clup went to work there when he was 14, and in 1995 he bought the place from Hap. Over the years nothing has changed. Greg chops onions in the morning, pats hamburgers, cooks chili, and gets hot dogs ready for the grill. The most popular item is hot dogs "all the way" (with chili, onions, and mustard). When Greg starts cooking, the aroma draws customers from blocks away, even when they might've had other plans. People form a line that extends far down the block, but it moves fast, and even strangers talk to each other as they wait. Greg works at the grill by the counter, where Vickie Carter wraps the orders, opens the sodas Ceerwine wine being the most popular), takes money, and makes change, all without breaking rhythm. There's no place to sit down. You can order to take out; eat inside, standing at a narrow shelf; or eat outside, standing at one of two rickety wood tables. When you're done with your drink, you deposit the glass bottle into a wood crate by the tables. Hap's is open 10 a.m. to 3 p.m. every day but Sun.

Wink's King Barbeque and Seafood (509 Faith Rd.; 704-637-2410) is another intensely local place to eat that is as large as Hap's is small. And, unlike Hap's, this sprawling, old-fashioned family restaurant serves everything from the barbecue and seafood in its name to meat loaf, prime rib, and fried eggs with country ham. In fact, you can order breakfast all day. At the rear of the building, you'll see huge stacks of slab wood that are burned to make pork barbecue. The aroma of roasting pork mingled with wood smoke fills the air. Waitresses here wear jeans and loose T-shirts emblazoned with the Wink's logo. The customers are an interesting mix—older folks, groups with kids,

Oink, Oink

As I headed back to my car after lunch at Wink's, a mooing sound attracted my attention. I saw a truck with an attached trailer cage in one of the pull-through parking spaces. A beautiful little brown calf in the cage was bleating its heart out. I just hoped veal wasn't on the menu.

The next time I went to Wink's, I ate barbecue and was happy to see no veal offered. But as I was leaving I heard baa-ing, which turned out to be goats in a trailer cage where the calf had been the previous week. I know Wink's does not serve goat. But I promise you, if that parking spot is filled with a cage of oinking pigs next time I'm there, I will order the vegetable plate instead.

It's a Carolina Thing

Q: What do folks who've had to move away from North Carolina miss most?

A: Cheerwine.

Cheerwine is a soft drink created in Salisbury in 1917 that has become such a local tradition, some people take it with them by the case when they travel. Every so often, the Cheerwine company invites people to describe how it differs from other soft drinks, and nobody can ever articulate it beyond mentioning the cherry taste. Its unique quality may be due to the fact that the flavoring is wild cherry. Don't underestimate nostalgia. Local people will tell you they like it because it's what they grew up with. And now, in the area, you can find Cheerwine doughnuts and truffles, too.

parents and grandchildren, black and white, working men with service trucks parked outside, men in business suits. This is clearly not where club ladies go to lunch; it's where real people go for a generous plateful of real food. Open Mon through Sat 5:30 a.m. to 9 p.m.

Another of the many barbecue restaurants in the area, *College Bar-B-Que* (117 Statesville Blvd.; 704-633-9953) is a long-established place where the waitresses have known some of the regulars for years. It's almost always busy, and don't be confused by the word "College" in its name. Old-timers, families with little kids, and "just folks" all come here, though it is close to Catawba College and attracts students, too. As you approach the restaurant, sometimes you can smell the wood smoke from the barbecue fire, and inside you will hear the steady thumping sound of knives against cutting boards as the pork is chopped. The restaurant serves all the breakfast standards—eggs, biscuits, sausage—as well as sandwiches and menu specials, and you can expect your glass of ice tea to be kept full until you leave, but barbecue is the defining offering. The restaurant opens every day at 7 a.m. and closes at 8 p.m. except on Mon, when it closes at 2 p.m., and Sat, when it closes at 3 p.m.

Almost any day you are in Salisbury, you'll see people wearing earphones and consulting booklets as they walk the streets, following one of the self-guided tours. You may borrow the brochures, tapes, and tape players for two of the tours, free, from the *Visitor Information Center* at 204 E. Innes St. (704-638-3100 or 800-332-2343; visitsalisburync.com). Brochures and guide maps for the African-American Heritage Trail are available at the Visitor Information Center and also at W. J. Walls Heritage Hall on the campus of Livingstone College. You can purchase a CD for a driving tour of the African-American Heritage Trail.

The **Salisbury Heritage Tour** (audio, walking) is a 1.3-mile walking tour that provides details about the history and architecture of Historic Downtown Salisbury and the large homes of the West Square Historic District. The **Civil War Heritage Tour** (audio, driving) provides insights into Salisbury's role during an infamous time, including a Union prisoner-of-war camp where 11,700 died. Nothing remains of the Salisbury Confederate Prison. The Union soldiers are memorialized at the Salisbury National Cemetery. The **African-American Heritage Trail** (brochure, driving) self-guided tour notes important moments, leaders, and lives of generations of African Americans who lived and worked in Salisbury.

When you are on Innes Street, orient yourself so the winged **Confederate Monument** in the center of town is to your back, turn left on Main Street (or turn right if you are facing the statue), and drive a few minutes into the neighboring town of **Spencer** to visit the **North Carolina Transportation Museum** (411 S. Salisbury Ave.; 704-636-2889; nctrans.org). This is the site of what was once the largest service facility or shops for Southern Railway Company. The museum's collection includes all kinds of transportation-related artifacts—antique automobiles, railroad cars, and an airplane. The roundhouse, with 37 bays, is an inevitable hit with train enthusiasts. You can watch a video about the railroad in the visitor center. Train rides in restored cars are popular. Admission to the museum is $6 for adults, $5 for active military and senior citizens, children 3 to 12 $4. The price doubles when train rides are included, March through May. Train rides and museum hours may vary seasonally. It is a good idea to call ahead. The museum also maintains an active schedule of special events related to transportation and you don't have to be a kid to enjoy them. Once, when there was a waiting line for train rides but not for helicopter rides, an 80-year-old woman climbed into the helicopter and had her picture taken just as the helicopter took off. Another time, a man who was interested in the working of old engines spent a couple of hours studying one. The website lists special events as they are scheduled.

Right across the street the **Little Choo Choo Shop** (500 S. Salisbury Ave.; 704-637-8717; littlechoochooshop.com) is a serious, well-stocked model-railroad shop handling supplies for scales from "G" to the tiny "Z." They buy, sell, trade, and repair. One room is devoted to books and videos about model railroading, and you can get top-notch advice from the people who work here, too. Another small room is filled with wooden toy trains to occupy kids while you browse among the grown-up toys. The store is open Tues through Sat 10 a.m. to 5:30 p.m.

Here's another side trip you can easily make from Salisbury for a glimpse of early mill life in the area, back when cotton and textiles were the center of commerce here. **Cooleemee** is a well-preserved but not gentrified mill town.

Humiliation

I had just begun exploring the area around Salisbury and Spencer. People kept asking me if I'd been to the Spencer Shops yet. I wasn't in a big hurry to find them, because shopping isn't my idea of a good time, but eventually I figured that anything so many people mentioned would be worth a visit. The idea of gift shops in an old transportation museum seemed OK.

I went into the museum office and after checking all the signs, asked the receptionist where the gift shops were. Was it like a row of specialty shops in converted train buildings or what? I asked.

Her face changed from polite-receptionist to local-citizen-horrified-at-such-ignorance. *The Shops at Spencer,* she said, are machine shops where mechanics once repaired Southern Railway's steam locomotives. Those trains hauled passengers and such freight as furniture, textiles, and tobacco, and the shops at one time employed nearly 3,000 people.

Gift shops, indeed! Sniff.

To get there, go to Jake Alexander Boulevard, which becomes US 601/70. Follow US 601 North into Davie County. At Greasy Corner, turn left onto NC 801 and drive about 1 mile to Cooleemee. Go right onto Marginal Street, then left onto Church Street. This will bring you to the *Mill Village Museum* in the Zachary-Holt House at Old 14 Church St. (336-284-6040; cooleemee.org.) It is well marked with signs. The Mill Village Museum offers an honest, down-to-earth look at life in a Piedmont cotton mill village a century ago, and the old homes in the town show how the town grew up around the *Cooleemee Cotton Mill.* The museum bills itself as "telling the story of Carolina cotton mill folks," and although the emphasis is on how the town developed around the Cooleemee Cotton Mill, later called Erwin Mills #3, the information about the people and the town gives you a good idea of what many mill towns in the Carolina Piedmont were like. The mill closed in 1969.

The Cooleemee Historical Society has actively collected artifacts, photographs, and stories from people who remember when the mill, which opened in 1898, was the center of life. Exhibits in the museum are organized under the categories Country Roots, Cooleemee Is Born, From Cotton to Cloth, Like One Big Family, Establishing a Society, The Old Square, A New South, Honoring Their Memory, and This Old House. A detailed and engagingly written museum guide explains each exhibit.

After looking around the main museum, check out the Mill House Museum, a 1903 mill house that has been restored to what it was in 1934. It shows what life would've been like for an ordinary mill family. Then a walk or slow drive around the town, where most of the mill houses are still occupied, gives you a further sense of what a mill village was like. For instance, the addresses of the houses used to be numbered so that the lowest numbers were for the houses closest to the mill.

The historical society wants to clear up what they consider misrepresentation of Southern mill towns by some historians. Michael Myerson, in his book, *Nothing Could Be Finer,* wrote about mill hands: "Tied to their machines day and night and housed in mill-owned shanty villages, the developing North Carolina lived an existence out of a Dickens nightmare." But that's not the picture drawn by the exhibits in the museum and the stories recalled by old-timers. The museum guide says the work was hard and dirty and ran into 66-hour workweeks for low pay, but it claims that wasn't out of line for rural people already used to hard work. The pace was relatively slow in the early days, and workers took breaks for drinks, snacks, or even a swim in the river. Looking around the town makes it clear the mill houses were never shanties, and old-timers' stories mention improvements such as indoor plumbing and electricity. The museum is open Wed through Sat 10 a.m. to 4 p.m., or by appointment. The museum is wheelchair accessible. Donations accepted at the main museum. Admission to the Mill House is $4 for adults, $3 for senior citizens, free to children age 12 and under.

Another side trip, to **Mooresville,** can be pure fun for kids and exhilarating for racing fans. Like Kannapolis, Mooresville was once a textile town. Today its economic base comes from motorsports. Some 40 race teams are based in Mooresville because the town is close to speedways in Charlotte, Wilmington, and Darlington, South Carolina. The town now calls itself Race City USA. To dip into the race and auto culture, check out the **Dale Earnhardt Inc. Showroom** (1675 Coddle Creek Hwy.; 877-334-9663; daleearnhardtinc .com), for displays of Dale Earnhardt Inc. drivers' achievements as well as a retail store where you will find memorabilia. Open Thur, Fri, and Sat 11 a.m. to 2 p.m., as well as during other hours for special events that you can find on the website. Admission is free.

JR Motorsports (349 Cayuga Dr.; 866-576-8883; jrmotorsport.com) introduces you to Dale Junior, who is making a name in his own right in racing. The building houses the management company and racing operation, but for visitors, a museum called "the Dale Jr. Fan Experience" tells the story of his life and racing career. A viewing window allows you to look into the shop. Open Mon through Fri 8:30 a.m. to 5 p.m., Sat 10 a.m. to 3 p.m. Admission is free.

Memory Lane Motorsports and Historic Automotive Museum (769 River Hwy.; 704-622-3673; memorylaneautomuseum.com) features exhibits

Remembering the Intimidator

North Carolina is home to more than 46 NASCAR (North American stock car racing) teams, more than any other state in the union. The state's focus on NASCAR racing became even stronger after the death of **Dale Earnhardt,** a Kannapolis native, who died in 2001 in a crash during the Daytona 500, just two months before his 50th birthday.

He was a high school dropout who became a racing legend, considered by experts the best ever in the sport.

When the road where Dale Earnhardt drove his 1956 Chevrolet as a teenager was named "Dale Earnhardt Boulevard" in 1993, 8,000 people turned out for the ceremony.

After Earnhardt's death, *Salisbury Post* sportswriter Mike London wrote, "Earnhardt did for racing what Arnold Palmer did for golf and Muhammad Ali for boxing."

Memorials to Dale Earnhardt stand in Cannon Village Park and in the Cannon Village Visitor Center.

showing the history of both racing and the automobile. Displays include one-of-a-kind vehicles, race cars, vintage automobiles, motorcycles, toys, and memorabilia. Open Mon through Sat 10 a.m. to 5 p.m. Longer hours during race weeks, shorter in winter. Admission is $10 for adults, $6 for children ages 6 to 12, children under 6 free.

The ***North Carolina Auto Racing Hall of Fame*** (119 Knob Hill Rd.; 704-663-5331; ncarhof.com) has an art gallery of work by motorsports artists, a museum with more than 35 cars, a gift shop with all kinds of racing memorabilia, and the Goodyear Mini-Theater, which shows 45-minute films about peak moments in racing. The hall of fame is open Mon through Fri 10 a.m. to 5 p.m., Sat 10 a.m. to 3 p.m. Closed Sun. Admission is $6 for adults, $4 for senior citizens and children ages 6 to 12.

The only thing ***Lazy 5 Ranch*** has to do with automobiles is that the owners want you to stay inside yours as you drive around the place looking at exotic animals. The ranch is between I-85 and I-77, on NC 150 East (15100 Mooresville Rd.; 704-663-5100; lazy5ranch.com). The ranch has about 750 animals from around the world, and you drive about 3.5 miles through pastures to see them: camels, Watusi cows from Africa with horn spreads of up to 12 feet, water buffalo, zebras, and so on. Although you have to stay in your car to see these animals, you can get out to enjoy the petting zoo and feed some of the animals there. This place is run with a sense of humor. Rules that make sense in any language are expressed with a grin: "You are not allowed to feed you children to the animals, no matter how bad they are behaving; don't honk your horn or turn on your lights unless you need help because it gives our animals heartburn; when you stop to take photos from your car, pull over to the side. This will allow other cars to drive around. It will also give the animals time to fluff their hair. So you get animal slobber all over your car . . . they're just trying to be friendly. You can wash it off later." You do need to know that you cannot take your pet here. Lazy 5 Ranch is open Mon through Sat from 9 a.m. to an hour before sunset, Sun from 1 p.m. until an hour before sunset. Admission is $11 for adults, $8 for senior citizens and children ages 2 to 12. You will need to pay in cash, not checks or credit cards.

If you're not in the mood for automobiles or cute critters, try a trip north on US 601 to US 64 to spend some time in Mocksville. This community of fewer than 6,000 people has done a great job with downtown historic restoration and offers a variety of interesting shops, from antiques to used books to dolls and toys. The town has some really good eating places, too. ***Ketchie Creek Bakery and Café*** at 844 Valley Road (336-751-9147; www.ketchiecreekbakery .com) has a huge selection of baked goods, from brownies to mini cheesecake and red velvet cake. From the café a broccoli and cheese quiche is so good that you start thinking you'll eat just half, saving the rest for later, and then finish the whole thing at once. Coffee to go with it comes from the coffee bar. This is a family run operation so there's no sense of a chain operation here. Open Mon through Fri 7 a.m. to 6 p.m., Sat 7 a.m. to 5 p.m. The deli closes at 4 p.m. on Sat.

An unlikely place for a little town like Mocksville with a miniscule Irish population is ***O'Callahan's Publickhaus Pub and Eatery*** at 115 N. Main St. (336-753-0011; o'callahan'snc.com). But, of course, it only takes one Irish person to do it. Local resident Dan Reynolds, with a strong Irish background, founded the place and, as it turns out, you don't have to be Irish to love it. Another local resident, Adam Ressa, who is half Irish, tried the offerings here and found them worthy. Much of the menu is traditional Irish food—bangers and mash, fish and chips, corned beef—but other offerings are eclectic. Teriyaki chicken salad and fried calamari are good examples. Then a few choices

Where's the Beef? Right here.

It's a point of pride with O'Callahan's that they corn their own beef, buying the briskets and adding the pickling spices, not just buying already corned beef and cooking it. Its popularity is demonstrated by the observation of a chef who used to work there that they use about 8,000 pounds of corned beef a year.

are sort of hybrids, like corned beef and sauerkraut fried in a wonton wrapper. Some of the drink specials, such as Sangria and Long Island Iced Tea are decidedly not Irish either. But this is a pub, after all, so you have a choice of a great variety of beers. Some are bottled but the staff can pull a beautiful pint from the tap, as well. O'Callahan's is closed Mon, open 11 a.m. to 10 p.m. Tues through Thur, 11 a.m. to midnight Fri and Sat, 10 a.m. to 9 p.m. Sun.

When you return to Salisbury, you could stay at one of two well-run B&Bs. Karen Windate rescued an old Victorian home at 529 South Fulton St., in the historic district, with a full-scale historic restoration that has won preservation prizes. *Turn of the Century Victorian Bed & Breakfast* offers 3 guest rooms and a 2-room suite, all with private baths, decorated and furnished in understated elegance with period antiques. Karen prides herself on serving a different full breakfast, on different china, each morning. Guests who've stayed for several days have sometimes made bets about how long she could go without repeating herself (704-642-1660 or 800-250-5349; turnofthecenturybb.com). A newer establishment, *Across the Pond* (324 N. Fulton St.; 866-296-7965; www.acrossthepondbandb.com), owned and operated by Mary and Andrew Walker, consistently wins rave reviews from guests. Its two rooms and a suite are all furnished in quiet luxury in a restored 1919 Colonial Revival house. The Walkers were originally from England but after having worked and lived on four continents, raising a family in Pittsburgh, Pa., they looked around for a small community with rich history where they wouldn't have to shovel snow. Salisbury won. They offer a full English country breakfast, including scones and homemade bread, though you could request something lighter if you wanted to. Each afternoon at 5 p.m., they host a reception with coffee, tea, sherry, wine or soft drinks, a time when guests can meet to share experiences as well as chat with the Walkers. Incidentally, the name of the B&B derives from an expression used by both Brits and Americans to refer to the country across the Atlantic Ocean from them. One observer says it's more used in England, rather like referring to America as "the Colonies." Leaving Salisbury, take US 52 South for an interesting drive that shows you the down-home, not the tourist, version of the Piedmont. In about 6 miles, almost before you've left Salisbury's environs, you come to Granite Quarry, where a big billboard on the left side of the road directs you to *Kluttz Piano Factory* (704-279-7237; kluttzpiano.com). Stop in and look around, even though you probably aren't planning to buy a piano while you're out tracking unbeaten paths. This place, which advertises more than 500 new and rebuilt pianos, is awesome. The showroom, where you try out new and reconditioned pianos, looks fairly standard, but you'll be dumbfounded by the work area, which seems roughly the size of a football field, filled with pianos—whole pianos and pieces of pianos in every make, model, and size. Ten minutes of just looking will tell you more about what's inside a piano than you've ever dreamed you could know. The people who work here talk as casually about the good and bad traits of grands, uprights, spinets, Yamahas, Wurlitzers, and Baldwins as the rest of us talk about the tomatoes in our gardens.

People who work here have noted that most of the folks who visit as a result of reading this guidebook are from Ohio and Pennsylvania. Nobody is sure why.

Outsiders, especially from "up North" sometimes get a chuckle out of the name Kluttz, but around here, Kluttz is just another family name, belonging not only to the owners of the piano factory but also to architects, contractors, and art shop proprietors. Some workers get there as early as 4 a.m., but regular hours for ordinary mortals are Mon through Fri from 9 a.m. to 5 p.m.

Also, on the same road, just 2 miles past Granite Quarry in a long stone building, you'll find **Old Stone Vineyard and Winery** (6245 US 52; 704-279-0930; osvwinery.com). The vineyards are beside and behind the building, while inside you'll find a state-of-the-art production facility, tasting bar, and salesroom, all managed by friendly, competent staff. The best-selling wines are the traditional, much-loved Muscadine wines of North Carolina. But over the years Old Stone's offerings have expanded to include some very nice dry reds, including a Sangiovese, a Merlot, and a Chambourcin. Many of Old Stone's wines have won gold and silver medals in competitions. If you'd like to taste a variety of wines here you have several options. It's $5 to taste 8 different wines and $10 to taste the full list of 16 wines. In each case you keep the glass as a souvenir. Depending on what is going on in the tank room, tours are offered. Even when they're not, you can see the action through large glass windows between the salesroom and the production area. Old Stone Vineyard and Winery is open Tues through Sat 11 a.m. to 6 p.m., Sun 1 to 5 p.m.

Continuing east on US 52, through Rockwell, you'll come next to **Gold Hill.** Orient yourself so that the Gold Hill Post Office and a convenience store stand on your left. On the right-hand side of the road, a sign carved

From the Grape Comes the Wine

The **Muscadine grape** is the oldest grape in America and native to this country. Muscadine wines are still a favorite among Southerners. As the state's wineries add and advertise "viniferous" wines, they refer to those made from grapes whose stock originated "in the old country," mainly Europe. And, as populations blend, the wineries are beginning to experiment with blends of Muscadine and viniferous grapes.

from wood and set in brick announces gold hill. Turn right through the gate and onto Doby Road. Cross the railroad tracks, turn left onto Old 80, and go a short block to a stop sign. At the sign, turn right onto St. Stephen's Church Road, follow it just a little more than a half mile, and you'll come to a section where banners welcome you to the ***Historic Village of Gold Hill.*** Gold Hill was once the largest mining district east of the Mississippi—a boomtown in the mid-1800s. But it was hard to extract ore from the soil here, and the gold rush moved on to other sites, leaving Gold Hill a sparsely populated rural community until community members began to rejuvenate the place.

The first thing you come to is a park bordered by fieldstone fences, complete with a pavilion shelter, a museum building, an outdoor stage, picnic tables, playground equipment, bike and walking paths, bridges, and information signs explaining the history of mining in Gold Hill, all the work of a community park committee. Across from the park, Gold Hill United Methodist Church, a simple white building with six columns, is a fully active church.

Boardwalks beginning here run the length of the "new" old village, past renovated, reproduced, and imported old buildings. One observer said this section looks like a Western movie set. The stores, which sell antiques, ice cream, pop, hot dogs, and Moon Pies, have varying hours of operation but are generally open weekends. As the village continues to attract small businesses and shops, it's also attracting more visitors looking for antiques, art, and crafts. Check the website at historicgoldhill.com to see what's going on in the village. Often special arts and pottery festivals take place over long weekends.

You won't need a schedule to enjoy the spacious park, which has good play space for children and places to enjoy a picnic. It's also become popular as a meeting place for people who want to get together for a quiet chat. The work of creating the park, refurbishing its walls and buildings, has been done by local volunteers.

allthatglitters

Even today it's possible to find pieces of rock in the area flecked with what appears to be gold. The names of such communities as Gold Hill, Rockwell, and Richfield reflect the early influence of gold, too.

When you're done in the village, if you drive straight on through, you'll come to Old Beatty Ford Road, which, if you turn left, will take you back to US 52 in a couple of minutes, or you can turn right for an hour's diversion down a different kind of entrepreneurial row.

Turn left onto a road that crosses the railroad tracks and runs past a large quarry operation. You'll drive about 12 miles along this road, past a Soil Conservation Service demonstration farm on the left; and a variety of small home-based businesses. Many yards have FOR SALE signs offering produce in season, a piece of used farm equipment, a boat, a camper "like new" with tow bar and a pickup (there must be a story in that one), firewood, oil paintings—it all changes with fortune and the seasons. You'll also pass a couple of uncommonly attractive older churches, the kind with their own manicured graveyards in back. Old Concord Road intersects Old Beatty Ford Road after about 12 miles. Turn left. Drive about 3 miles more, passing Roy Cline Road and Irish Potato Road, and turn right immediately onto Goldfish Road. You're at *Greendale,* 6465 Goldfish Rd., Kannapolis, which from the outside looks like one more sprawling roadside building. Inside you'll find wonder and the ultimate rural entrepreneurial enterprise.

Long rows of beautifully clear, brightly lighted aquariums gleam in the dim room, covering 44,000 square feet of display space. Here in the boonies, where if you tell your mother you're going to the fish store she assumes you're going to buy flounder, you discover gouramis and guppies, oscars, cichlids, corals, and saltwater exotics whose names you don't even know, all apparently thriving. OK, you can't keep goldfish on the road, but just looking beats watching television, and you may find the selection and prices on aquarium equipment appealing enough to make a purchase.

Greendale started out as a goldfish farm back in 1929, when Rufus Green got laid off by Cannon Mills and decided to make his living raising goldfish in outdoor ponds to sell to dime stores. One of his first sales was to get money to buy a shirt for church. The years passed, Rufus died, and his wife maintained the business as well as she could. Rufus's son, George, returned in 1978 from another war that wasn't called one, with his wife, Gaysorn, a classical dancer from Bangkok. By now hobbyists had turned enthusiastically to exotic tropical fish, so it made sense for Greendale to develop accordingly. The whole story, in a yellowing newspaper clipping, is taped to the front wall.

It's hard to imagine there would be enough customers to keep the business going, but they come from all directions: Concord, Kannapolis, Salisbury, Albemarle. The store is closed on Monday and Tuesday, partly because new shipments of plants and fish come then. On Wednesday it's so busy that, as one employee put it, "People just come in and throw money at you." You can always find someone to chat with about the troublesome habits of live bearers and how hard it is not to disrupt a gourami's bubble nest. Open Wed through Sat from 10 a.m. to 6 p.m., and Sun from 2 to 6 p.m. Closed Mon and Tues (704-933-1798; carolinacorner.com/attractions/exotic-fish-store.htm.) When you leave, depending on which way you turn, you may see a large block-lettered sign inside a cul-de-sac in front of a mobile home: IF YOU DON'T HAVE BUSINESS HERE, THIS IS A GOOD PLACE FOR YOU TO TURN AROUND. This may be the only guy in the county who isn't looking for customers at home. The best way to return to US 52 is the way you came in. Since everything looks different going in the opposite direction, you'll see things you missed the first time and won't feel that you're backtracking.

Coming into Misenhiemer, US 52 runs through the middle of the small **Pfeiffer University** campus, where all the classroom buildings, administration buildings, dormitories, and faculty houses are made of red brick. You might think that this is the kind of place a film director would like to shoot *Who's Afraid of Virginia Woolf?*, although a director would never get approval in this Bible pocket.

Farm Country

From Pfeiffer University it's only a couple of miles to the intersection of US 52 and NC 49 at **Richfield.** By the way, take the 35 mph signs here seriously. A lot of people who didn't have paid hefty fines. Going north on NC 49 for about as long as you need to take a couple of deep breaths, you will find a lot of development at the corner of NC 49 and US 52 in Richfield has sprung up fairly rapidly, creating an area with a supermarket, drug store, bank, and several fast food chains. But somehow there's always support for something distinctly unchain like. In this case, it's **Coffee Central** at 114 NC 49 just across from all that corner development (704-463-5551; www.facebook.com/pages/Coffee-Central). This is a coffee shop that has become popular not only with local people but also as a great stop for folks traveling from the Charlotte area to the Piedmont. And the building didn't start out as a coffee shop; it was the home of First Bank, which is now in new quarters across the street in the busy corner. Jay and Beverly Patel turned it into a shop that sells beverages and hand dipped Hershey's ice cream. The repurposing has worked really well

Old-Timers

They still tell the story in Richfield about a bet two of the men once made. Nobody remembers for sure what it was about, though it may have had something to do with whether or not a kid could steal some chickens and then sell them back to the owner, but they do know that the loser had to push the winner to Albemarle, about 10 miles away, in a wheelbarrow.

How long did it take?

Didn't keep time, exactly, but it definitely took most of the day.

because the drive through that used to serve the bank now works the same as those of major coffee chains for Coffee Central, though most customers seem to prefer sitting inside, meeting friends, chatting with the owners, Jay and Beverly Patel. Here's another fun observation—one of the most popular beverages Coffee Central sells is chai latte. Chai is a spiced tea with milk going back to the 1800s in India. Jay and Beverly don't use any sort of instant product, they make their own with their own blend of spices. One customer explained his fondness for chai latte, rather than coffee, "Coffee gives you a jolt; tea gives you a lift." It seems unlikely, though, that the Patels will ever change the name of their shop to Chai Central. The shop is open Mon through Fri, 7 a.m. to 9 p.m., Sat 9 a.m. to 9 p.m.

Returning to US 52 and continuing a few miles south, you'll come to Austin Road on the right, right after the Mauney Feed Company. Turning onto this road and following it across the railroad tracks and through some rural countryside for a few miles brings you to the **Uwharrie Vineyards and Winery** (28030 Austin Rd.; 704-982-9463; uwharrievineyards.com), the fifth-largest winery in North Carolina. The sign is fairly inconspicuous and you might pass by, but you can't miss the expanse of vineyard, all neatly surrounded with white fence, or the 14,000-square-foot building that includes production rooms, salesroom and gift shop, tasting bar, and a banquet hall as well as a patio under roof where you can enjoy a glass of wine. The gift shop area features the work of various Seagrove Potters as well as T-shirts and other items. You can taste fifteen wines with crackers for $5. If you'd like to keep the large, 15.5 ounce wine glass as a souvenir, it's $3 more. Wine, especially red wines, tastes better in a large glass because it allows you to swirl and and enjoy the aromas. Winemaker Chad Andrews is thoroughly knowledgeable about making wine and can explain in minute detail how his sophisticated equipment works; much of the process requires his close monitoring, which sometimes means minimal sleeping. Uwharrie Vineyards' wines, some of which have won prestigious awards, range from a substantial Merlot and a very dry Cabernet Sauvignon and a Riseling that is dry, not sweet, to the sweeter Muscat, Magnolia, and Autumn Blush. Because of Chad's understanding of the relationship between quality of winemaking procedures and the quantity of sulfites needed, he can

learningthe lingo

If a North Carolinian tells you he's ill, don't call the doctor. He means he is in bad humor. If he says he's "ill as a hornet," try not to make him mad because, if you do, he'll pitch a hissy fit. This differs from throwing a conniption fit, but it's tough to get anybody to explain how.

Southern Sweets

Chad Andrews, winemaker at Uwharrie Vineyards, says you can predict the kinds of wines you'll find in North Carolina by geography. "Remember the Southern sweet tooth," he says. The closer to the coast you get, the sweeter beverages will be. So, while some regions have sweet and unsweet iced tea, the coastal region has sweet tea and sweeter tea. Chad says, "Don't expect them to drink dry wine there."

almost promise you a bottle of wine that won't induce a headache, if you're sensitive to sulfites. "It can make you drunk," he says, "but it won't give you a headache." The winery is open Tues through Sat 10 a.m. to 6 p.m., Sun noon to 5 p.m.

If you return to US 52 in a few miles you come to *Lucky Tusk* at 1465 US 52. This is another example of a repurposed building. It used to be a KFC franchise, complete with drive-through window. From the outside it doesn't look like much. But inside it's pleasantly appointed with booths and tables. And you can call in an order and pick it up about half an hour later at the drive-through. The menu is huge, including fried rice, Thai noodles and stir fry, as well as many sushi choices. (The combination of sushi with Thai food is common in this area.) One man who knows his Thai food said the Crispy Duck here was the best he'd ever had. A popular appetizer is the fresh roll, with shredded lettuce, bean sprouts, shrimp and herbs in a rice paper wrapper. Note, if you have the gene that makes cilantro taste like soap, be sure to specify "no cilantro." Lucky Tusk is open 11 a.m. to 3 p.m. and 5 p.m. to 9 p.m., Mon through Sat (704-985-1127; www.facebook.com/Pages/Lucky-Tusk/20054634338).

Continuing on US 52, go past Albemarle where you can pick up NC 740, which takes you to the little town of *Badin* another place in the state that is reinventing itself after the loss of manufacturing. Its history goes back to 1913, when a French company, L'Aluminium Français, began building a dam on the Yadkin River, which created *Badin Lake.* Next, a town for company workers was built alongside the lake and named for the company president, Adrien Badin. Eventually the French company went on to other projects, and ALCOA bought the town. Badin was soon a thriving company town, with the ALCOA plant at its entrance, across from the lake. The plant shut down, but it remains the dominant visual feature of the area. At least until you drive on up the hill to *Badin Inn Golf Resort and Club* (107 Spruce St.; 704-422-3683; badininn .com). In an earlier time, it was the Badin Country Club and Golf Course. Before that it served as a residence hall for single males and, on another floor, female schoolteachers. When the admittedly worn building was renovated, managers preserved some historical accoutrements such as the original windowpanes, woodwork, and hardware but added large windows and open spaces to create a lighter environment that is popular for special events. The greens have been refurbished and a swimming pool added. Six guest suites upstairs feature antique-style furnishings that pay homage to the history of the place, as well as small refrigerator and microwave units acknowledging today's fondness for convenience. Some of the suites have fold-out sofas to accommodate extra guests. Views of the golf course and woods from the windows seem timeless. Room rates vary with the season from $85 to $105, with the highest April through October. These rates include use of the golf course and swimming pool (in season) and a continental breakfast. The inn has a grill also with hours that vary. In addition to the amusements of the inn and resort, the village offers diversion with small shops, local museums, and pretty gardens. It's interesting to see the way many of the old mill duplex houses have been refurbished and landscaped for a new generation. Town rules allow golf carts in the village, which the inn will provide. Badin Lake, which you pass as you drive into town, has a place for putting in boats and a sandy beach area where the water is shallow and only gradually deepens. Most of the people who spend time at the lake live somewhere in the area.

Badin is at the foot of **Morrow Mountain State Park** (49104 Morrow Mountain Rd.; 704-982-4402; stateparks.com/morrow_mountain.html), which technically has an Albemarle address because Albemarle and Badin are pretty much side-by-side. You could say that Badin is a suburb of Albemarle, but Badin residents might say just the opposite. The park is much loved by folks in the area as a place for picnics, family parties, walking, hiking, and horseback riding. For many, it's a spot to spend an afternoon or a day in the woods. The park has camping and cabin sites, RV accommodations, a lake for boating, and a pool. It's open at 8 a.m. and closes in the evening at about dark, depending on the time of year.

A few miles out of town, **Badin Road Drive-in Theater** (2411 Badin Rd.; 704-983-2900; badinroaddrivein.com) is an attraction people associate with an earlier time, when loading pickups with people settled against bales of hay or driving in with a carful of kids was standard Saturday-night entertainment. Here it still is, although the movies are contemporary. This is one of just six drive-in theaters left in North Carolina. The theater has 2 screens, one typically featuring a movie for kids and another for adults. Admission is $5 for adults, free for children ages 11 and under. The drive-in has Wi-Fi access (though what would you want with that when you're watching a movie?) and bathrooms.

Consider another side trip from Albemarle, going southeast on NC 73 about 15 miles to **Mount Gilead** to see **Town Creek Indian Mound** (509

Town Creek Mound Rd.; 910-439-6802; towncreek.nchistoricsites.org). This site, which is in the middle of farmland and undeveloped countryside, deserves more attention than its remote location affords. Based on information from excavations that have been in progress since 1937, two temple buildings, a burial hut, and a stockade have been reconstructed, giving visitors a glimpse of the Pee Dee culture as it developed beginning sometime in the 11th century. It's the only state historic site in North Carolina dedicated to Native American culture. With state funds skimpy, volunteers contribute a great deal to keep the research going and to explain the site to visitors. As interesting as the outside structures are, maps and photographs inside the visitor center showing what's been learned from excavations are equally fascinating. Guides explain how as one structure collapsed it was covered with earth and another built on top of it. Each phase left behind artifacts that archaeologists use to interpret the development of the culture. The site is open Tues through Sat 9 a.m. to 5 p.m., Sun 1 to 5 p.m. Closed major holidays. Admission is free, but donations are appreciated. There's a picnic area here, which you might enjoy in good weather.

thetarheelstate

North Carolina got its nickname because of its large forests of long-needle pine trees, which were the source of tar, pitch, and turpentine. According to local lore, stepping into the tar left it stuck to the heels of your feet or shoes.

Downtown Mount Gilead comes as a bit of a surprise. The community occupies less than 4 square miles of land and has fewer than 1,500 residents, but it's a lively place celebrating local artists, musicians, crafters, and history (mt.gileadnc.com). The shops vary and change from time to time, so it's a fun place to explore no matter when you visit.

A Lifetime Passion

Dr. Pressley R. Rankin Jr. practiced medicine in the town of Ellerbe for more than 40 years. The **Rankin Museum** is the direct result of a lifetime of collecting and studying. He began collecting birds' eggs when he was 8 years old. (Although that's illegal now, it wasn't back then.) By the time Dr. Rankin was a teenager, he'd become interested in Native American artifacts. As his interests continued to expand, the items he collected filled his home, which was one impetus for starting the museum. People in Ellerbe raised money for the building, and the museum continues to be a project the community supports actively.

Driving about 15 miles farther south on NC 73 brings you to the ***Rankin Museum of American Heritage*** (131 W. Church St.; 910-652-6378; rankin museum.com). The museum is attached to the library, a simple brick building that, from the outside, isn't impressive. But once you are inside and begin to study the exhibits, it's enough to take your breath away. The museum was begun more than 20 years ago with the personal collection of Dr. Pressley R. Rankin Jr. Exhibits range from a collection of Native American artifacts and a collection of South American art to the work of early potters in the Piedmont area of North Carolina. In one large display, you'll see what the museum claims is "the most well-preserved 500 gallon turpentine still on display anywhere."

Other exhibits contain relics from the Civil War, ivory carvings by Eskimos, and a fossil collection dating from the Cambrian Period, covering 500 million years. Each display is artistically arranged and accompanied by signs explaining the significance of the artifacts. The museum includes a reference library, an interactive zone for students, and a self-guided scavenger hunt.

The museum is open Mon, Tues, Thurs, Fri, and Sat 9 a.m. to 5 p.m., and Sun 2 to 5 p.m. Closed Wed. Admission is $4 for adults, $1 for students. Children ages 4 and under are free.

An eating place at Mt. Gilead that has been long popular with residents in the area, ***Lefler's Place Café and Grocery,*** at 6423 Highway West, is just where 73 turns to Mt. Gilead. The café's most popular offering is barbeque, with hot dogs running a close second along with daily specials. The barbeque isn't really pulled or sliced but more diced. Fans say that increases the flavor. Thursday is fried chicken day, which may trump all the other specials.However they tend to sell out early. The grocery store sells a few household items and lots of old-timey candies. Open 7 a.m.to 2 p.m. Mon, Tues, Wed, 7 a.m. to 8 p.m. Thurs and Fri, 7 a.m. to 3 p.m. Sat. (919-439-5451; leflersplace.com.)

golden opportunity wasted

The gold nugget Conrad Reed found in 1799 weighed 17 pounds, but he was only 12 and everybody figured the kid was just hauling a big rock home. The family used it as a doorstop for three years before the boy's father sold it for $3.50.

Back at the intersection of NC 49 and US 52, you can also take NC 49 North through the ***Uwharrie Forest*** up to Asheboro, or you could go south for an interesting drive to Charlotte.

Headed toward Charlotte, when you get to where US 601 meets NC 49, you may decide to make a side trip on US 601 South to NC 200 and follow the signs to the ***Reed Gold Mine*** at Midland, about 10 miles east of Concord (704-721-4653; reedmine.com). This is the site of the first authenticated gold find in the United States. It seems that Conrad Reed found a gold nugget the size of a brick on the family farm, and after that the family sort of lost interest in farming. We tend to associate the gold rushes with Alaska and California, but the fever burned here in North Carolina back in the late 1820s. For a time more people worked at gold mining than any other occupation except farming.

At the Reed Gold Mine State Historic Site, you can pan for gold in the spring and summer and tour the mining area year-round. In the visitor center, exhibits and a film explain the history and mining process. Admission is free, but you must pay a modest fee to pan for gold. Open for tours Tues through Sat from 9 a.m. to 5 p.m. year-round. Panning is available April 1 to October 31.

Land of the New

In the beginning **Charlotte** was all about gold, and it's still about money today, having become a center for banking and commerce. And, as both gold and money will do, the city attracts people—lots of people—and traffic. You could say that here the path has been not only beaten, but flailed. However there are a couple of places that aren't widely known and deserve more attention. One is the *Hezekiah Alexander Homesite and Museum of History* (3500 Shamrock Dr.; 704-568-1774; charlottemuseum.org). The Hezekiah Alexander house is the oldest dwelling still standing in Mecklenburg County. It was built of local quarry stone in 1774 and has been restored. Costumed guides lead tours of the house, log kitchen, barn, and gardens. The history museum displays local crafts and artifacts. Hezekiah was a delegate to the Fifth Provincial Congress and served on the committee that drafted the North Carolina State Constitution and Bill of Rights. The site has a number of fascinating details. The house is known as "the Rockhouse." Its doors are unusually low by today's standards, a feature intended to keep heat inside when people opened the doors—and a feature tall people should keep in mind.

In the re-created springhouse behind the house, you can see how milk and butter were cooled in the late 1700s. Open Tues through Sat from 11 a.m. to 5 p.m. Admission is $10 adults, $7 senior citizens, students, and children ages 6 to 12. Guided tours are at 1, 2, 3 and 4 p.m.

On the north side of Charlotte, on NC 49, the botanical gardens at the University of North Carolina at Charlotte deserve a lot more attention than they receive. The *UNC Charlotte Botanical Gardens* (704-687-2364; http:// gardens.uncc.edu) have three parts: the McMillan Greenhouse, the Van Landingham Glen, and the Susie Harwood Garden. The greenhouse has one of the best collections of tropical orchids in the South, with something like 800

> ## Old Sayings
>
> In the master bedroom of the Rockhouse, a rope bed dominates the room. In this kind of bed a latticework of ropes supported the mattress. Every so often the ropes had to be tightened—giving rise to the old phrase, "Sleep tight." Don't even think about the origins of the rest of the phrase, "Don't let the bedbugs bite."

species. The tropical rain forest conservatory is a convincing simulation of a real rain forest. Other greenhouse rooms include a cactus room and a cool room. A great variety of carnivorous plants grow in a protected outside area by the greenhouses. The Van Landingham Glen started as a rhododendron garden in 1966 and has expanded to include more than 4,000 rhododendrons, mostly hybrids. Another interesting feature is the 1,000 species of Carolina-native plants growing in the gardens. The Harwood garden, with gravel paths, is more formal and includes exotic plants from around the world. The collection of Japanese maples is noteworthy, as is the winter garden. The greenhouse is open Mon through Sat 9 a.m. to 4 p.m., Sun 1 p.m. to 4 p.m. but you can visit the gardens any time dawn to dusk. The best way to find the gardens is to go onto campus through the main gate on NC 49 and follow the signs to the visitor parking garage and ask for directions from there.

It takes about 15 minutes driving north on I-77 to reach **Davidson,** home of Davidson College, a small liberal arts school with outstanding music and arts programs. The little town covers less than 5 miles and, even though it's at Lake Norman, a popular destination, the community rarely makes it into guidebooks. It's an agreeable retreat from the city atmosphere of Charlotte, though you do want to avoid graduation day in mid-May and homecoming at the end of April, when the place is packed.

Davidson Village Inn (117 Depot St.; 704-892-8044 or toll-free 800-892-0796; davidsoninn.com) is a comfortable 18-room inn directly across from the college campus, in the historic district. The building, though relatively new, was built on the site of the old Chambers Hotel, and brick sidewalks help the brick inn fit in visually. The common areas are spacious and bright, with a big library—a real one—complete with comfortable reading chairs and a fireplace. From this location you can cross the street to tour the campus, walk quickly to popular restaurants, visit an independent bookstore, and check the offerings in a knitting and needlework shop.

You're also just steps away from the Belk Visual Arts Center, which is flanked by the **Every/Smith Galleries** (315 N. Main St.; 704-894-2575; david son.edu), part of Davidson College. The galleries, completed in 1993, cover

2,000 square feet and house a permanent collection of nearly 3,000 pieces. The spaces were designed to accommodate large-scale paintings and sculpture as well as smaller work. In addition to the permanent collections, the galleries feature changing professional exhibits and also student exhibits. The galleries are open Mon through Fri 10 a.m. to 5 p.m. and Sat and Sun noon to 4 p.m. when college is in session.

A block away, at 423 N. Main St., you come to the studios of **WDAV**, the college's all-classical public radio station. Found at 89.9 on the FM dial and wdav.org online, the station offers better-than-average programming, including live broadcasts and recordings of performances in the area (704-894-8900; wdav.org).

Even closer to Charlotte than Davidson, *Belmont,* off NC 273, has somehow managed to avoid being swallowed up by Charlotte development and retains its distinctive feel as a community of fewer than 10,000 people. Catawba Mills, makers of knitwear, was a major employer here, and in the area around Sixth Street, modest two- and three-bedroom homes that were mill houses still show pride of ownership on properties that typically have well-clipped grass and carefully tended shrubs in the front, with the backyards variously given over to more grass or perennial gardens or vegetable gardens. The old brick mill building has been rescued and renovated and now houses upscale condominiums. From all these locations, people walk to restaurants, a library, small stores, and the post office. A small restaurant at 23 N. Main St., *Cherubs' Cafe* (704-825-0414; holyangelsnc.org/cherubs), serves sandwiches, soups, salads, and desserts from 7 a.m. to 5 p.m. Mon through Fri, closes at 4 p.m. Sat. It is run by the Sisters of Mercy and volunteers to provide money for care, vocational training, and jobs, as well as work experience for children and adults with mental retardation and other disabilities. The restaurant has its share of church humor, with names on the menu such as "Divine Desserts" and, for coffee concoctions, "Holy Grounds."

The Roman Catholic Church has another presence at *Belmont Abbey College and Monastery Historic District,* 100 Belmont-Mount Holly Rd. (888-222-0110; belmontabbeycollege.edu). The college was founded by Benedictine monks in 1876, on land that had been a plantation. Today the grounds include the oldest liberal arts college in the Southeast, a monastery, the 1892 Our Lady of Lourdes Pilgrimage Shrine, a cemetery dating to 1890, and a library with a large collection of rare books. Classes are small, typically fewer than 20 students per teacher, and although not all teachers are Benedictine monks, many are. Teachers also come from other countries, other schools, and other religious orders. But the spirit of the school is distinctly Benedictine, trying to follow Benedict's instructions to the early monks to welcome each person as Christ.

The other major attraction in the Belmont area, ***Daniel Stowe Botanical Garden*** (6500 S. New Hope Rd.; 704-568-1774; dsbg.org) could be attributed to both divine providence and corporate generosity. In 1989 a retired Belmont textile executive, Daniel Jonathan Stowe, set aside 450 acres of land and lakefront property and $14 million to develop a world-class botanical garden. Since then, volunteers and employees have worked to develop formal gardens as well as woodland, meadow, and wetland areas. The Robert Lee Stowe Visitors Pavilion houses a gift shop and areas for displays, meetings, and classes. The garden maintains ongoing educational programs, plant sales, and seasonal exhibits. In nice weather, picnicking on the grounds is welcome. A notable addition to the property is an 8,000-square-foot orchid conservatory, billed as "the Carolinas' only glass house." In addition to a stunning variety of orchids, you'll find many other warmth-loving plants here, including bromeliads and succulents, in artfully arranged, changing exhibits set off by a waterfall. The garden is open every day from 9 a.m. to 5 p.m.; closed Thanksgiving, Christmas, and January 1. Admission is $10 for adults, $9 for senior citizens, $5 for children ages 4 to 12.

About 20 miles west of Charlotte, in Gastonia, which you can reach quickly on I-85, the ***Schiele Museum of Natural History and Planetarium,*** at 1500 E. Garrison Blvd., attracts large numbers of visitors, especially schoolchildren, with its collection of North American mammals in habitat settings, a 100-seat planetarium, a restored pioneer site of the 1700s, and a reconstructed Catawba Indian village. Other exhibits deal with everything from forestry to archaeology. A brochure maps out several self-guided tour suggestions for the outside grounds. Don't skip this one because it's popular; it has good reason for being so. Open Mon through Sat from 9 a.m. to 5 p.m. and Sun from 1 to 5 p.m. Call for planetarium show times, (704) 866-6900; schielemuseum.org. Admission fee is $7 for adults, $6 for senior citizens and students. To get there, take the New Hope Road exit from I-85 and follow the signs.

Places to Stay in the Lower Piedmont

CHARLOTTE

The Dunhill Hotel
237 North Tryon St.
(704) 332-4141
dunhillhotel.com
The city's only National
Historic Landmark hotel.
Moderate to expensive

The Morehead Inn
1122 E. Morehead St.
(704) 376-3357
moreheadinn.com
A well-established, well-
run bed-and-breakfast in
a renovated home in the
Dilworth area.
Expensive

SALISBURY

Across the Pond
324 N. Fulton St.
(866) 296-7965
www.acrossthepondbandb
.com
A couple originally from
England opened this B&B
in a historic home. They
offer a full, traditional
English breakfast.

**Turn of the Century
Victorian Bed & Breakfast**
529 S. Fulton St.
(704) 642-1660
turnofthecenturybb.com
Tasteful, restrained
Victorian restoration and
furnishings.
Moderate

Places to Eat in the Lower Piedmont

CHARLOTTE

Amalfi's Pasta and Pizza
8542 University City Blvd.
(704) 547-8651
amalfi-charlotte.com
Great pizza, but try the
fried calamari!
Inexpensive

Price's Chicken Coop
1614 Camden Rd.
(704) 336-9866
priceschickencoop.com
Famous for fried chicken
Inexpensive; cash only

Thai Taste
324 East Blvd.
(704) 332-0001
thaitastecharlotte.com
This was the first Thai
restaurant in Charlotte and
is still a favorite with serious
foodies.
Moderate

MOCKSVILLE

**Ketchie Creek Bakery
and Café**
844 Valley Rd.
(336) 751-9147
www.ketchiecreek-bakery
.com
Of the many café offerings,
the broccoli and cheese
quiche Is wonderful and
you can't go wrong with a
brownie.

O'Callahan's Pub
115 N. Main St.
(336) 753-0011
o'callahan'snc.com
A genuine Irish pub with
some additional cullinary
quirks but the corned beef
is legendary.

SALISBURY

Sweet Meadow Cafe
111 N. Main St.
(704) 637-8715
www.facebook.com/
SweetMeadowCafe
The crab cakes are to die
for! And for vegetarians, so
are the black bean burgers.
Moderate to expensive

The Northern Coast & Islands

Peaceful Places

Your next major stop as you head north along the coast is Morehead City, a deep port where the Intracoastal Waterway joins the Atlantic Ocean. It is both a commercial fishing town and a summer resort area, appealing especially to sport fishers. The waterfront is more devoted to commerce than tourism, has more than 5,000 square feet of continuous wharf, and includes a lot of shipping storage space. That means the waterfront isn't really pretty; it's too commercial and busy, but the activity is authentic and interesting. As a traveler, if you aren't here to fish, you're probably here to eat fish. The area has plenty of moderately priced motels and more seafood restaurants than you could patronize in two weeks' hard eating. If you ask people where to go, they'll most often make the unlikely sounding recommendation of the ***Sanitary Fish Market and Restaurant*** (501 Evans St.; 252-247-3111; sanitaryfishmarket .com). It's just a block from US 70, on Bogue Sound. Some reviewers have speculated that the name was intended to reassure customers that this place is sanitary, even though some seafood restaurants are not, but that's not quite accurate. The

THE NORTHERN COAST & ISLANDS

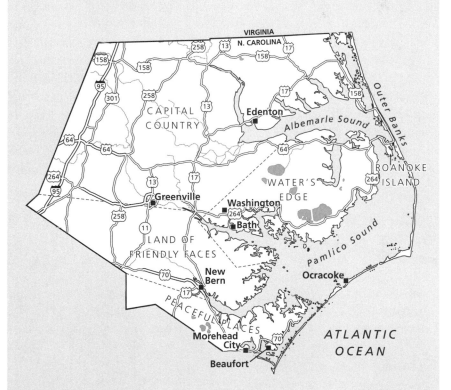

N

0 ——— 30 mi

0 ——— 30 km

VIRGINIA
N. CAROLINA

258
13
17

158
158

158

95

301
258

CAPITAL
COUNTRY
13
Edenton

Albemarle Sound

64

17

Outer Banks

158

264
64

WATER'S
EDGE
264
ROANOKE
ISLAND

13
17

Greenville

Washington
264
Bath

95
264

258

11
LAND OF
FRIENDLY FACES

Pamlico Sound

70
New
Bern
Ocracoke

17

PEACEFUL PLACES

Morehead
City
70

ATLANTIC
OCEAN

Beaufort

name was originally coined to signify an understanding between the man who rented out the first small market building and the partners who started their fresh seafood market there, that they'd sell no beer or wine and they would keep the place clean and neat. When the market also became a restaurant, it was with 12 stools at a counter and a two-burner kerosene stove. People liked the fresh seafood, and the market and restaurant kept growing. Now it's a big, casual, family-oriented place that seats more than 600 people and serves all kinds of seafood, with seating on an outdoor deck in good weather. Although sweet tea remains the beverage of choice for many customers, you can order wine or beer now, or sit at the Tall Tales bar. Owners estimate that over the years the place had fed more than 15 million people. While shrimp and flounder are invariably popular, the hushpuppies are downright legendary. This is, after all, the South. The restaurant is open every day from 11:30 a.m. to 3 p.m. for lunch, and 3 p.m. to 8:30 p.m. for dinner. Breakfast is served Sat and Sun from 8 to 11 a.m. *The History Place* (1008 Arendell St.; 252-247-7533; carterethistory.org), is the kind of place that makes you feel good about people, just regular folks, and what they can accomplish when they set their minds to it. The Carteret County Historical and Genealogical Society owns and operates the museum almost entirely on volunteer help and donated funds. The museum opened in 1988 in a building that had served at various times as a school and a church, but in 2001 the museum moved to its new, greatly expanded space on Arendell Street. For tourists the displays of county artifacts, including Native

ANNUAL EVENTS IN THE NORTHERN COAST & ISLANDS

KILL DEVIL HILLS

Annual Artful Gala
(late February)
(252) 473-5558

MANTEO

Virginia Dare's Birthday Celebration
August 18
(252) 473-2127

National Aviation Day–Orville Wright Birthday
August 19
(252) 441-7430

MOREHEAD CITY

Annual NC Seafood Festival
Waterfront
(mid-October)
(252) 726-6273

OUTER BANKS

Annual Stunt Kite Competition
Jockey's Ridge State Park
(mid-October)
(252) 441-4124 or
(800) 334-4777

Odd Burials

People in Beaufort like to tell stories. Unquestionably their favorites are those about the *Old Burying Ground.* The oldest date you can make out on a grave marker is 1756, but the cemetery was deeded to the town in 1731. One story is about the English soldier who was buried standing up because he swore he would never lie down on foreign soil.

And then there's the little girl buried in a barrel of rum. Seems that before her father took her off to England on a ship, he promised her mother that he would bring the child back again. Unfortunately, she died aboard the ship, and embalming her in rum was the only way he could think of to keep his promise.

American items, pieces from the Civil War and World War II, a fully furnished Victorian parlor, and clothing from the 1800s, is probably the most interesting aspect of the museum. But the facilities for historical research and genealogical study are also widely used and richly detailed. The museum is open Tues through Fri and the first Saturday of every month, 10 a.m. to 4 p.m. Admission is $3 for adults, $1.00 children 5 to 18, under 5 free.

From Morehead City it's just a short drive over the Paul Graydon Bridge to *Beaufort.* The first step to having fun in Beaufort is learning to say it properly—*BOW-ford.* This separates it from that place in South Carolina spelled the same way but pronounced to rhyme with "phew." People in Beaufort, North Carolina, care and respond accordingly.

This was once a fishing village, settled by French Huguenots and English sailors more than 275 years ago. The port was active during three wars: the American Revolution, the War of 1812, and the Civil War. Today Beaufort is a laid-back vacation area in which historic preservation and restoration have been impressive. Much of the downtown has been designated a National Historic Landmark, and the Beaufort Historical Association has restored a number of early buildings that are open to the public.

Local art is offered in the *Mattie King Davis Art Gallery* on the grounds of the Old Town Beaufort Restoration Complex, where local artists and craftspeople display their pottery, weaving, oil paintings, watercolors, and other original art, juried by the art gallery committee. The gallery is open Mon through Sat from 10 a.m. to 4 p.m., or until 5 p.m. from Mar through Nov. No admission fee (beauforthistoricsite.org/MKD.html).

The *North Carolina Maritime Museum* (315 Front St.; 252-728-7317; ncmaritimemuseums.com) contains artifacts ranging from fish and fossils to ships, including a model-ship collection and a collection of 5,000 seashells from

AUTHOR'S FAVORITE PLACES
IN THE NORTHERN COAST & ISLANDS

Beaufort	Mattamuskeet National Wildlife Refuge
North Carolina Maritime Museum	
Portsmouth Island	Wanchese
Aurora Fossil Museum	Hope Plantation
	Somerset Place

all over the world. Serious boat people visit here to watch wooden boats being built and restored. Open Mon through Fri from 9 a.m. to 5 p.m., Sat from 10 a.m. to 5 p.m., Sun from 1 to 5 p.m. Closed Thanksgiving, Christmas, and New Year's days. For a schedule of special events, write the museum at 315 Front St., Beaufort 28516, or check the website. No admission fee.

One way to see the sights and learn a lot about local lore is by taking one of the **Beaufort Historic Site Tours** operated by the historical association. All tours leave from the welcome center at 130 Turner St. Call ahead for all tour arrangements (252-728-5225 or 800-575-7483; historicbeaufort.com). Hours and days of tours vary depending on the time of year and, sometimes, on the weather.

The home tour includes not only old homes but also the jail, courthouse, and apothecary shop. Admission is $10 for adults, $5 for children.

From April 11 through October, the narrated English double-decker bus tours cover the downtown district and go out past a house that is reputed to have been a hangout for Blackbeard and his pirates (see "Shiver Me Timbers!" sidebar on p. 137). The tour narrator gives a lively mix of fact and folklore. These tours cost $10 per seat for adults, $5 for children ages 7 to 12.

Narrated tours of the Old Burying Ground at Ann Street, where stones date back to 1709 and possibly earlier, are offered in summer and fall. The narrator tells colorful stories about unusual circumstances through which people came to be buried here. Admission is $10 for adults, $5 for children 7 to 12. You may walk around the grounds anytime for free.

A nice place to stay in Beaufort is the **Pecan Tree Inn** (116 Queen St.; 252-728-6733 or toll-free 800-728-7871; pecantree.com). Innkeepers Stan and Christine Lamb are working on improvements in what was already a nice B&B. Pecan Tree Inn is the kind of place you stay for a special getaway in surroundings nothing like home. The 1860s Victorian inn was originally built to serve as a Masonic lodge. Now it is furnished with period antiques and bed styles ranging from romantic canopies to brass, iron, and wicker. It has 7 rooms, 2 of them with 2-person Jacuzzis. WiFi and wireless Internet connections are available throughout the inn. On the second floor, one of the inn's 2 suites has a private entrance with stairs to the brick courtyard and gardens below, so that lavish blooms complement the lavishly decorated room inside. Breakfast is a big deal here, with a buffet including everything from homemade granola and scones to frittatas, bacon, sausage and eggs. A variety of snacks and beverages is available afternoons in the dining room. This inn anchors more than two and a half acres of gardens, paths, and water features. No matter the time of year, you'll always find something pretty in these gardens.

Another B&B in a historic home is ***Langdon House*** (135 Craven St.; 252-728-5499; langdonhouse.com), a building with fascinating history. The initial structure was built in 1732. The ballast stones in its foundation were transported from England, giving innkeepers the opportunity to joke that the house is built on British soil. Additions were built in the 1700s, 1860s, and 1920s. After Jimm Prest turned it into a B&B he made some changes in how the rooms were used. He was married more than 17 years ago to Lizzette. She has maintained the B&B in the spirit of Jimm, who passed away in 2008 when he was only in his mid-50s. She has kept much of his commentary in Langdon House descriptions, and still serves breakfasts as they were in his day with a choice of a full breakfast, a lighter continental breakfast, or just early morning coffee if you're in a hurry to get out and explore. Langdon House has five rooms, each with private bath, in varying degrees of luxury. The most sumptuous, on the second floor, has a huge, four- by six-foot jetted tub that easily accommodates two people, side by side. The simpler rooms have showers.

Shiver Me Timbers!

Most of the coastal towns and islands in the area lay some claim to Blackbeard, the notorious pirate who built a fleet of captured ships and terrorized the seas in the 1700s. He captured a French Guinea ship in 1717, renamed it *Queen Anne's Revenge,* and put 40 huge guns, called blunderbusses, aboard. Later he deliberately ran the sailing vessel aground near Beaufort, which was known as Fishtown in those early days, as part of a plan to dump his fleet and crew, while escaping with his loot and getting a pardon from England. In 1997 salvage crews found what they believe to be the remains of *Queen Anne's Revenge* in about 20 feet of water at Beaufort Inlet. They found a blunderbuss barrel, a ship's bell, and a cannon ball. All these items now belong to the state of North Carolina.

But perhaps one of the greatest delights here is sitting in rockers on the front porch, sipping iced tea or perhaps an "adult" beverage, chatting and watching people wander by.

You'll find yet another kind of lodging at **Beaufort Inn** (101 Ann St.; 252-728-2600 or toll-free 800-726-0321; beaufort-inn.com). This is a small-scale hotel that the owners, Bruce and Katie Ethridge, like to say combines the privacy of a hotel with the ambience of a bed-and-breakfast. The inn, which has three stories and 44 rooms, each with private bath, telephone, and TV, is an attractive, well-settled place, with nice furnishings, a dining room with a fireplace, and an outdoor hot tub. The Ethridges have had the inn for more than 20 years and are definitely not impersonal absentee owners—they're there. In addition to a full breakfast served in the dining room anytime between 7 and 10 a.m., they offer refreshments on weekends from 3 to 6 p.m.

Beaufort has a number of restaurants, all within walking distance of the town's lodgings. Two of them have what one innkeeper calls "best kept secret allure."

Blue Moon Bistro (119 Queen St.; 252-728-5800; bluemoonbistro.biz), serves dinner Mon through Sat. Call for reservations. The atmosphere here is deliberately funky, the menu sophisticated, the wine list extensive. Appetizers range from steamed pork dumplings to pan-seared scallops au poivre. The entrees can be as simple as grilled Angus steak and as exotic as a risotto of white beans, sun-dried tomatoes, and chèvre over grilled eggplant.

Wet Adventure

I paddled my first sea kayak in Beaufort. This is not something you start out doing gracefully. Getting into a life vest and wet suit takes some squirming. Crawling into the small open area of the kayak becomes an exercise in humility. And sitting with your legs stretched straight out in front of you seems an impossibility.

But then somebody gives you a shove off the sloped ramp and into the water, and after a few tentative strokes, paddling this thing across the waterway to an island seems doable.

It takes a while to remember which rudder to push and even longer to get really proficient at paddling so the boat goes where you want it to. Then it all comes together, the kayak moves silently and efficiently across the water, and except for avoiding other boats and catching glimpses of the wild ponies and the birds on the islands, nothing else matters.

Be warned: Sea kayaking is addictive.

Dance Wherever You May Be

The folks devoted to preserving Ocracoke Island and its history say it's not about the buildings so much as it's about the people. One oft-mentioned example is Sam Tolson, who earned his living as a waterman, but was loved for his dancing. He entertained at most celebrations on the island and is reputed to have been able to dance for hours while balancing a glass of water on his head.

Aqua (114 Middle Ln.; 252-728-7777; aquaexperience.com) is a Spanish tapas–style restaurant, with the slogan "Small plates, big wines." Everything comes to you in small portions, so you can order several to make a meal or pass around the table. The idea is to sample lots of different appetizers, and these can be paired with appropriate wines by the staff, or you can make your own choices. Artful arrangement of the food on each plate is an important part of the presentation. You might order something like lump crab cake on citrus fennel slaw with a chipotle glaze or a cheese plate with assorted condiments. However, full-size dinners are served too. Foods in season influence the menu. The wines are not off the grocery store shelf, either. Aqua has a sort of hidden feel, as it is located on Middle Lane just west of and next door to the Back Street Pub. The restaurant serves dinner Tues through Sat.

One could stay in Beaufort a long time just wandering around, eating seafood, and sitting on the porch reading trashy novels. But you can find more adventure if you want it, too. On the waterfront, near the North Carolina Maritime Museum on Front Street, you'll find *Outer Banks Ferry Service* (252-728-4129; outerbanksferry.com), which will take you to *Shackleford Banks,* an island populated only with wild horses; *Carrot Island,* a good place for shelling, as well as *Bird Shoal* and *Sand Dollar Islands;* and to *Cape Lookout* for tours to visit the lighthouse and keepers' quarters and a jeep ride to the cape point. These are great activities in good weather but miserable places on cold, stormy days—assuming you could even get a ferry to take you over then—so it's better to arrange a trip once you see how the weather is going to be.

Assuming you are ready, eventually, to leave Beaufort, you should push on north almost to the end of US 70 East, to the little town of *Atlantic* (not to be confused with Atlantic Beach), where you can catch the ferry to the Outer Banks. Looking at your map, you will see that the Outer Banks is a long series of islands off the North Carolina coast. Some of them are fully developed resort areas; others have no concessions or services at all.

In particular, visit **Portsmouth Island.** It's uninhabited now, but 635 people once lived on the 30-mile-long island in the village of Portsmouth. Ultimately, they couldn't survive the weather, especially hurricanes. A particularly bad one in 1846 opened Hatteras and Oregon Inlets and changed shipping patterns, which cut off future economic development for the village. Gradually the people left, first the young and then the old. According to Joel Arrington, writing in the magazine *Wildlife in North Carolina,* only 14 people remained on the island in 1950; the last male resident died in 1971, after which the remaining two women gave up and moved to the mainland. The buildings of the village remain a little beat-up but intact, maintained by the National Park Service.

Your difficulty in seeing the village will be that, even after you've ferried across to the island, if you want to cover any distance, you'll need a four-wheel-drive or all-terrain vehicle to travel the 18 miles up the beach from the ferry landing to the village, because there are no roads. In addition to ferry services, two reliable companies offer tours and transportation.

One of the most lovingly cared for buildings is the Portsmouth Village Methodist Church. Indeed, the sight of half a dozen or so men in fishing clothes, sitting quietly on the benches inside the old church when they're supposed to be at water's edge fishing, may be as special an experience as visiting the village. For information about ferry hours, call **Morris Marina** (252-225-4261; portsmouthislandfishing.com). For information about land transportation, contact **Portsmouth Island ATV Excursions** (252-982-4484; portsmouth islandatvs.com). These tours leave from Ocracoke Island.

A simpler way to visit the village, though less colorful and a bit more on the beaten (or should it be rowed, in this case?) path, is to take a boat tour beginning at **Ocracoke Island.** Contact **Austin Boat Tours** (252-928-4361 or 252-928-5431; portsmouthnc.com). If you're not sure how to manage the trip and would like more information and advice, call the ranger station (252-728-2250) for enthusiastic, knowledgeable help. They have a list of all the ferrying services and can put you in touch with the one that will work best for you.

Harkers Island is another "people place" that doesn't attract a lot of tourists. Here some people still remember when hunting waterfowl for food was a natural part of daily existence, not a recreational sport. They remember carving decoys because they needed them to attract ducks, not to set up on the mantel as decorator items. The **Core Sound Waterfowl Museum and Heritage Center** (1785 Island Rd.) honors that Down East heritage and provides a place for carvers to practice the old art and younger people to learn it, or at least see it in action. Most days you'll find two or three local wood-carvers at work on the porch, telling stories about the days when waterfowl were so plentiful their clusters looked like islands out on the sound. When decoys got lost or drifted away, it wasn't a big deal. They just carved more as part of the daily routine. Nothing fancy about it. The early decoys didn't have to fool anybody but the flocks of birds high overhead.

The museum is actively working on all kinds of other historical projects, with an emphasis on teaching and preserving the old ways. This includes quilting bees. A finished quilt is raffled off to raise money for work on the museum. A new, much larger museum is in the works—on 16 acres at Shell Point, next to the National Park Service's Cape Lookout National Seashore headquarters near the tip of the island. It's a community effort, the money being raised by local people, with such attractions as a viewing platform on Willow Pond built by volunteers with donated materials. Whatever state the place is in when you get to Harkers, it's a heartwarming stop. The museum is open year-round, 10 a.m. to 5 p.m. Mon through Sat and 2 to 5 p.m. Sun. Admission $5 for adults, students and children free. For more information call (252) 728-1500; core sound.com.

Portsmouth Island and Harkers Island are part of the 56-mile-long ***Cape Lookout National Seashore*** (252-728-2250; nps.gov/calo), which comprises North Core Banks, South Core Banks, and Shackleford Banks. A good place to sort out all the possibilities is at the visitor center at the end of Harkers Island, in a house that used to be the keepers' quarters near the Cape Lookout Lighthouse, at the end of the island. The lighthouse itself is not open for visitors, but it's a great subject for photographs and sketching. The center is open 9 a.m. to 5 p.m. 7 days a week. Closed Christmas and New Year's Day. A variety of tours and camping arrangements are available, but before you sign up for anything, remember that the undeveloped islands don't have roads, bathrooms, or water, so you must be able to climb in and out of boats and walk a reasonable distance to spend time on them. You also need to carry in your own drinking water. As one park ranger says, "It's really a backcountry experience." It doesn't hurt to take along a good insect repellent, either. One reliable concessionaire affiliated with the National Park Service providing ferry, tour, and camping options is ***Morris Marina Kabin Kamps Ferry Service, Inc.*** (252-225-4261) on North Core. Since the companies providing such services change, check the National Seashore website for current information.

Land of Friendly Faces

The entire area along the northern coast, the barrier islands, and the Outer Banks is a maze of toll ferries, free ferries, private ferries, and bridges. The way you organize your trips here depends on everything from the weather to how much time you want to spend driving or being ferried. Remember that a ferry is

Crossing the Water

The North Carolina ferry system links many coastal and island communities that would otherwise take hours to reach by road or be completely inaccessible except by private boat. The system, which has been running since the mid-1940s, is operated by the North Carolina Department of Transportation. It is one of the largest ferry systems in the nation.

Crossing times range from 20 minutes to get from Cherry Branch to Minnesota to 2.5 hours for the trip from Ocracoke to Swan Quarter. Schedules vary with the seasons. For full details call (800) BY-FERRY or check the website: ncdot.org/ferry.

not a fast way to travel. In planning trips in this area, it sometimes works better to find a pleasant base to which you return after each foray in a new direction. Try *New Bern* as a slightly inland base from which, one way or another, you can get to a wonderful variety of places to spend a day or so. Everyone in New Bern will have ideas for you, which will certainly include Oriental.

Oriental is about 25 miles east of New Bern on NC 55. It has won a reputation as the sailing capital of the East Coast and almost always has a sailing school or camp in progress. Except for some antiques shops, a modest motel or two, and some restaurants, there's not much here except nice people.

For a fascinating glimpse of this town's activities and people, check the website, towndock.com, for information about recent local weather, news and events.

Then again, once you're in New Bern, you may not want to go anywhere else at all—not just because there's so much to see and do but also because this is one of the friendliest towns anywhere. To give you an idea, a couple staying at a bed-and-breakfast inn in the historic district was walking to a nearby restaurant where they had dinner reservations when they stopped to admire an especially nicely restored house. The owners, who happened to be on the porch, invited the couple in for a drink and showed them around. They spent so much time chatting that the couple never did make it to the restaurant.

On the outside chance that you might not be so generously befriended by strangers, stop in at the New Bern-Craven County Convention and Visitor Center (203 S. Front St.; 252-637-1551; visitnewbern.com) to pick up brochures and information about shopping and local attractions. The center is open Mon through Fri 8 a.m. to 5 p.m., Sat 10 a.m. to 4 p.m.

You'll be able to pick up full details on Tryon Palace Restorations and Garden Complex, where first a royal government and then an independent state government were housed. In colonial times *Tryon Palace,* at 610 Pollack

St., was known as the most beautiful building in America. The elaborate formal gardens as well as the elegant buildings and furnishings have been restored.

Tours conducted by guides in costume lead you through the rooms; give you a look at demonstrations of candle making, cloth making, cooking, and other period activities; and fill you in on specific facts about the buildings and their earlier, illustrious occupants. If you just want to walk around in the gardens, you can take a self-guided tour. The complex (252-514-4900 or 800-767-1560; tryonpalace.org) is open year-round, Mon through Sat from 9 a.m. to 5 p.m. and Sun from noon to 5 p.m. Closed Thanksgiving Day, December 23 through 25, and January 1. Admission for everything in the complex is $20 for adults, $10 for students with identification. Hours vary seasonally for individual features in the complex, and prices do too, depending on what you want to see. Check the website for the specific times you might visit. Much less well known than the Tryon Palace are two small museums, each within walking distance of the other.

The *New Bern Firemen's Museum,* across the corner at 420 Broad St., houses a collection of memorabilia of North Carolina's earliest fire company, from 1845, and of the Button Company, a rival volunteer company. The New Bern Firemen's Museum claims the title of "oldest volunteer fire company in North Carolina." The displays include early steamers and pump wagons, large photographs, and the mounted head of an old fire horse named Fred, who, at least according to publicists, died in harness answering a false alarm in 1925. No information is offered about what happened to the rest of the horse. Open Mon through Sat from 10 a.m. to 4 p.m. Closed Thanksgiving, Christmas, and New Year's Day. Admission is $5 for adults, $2.50 for children (252-636-4087; firemensmuseum.com).

At *Bank of the Arts* (317 Middle St.; 252-638-2577; cravenarts.org), about a block away, you'll find artists' exhibits in sculpture, oil, watercolor, pottery, and photography. The exhibits change every month. Originally a neoclassical bank building, it is now home to the Craven Arts Council and Gallery. The gallery has 30-foot-high ceilings with ornate colored plaster in the Beaux Arts style. Sometimes afternoon concerts, storytellers, and folksingers are featured. Open Tues through Sat 10 a.m. to 5 p.m.

The *New Bern Trolley Cars* (252-637-7316 or 800-849-7316; newbern tours.com) combine the fun of motion with the expertise of tour guides who know the history of New Bern and tell it well. You can choose from several different tour options: walking, horse-and-carriage, and the traditional trolley tours. Tour hours vary with the seasons, and prices with the options, so you'll do better by calling to find out what's happening during your visit to the area. Oh yes, if you wanted to book a trolley for your wedding, you'd need to arrange it ahead of time, but it *can* be done! Office hours 8 a.m. to 4 p.m. Mon through Fri.

In a town as historically significant as New Bern, you could easily get overwhelmed by more historical data than you really want on a vacation, but to enjoy the area you should know at least a few basic facts. The community was first settled in 1710 by Swiss and German immigrants, who named it for Bern, Switzerland. It was capital of the colonies from 1766 to 1776 and then state capital. Economically, the area flourished mostly because of its port at the time of the Revolution, slumped during the Civil War, then recovered fairly quickly. From about the time of World War II, it has gradually restored its historical spots and become a comfortably established, low-key attraction.

Irrelevant but fun to know: Pepsi-Cola was invented here, but the inventor went bankrupt during a sugar scarcity. Caleb Bradham created a drink in 1898 at his pharmacy that he said did not contain the "impurities" found in bottled health tonics and other drinks, referring to the alcohol and narcotics some of them contained. People liked it and started calling it "Brad's drink." Bradham's photograph shows a good-looking man with dark hair, a long face, high arching eyebrows, and a quirky smile under a narrow mustache. He looks like the drink made him happy. He made the stuff in the cramped basement of his store, bottling the syrup for his fountain and other pharmacies in the area. In a few years he was doing enough business to realize he was on to something, and incorporated as Pepsi-Cola on December 24, 1902. Today the ***Birthplace of Pepsi-Cola*** (256 Middle St.; 252-636-5898; pepsistore.com) is a memorabilia gift shop in the same location, owned by the Pepsi-Cola Bottling Company. You can buy a fountain Pepsi and drink it sitting at a table surrounded by Pepsi memorabilia—signs and shirts and lamps and key rings and magnets and limited-edition displays. A video narrated by Walter Cronkite telling the Pepsi-Cola story is available to watch while you're in the store. An employee says

Showing the Colors

During the summer and into autumn in New Bern, you'll notice the streets are lined with trees blooming in a range of colors from palest pink to bright red to dark purple. *Lagerstroemia indicia,* commonly known as crape myrtle, is the official shrub of New Bern. Originally native to China and tropical and subtropical countries, **crape myrtle** is popular throughout the South and not hardy north of Baltimore. Hybridizers have created dwarf versions of the plant for smaller gardens. The bark on *Lagerstroemia* flakes away from the wood in patches, showing a lighter color underneath that attracts the eye in winter after the tree has shed its leaves and branches.

BETTER KNOWN ATTRACTIONS
IN THE NORTHERN COAST & ISLANDS

KILL DEVIL HILLS

Wright Brothers National Memorial
(252) 441-7430
nps.gov/wrbr

MANTEO

Lost Colony Outdoor Drama
(252) 473-2127
(800) 488-5012
thelostcolony.org

NAGS HEAD

Jockey's Ridge State Park
(252) 441-7132
jockeysridgestatepark.com

NEW BERN

Tryon Palace
(800) 767-1560
tryonpalace.org

ROANOKE ISLAND

North Carolina Aquariums
(252) 473-3493
ncaquariums.com

that for those who work there hearing the narration over and over gets a little old ("ad nauseum"), but visitors enjoy it, though hearing Walter Cronkite is a bit like hearing the ghosts of Christmas Past. The store is open year-round Mon through Sat 10 a.m. to 6 p.m., and noon to 4 p.m. Sun.

Water's Edge

One interesting trip from New Bern is the drive north on US 17 to Washington, where you pick up US 264 to Bath, Belhaven, and Swan Quarter. The trip winds through mostly rural areas.

You'll find a lot of local color just before you come to Washington, at *Chocowinity,* billed as "Home of the Indians," where the high school boasts various athletic triumphs each year. Chocowinity is a crossroads community, not set up to lure or serve tourists, so don't count on it as a place to stop, fuel up, eat, and so on. Look at it as an absolutely honest glimpse of small-town coastal North Carolina.

From here you can drive on through Washington to Bath or get to Bath by crossing the Pamlico River on the ferry, which you approach by following NC 33 East from Chocowinity through corn and tobacco country, past a brick house with a stonework chimney that's bigger than the house, past Possum Track Road, and on to Aurora—a drive of about 33 miles. This route actually backtracks some, and you could get to Aurora faster by taking NC 1003 from US 17 just outside New Bern, but then you'd miss Chocowinity. It all depends on how much exploring you want to do.

Twin Lakes Resort (1618 Memory Ln.; 252-946-5700; twinlakesnc.com) in Chocowinity offers swanky camping. You have a choice of trailer sites (some shaded), tent sites, and pull-throughs, supplying water and electricity. Also on the grounds are hot showers, campfires, laundry facilities, pay phones, ice, firewood, church services, a boat ramp, a fishing pier, waterskiing, a playground, recreational facilities, a camp store, and a picnic area. People sometimes bring big tents, refrigerators, and small television sets—everything they need to stay for a long time. Call to check rates and make reservations.

Close to the juncture of NC 33 and NC 306, the little town of *Aurora*—population about 500—is home to the *Aurora Fossil Museum* (400 Main St.; 252-322-4238; aurorafossilmuseum.com). This museum is great for kids who are turned on by hunting for artifacts and equally rewarding for anyone looking for a better understanding of the geological history of eastern North Carolina, from the birth of the Atlantic Ocean to the present.

Millions of years ago this part of the state lay under the ocean. Fossils anywhere from 5 to 22 million years old are on display in the museum, along with a variety of murals and an 18-minute video explaining the history of the region. The fossils include giant teeth from 40-foot sharks, bones from extinct birds, and skeletons of dolphins that had necks. Some scientists speculate that the existence of the neck proves dolphins once lived on land and evolved to adapt to the sea.

The museum gets its artifacts from a large phosphate mine a few miles north of town. An exhibit in the museum shows a mock phosphate pit to illustrate how phosphate is mined and where the fossils come from. And outside the museum stands a huge pile of coarse phosphate materials through which visitors may sift for fossils. What you're most likely to find here are prehistoric shark's teeth.

The museum is about more than fossils and prehistoric times and now includes such exhibits as a collection of Native American artifacts. A learning center next to the museum features fossil and mineral displays with videos and educational programs. The museum is open 9 a.m. to 4:30 p.m. Mon through Sat and from March 1 through Labor Day, also 2:30 p.m.to 4:30 p.m. on Sun. Closed on holidays. You can dig in the outside phosphate/fossil pile any time. Admission is free.

From Aurora, NC 306 North runs to the Pamlico River Ferry. The ferry is free. The crossing takes about 25 minutes. From the ferry landing, go left on NC 92 into historic *Bath,* where you come first to the visitor center.

Whitfield's Curse

Bath opened the first public library in the American colonies in the early 1700s, started the first shipyard in the state in 1701, and was the state's first capital in 1744. So why did such a forward-looking town never grow the way some other seaport towns did?

Local legend has it that the townspeople rejected Methodist evangelist George Whitfield when he came in 1774 to save their souls. They didn't want to hear his preaching, and they wouldn't give him a place to stay in town. Whitfield got back at them by placing a curse on the village: ". . . you shall remain, now and forever, forgotten by men and nations. . . . "

After that the town burned three times, and even today the population stays at about 200 souls, which may or may not be saved.

Bath is the kind of place you fantasize about when you dream of leaving the rat race for a simpler way of life. The town, with a population not much over 200, only 3 blocks long and 2 blocks wide, is friendly and without guile; people cutting their grass or working in their gardens wave as you walk or drive by. They're proud of their history but see it with enough humor to name the state liquor store "Ye Olde ABC Package Store."

The folks in the **Historic Bath Visitor Center** (207 Carteret St.; 252-923-3971; nchistoricsites.org/bath) encourage you to see the 25-minute orientation film, "A Town Called Bath," before you begin a self-guided walking tour or take one of the guided tours. These tours are given on the hour, with the last tour leaving an hour before closing time. Hours are 9 a.m. to 5 p.m. Tues through Sat and from 1 to 5 p.m. Sun. Tours take about 1.5 hours. Adults $2, students $1.

You can approach the history a couple of different ways. Bath was the home of Blackbeard, the pirate, and some of his loot is still supposed to be buried somewhere in the area. It's also the oldest incorporated town in North Carolina. The Palmer-Marsh House, from the colonial period, dates back to about 1740. The St. Thomas Church, which was begun in 1734, is the oldest church in the state. It has been restored and is still used by the Episcopal Diocese as an active place of worship, although visitors are allowed to come in anytime for a self-guided tour. The St. Thomas parish had a collection in the early 1700s of more than 1,000 books and pamphlets from England, and that collection became the first public library in North Carolina.

From Bath, it's a pretty drive of 11 miles on NC 99 to **Belhaven.** Here you can visit **Belhaven Memorial Museum,** in Old City Hall (211 E. Main St.; 252-943-6817; beaufort-county.com/Belhaven/museum/Belhaven.htm). The collection represents the idiosyncratic personal interests of Eva Blount Way in collections she began about 1900, when she would have been about 30 years old. She began with buttons, ending up with about 30,000 of them. This won't make much sense if you're so young you've seen only standard plastic buttons found on most clothing today. But before plastic, buttons were made from all kinds of materials: precious metals, gemstones, wood, shells. They were often highly ornate, hand produced, and beautiful. In Eva's day, practically all women had jars full of buttons or kept buttons on long strings. Eva's collection just got a little out of hand. She also got interested in old coins, early American kitchenware, coffee grinders, antique dolls, and toys. The displays now include Civil War items, military memorabilia from two world wars, farming tools, and so on. One quirky addition is an X-ray machine from the 1920s that looks like something from a Flash Gordon serial. According to the museum's advertising, "It's like spending a day in your grandmother's attic." Belhaven Memorial Museum is open every day but Wed 1 to 5 p.m. Admission is free; donations are appreciated.

At Belhaven pick up US 264 East, crossing the Intracoastal Waterway to Swan Quarter—a nature lover's paradise—filled with water, woods, and wildlife, where people so far have made only the lightest noticeable mark. Most of this distance is lovely, although you'll probably see a lot of heavy equipment in some areas. In early summer hibiscus bushes bloom along the road, red and yellow cannas adorn the lawns of farmhouses and mobile homes, and apple trees bear so heavily that the fruit seems to be dripping from the laden and drooping branches.

miss eva's cough syrup

2 tablespoons castor oil

1 tablespoon lemon juice

2 tablespoons paregoric

1 cup brown sugar

Mix all ingredients well.

Seems like this needs more liquid, but maybe just the threat of having to take it was enough to stop a cough.

At Swan Quarter you can either take the ferry to Ocracoke, probably the best known of the barrier islands, or you can continue driving up the coast along US 264 to Manns Harbor, where you cross the bridge to Roanoke Island and continue on over the **Outer Banks** islands. If you plan to take the ferry, a 2.5-hour ride, call the Ocracoke Visitor Center (252-928-4531) ahead of time to check on current schedules and weather conditions.

Ocracoke, an old fishing village, is fun if you're willing to take a couple of days and just hang out; if all you do is drive through, you'll miss most of what it has to offer. Of course there's history. As early as 1715, Ocracoke was a port of the North Carolina colony, where Blackbeard, the pirate, buried his treasure and lost his head. The head got carried off to Bath; presumably the treasure's still somewhere on the island. These days, fishing, bicycling (you can rent bicycles here), and bird hunting are bigger attractions than treasure hunting. But mostly Ocracoke is a place to escape the chrome-and-plastic world of commercial tourism. For full information about the island, ferries, and marina, contact the Ocracoke Visitor Center (252-928-4531). ***Ocracoke Island Lighthouse*** (888-493-3826; ocracoke-nc.com/light), on Point Road, is the oldest lighthouse still in use in North Carolina. It was built in 1823. The tower is 75 feet tall, built of brick and concrete, with 5-foot-thick base walls. The white tower serves as an entrance beacon to Ocracoke Inlet. The tower is not open to the public, but you may tour the grounds. Admission is free.

Fair warning here—Ocracoke gains in popularity as a tourist destination every year, and to enjoy it as a slower-paced place, you need to plan a trip that doesn't land you on the island at the peak of the summer season in July and August. Although you can still enjoy the island's 16 miles of clean, unspoiled beaches without crowding or concessions then, you'll find the area around the harbor full of people wandering about, gaping, and filling the restaurants. Not that there's anything wrong with that. Ocracoke, after all, has set itself up to serve tourists. But you'll get a much better sense of the place and its people during the slower times.

A good example of this is ***Edwards of Ocracoke*** (226 Back Rd.; 800-254-1359; edwardsofocracoke.com), a place to stay in the village. This is one of the long-established lodgings, with motel rooms and efficiencies, cottage apartments, and a couple of private cottages all clustered around a tree-shaded yard with lawn chairs, grills, and a place to clean fish. The accommodations are relatively inexpensive and quite plain, but comfortable. It's a place with no affectations, run by Wayne, Trudy, Bert, and Sara Clark, all of whom came to the place after leaving more high-powered jobs and education. It's friendly and homey. But in the busiest times, such as mid-July, it's also full of people, so you definitely won't have any sense of privacy and silence on a tiny island.

Virtually everyone who visits the island ends up having at least one meal at ***Howard's Pub and Raw Bar Restaurant*** on NC 12 at the north end of the village (1175 Irvin Garrish Hwy.). This is a big, clattering place with a menu that has everything from thick, hand-shaped burgers to oysters on the half shell. Portions are generous, service is friendly, and the atmosphere is casual. People seem to be having a good time, especially those seated on the screened porch. In addition to a wine list, Howard's has a huge line-up of beers, more than 200 of them, from domestic Coors and Rolling Rock to microbrewery organic beers such as Butte Creek Pale Ale to regional microbrewery specialties. Also, Howard's has a line of T-shirts, hats, sweatshirts, mugs, magnets, and the like emblazoned with its logo. For all the commotion, you don't get the feeling of being churned through a corporate eating place here, and especially in the off-season, it's fun. The restaurant is open every day of the year, beginning at 11 a.m. (252-928-4441; howardspub.com).

No matter how much you like it, sooner or later you'll have to leave Ocracoke. A free ferry will take you from Ocracoke to Cape Hatteras. Hatteras is pretty well built up and can have heavy traffic on its main highway, but you should plan on a visit to the *Pea Island National Wildlife Refuge,* south of the Oregon Inlet, where you can see more birds than you even knew existed—more than 250 different species. Serious birders spend days here. You need a good insect repellent, a shirt with long sleeves, a hat with a brim, suntan lotion, and drinking water to make the experience comfortable. Binoculars help, too. Some observation decks let you see not only the ocean and wildlife but also shipwrecks on the shore. The refuge is open every day from dawn to dusk. The information office is open daily 9 a.m. to 4 p.m., year-round, and admission is free (252-987-2394 or 252-473-1131; fws.gov/peaisland).

Next, still along the Outer Banks, at Frisco, you'll find the *Native American Museum and Natural History Center* (53536 NC 12; 252-995-4440; nativeamericanmuseum.org). The museum has a nationally recognized but too-seldom-seen collection of Native American artifacts and exhibits. In the natural history center, you'll find educational displays, special films, live exhibits, and a nature trail winding through the maritime forest. The people who work here say it's impossible to tell what the most popular exhibits are because favorites vary with each individual, but the stone artifacts attract a lot of attention, the Hopi wishing drum really does work, and people who commune with nature in the maritime forest claim some unusual experiences. The gift shop is popular, too, because it sells genuine Native American crafts. The museum is open Tues through Sun 10:30 a.m. to 5 p.m. Winter hours will be shorter. To request information by mail, write the museum at P.O. Box 399, Frisco, NC 27936. Admission $5 for adults, $15 per family, $3 for seniors.

It's possible to drive on up the Outer Banks, but it's monotonous in some undeveloped areas, full of traffic elsewhere, and generally just not as interesting as you'd expect it to be. You might do better to ferry back across to Swan Quarter and from there drive north on US 264, toward Manns Harbor, where the bridge takes you across to Manteo on Roanoke Island. This trip takes you into the *Mattamuskeet National Wildlife Refuge,* a breathtaking wilderness of 50,000 acres comprising Lake Mattamuskeet, marshland, timber, and cropland. The lake is 18 miles long and about 6 miles wide, the largest natural lake in North Carolina.

In parts of the acreage, water levels are controlled mechanically to allow local farmers to plant corn and soybeans and to allow for overseeding some acres to provide food for the wildlife. The wooded areas along the boundaries of the refuge contain pine and mixed hardwoods. Some commercial logging and controlled burning are used to keep the woodlands healthy.

Headquarters for the refuge (38 Mattamuskett Rd.; 252-926-4021; fws.gov/mattamuskeet) is off NC 94, 1.5 miles north of US 264, between Swan Quarter and Englehard. Stopping in is a good way to learn all the possibilities of the place. At various points you can crab, fish in fresh- or saltwater, and hunt. The area begs for bird watching, photographing, and painting. Depending on the time of year, you might spot swans, Canada geese, song- and marsh birds, and even bald eagles, as well as deer, bobcats, and river otters. Some hunting of swans, ducks, coots, and occasionally deer is allowed.

But this is a refuge administered by the US Fish and Wildlife Service of the Department of the Interior and operates by its rules. You can't camp, swim, or collect exotic plants here. There are restrictions on firearms. The refuge is open for daylight use daily. For full details on how to enjoy the place and lists of lodgings available nearby, write Refuge Manager, Mattamuskeet National Wildlife Refuge, Route 1, Box N-2, Swan Quarter 27885, or e-mail mattamuskeet@fws.gov.

Mattamuskeet Lodge on the property is no longer open for visitors inside because of structural problems, but it's still an interesting place to take pictures of from the outside, and the story of the lodge stands as proof that people have been messing with the environment to make money for a long time. Beginning in 1911, three different investors tried to drain Lake Mattamuskeet to build a community they wanted to call New Holland and farm what would be rich soil once the water was gone. They built a pumping station in 1915, where four coal-fueled steam pumps moved 2,000 gallons of water per second. This was the largest pumping station in the world. But the whole enterprise was so expensive that each of the investors ultimately gave up on the idea and the US government took over the land in 1934, establishing a waterfowl sanctuary. The Civilian Conservation Corps turned the pumping plant into a lodge, with an observation deck in the tower that had been a smokestack. The lodge has been empty since 1974, but local volunteer groups, the nonprofit group Partnership for the Sounds, and the US Fish and Wildlife Service are raising money to restore the lodge so it can be used for research and education about migratory waterfowl. The first weekend in December, the *Swan Days Festival,* with local craft and food vendors, guided tours of the refuge areas, and workshops, focuses attention on the lodge and the refuge. The refuge office and lodge website (albemarle-nc.com/mattamuskeet/refuge/) provide details.

From Mattamuskeet Lake, US 264 continues through lonely marsh and woodland up to Manns Harbor and across to Roanoke Island. The main community here, Manteo, used to be a small resort area. It's growing now, not excessively, but too much to suit the longtime residents, who remember when the road through town didn't turn into bumper-to-bumper ribbons of automobiles during rush hour.

Roanoke Island

You'll remember from your grade-school history lessons that **Roanoke Island** is where the English first tried to establish a colony in the New World in 1585, encouraged by Queen Elizabeth I and led by Sir Walter Raleigh. They named it for Raleigh but couldn't keep it going. A year later those who had survived returned to England. In 1587 Raleigh tried again, this time including women and children in the group led by John White. Virginia Dare was born here. Then Sir Walter went sailing away for supplies. By the time he got back, three years later, the colony had vanished, leaving no signs of what might have happened to it. The **Fort Raleigh National Historic Site** (thelostcolony.org) memorializes the lost colony with a restoration of the old fort and a granite marker commemorating Virginia Dare's birth as the first English child born here. From June through Aug, the drama *The Lost Colony*, performed outdoors at the Waterford Theatre on the site, tells the story. (Long before he appeared as Andy Taylor in the Mayberry television shows, Andy Griffith played Sir Walter Raleigh in this production.) Everything about this outdoor drama happens on a grand scale, on a stage in front of the bay so the water almost seems to be a backdrop. Many of the effects are marvels of engineering. For instance, three ships "sail" in front of the stage, moved by a combination of ropes and human energy. Tickets begin at about $30 for adults, $25 for teens, $13 to $18 for children. Phone (800) 488-5012 for exact schedules. Be sure to ask what the current policy is regarding bad weather.

Next to the theater, the **Elizabethan Gardens** (252-473-3234; elizabethangardens.org), created by the Garden Club of North Carolina as a memorial to the lost colonists, bloom from spring until fall, with roses, crape myrtle, lilies, hydrangeas, and summer annuals. The gardens feature an extensive collection of old garden ornaments, some dating back to the time of the first Queen Elizabeth, as well as a sunken garden, a wildflower garden, an herb garden, and camellias and azaleas in season. Open Apr and May 9 a.m. to 6 p.m.; June, July, and Aug to 7 p.m.; Sept and Oct to 6 p.m.; Nov to 5 p.m.; Dec, Jan, and

Feb to 4 p.m.; Mar to 5 p.m. Admission is $9 for adults, $7 for senior citizens, $6 for children ages 6 to 17; children under 5 $2.

Complete your history lesson by visiting the **Roanoke Island Festival Park** (1 Festival Park; 252-475-1500; roanokeisland.com) across the bridge and opposite the Manteo waterfront. The museum contains exhibits depicting life in the 16th century, including a reproduction of a sailing vessel similar to what would have been used to bring the first colonists to Roanoke in 1585. A 20-minute multimedia program gives you the feel of those early voyages and what it would have been like to live on the ship. In the summer costumed actors portray early mariners and colonists. After seeing the film, you may tour the ship. Other exhibits include the American Indian Town, and a depiction of the settlement site. Operating hours vary seasonally. Open March 1 to December 31, 9 a.m. to 5 p.m. daily. Admission $8 for adults, $5 for children 6 to 17, under 6 admitted free.

In downtown **Manteo** (named for an Indian of Roanoke who went back to England with the early sailors) on US 64/264, you can pick up a bit of local family history by staying at **Scarborough Inn** (524 US 64; 252-473-3979; www .scarboroughhhouseinn.com), which is run by longtime residents of the island. The 14 rooms in the inn and annex are furnished with antiques and collectibles that have been in the family, or at least in the community, for generations. It's not fancy stuff but the kind of things you remember from visiting old Aunt Lizzie or Great-Grandma. The rooms are simple but comfortable. Two units over the barn are outfitted with king-size beds. Each room has a private bath, a small refrigerator, and a coffeemaker with coffee provided. Rates include continental breakfast and the use of bicycles for exploring the island.

For a special occasion, you might try the **Tranquil House Inn** (405 Queen Elizabeth Ave.; 800-458-7069; tranquil houseinn.com). Located on the Shallowbag Bay waterfront in downtown Manteo, the inn whispers "luxury" when you enter. The building is a reproduction of a typical 19th-century Outer Banks inn, with added contemporary conveniences a 19th-century traveler wouldn't even have dreamed about. Because of the pale cypress woodwork, glass, and stained glass throughout, the inn's interior seems almost as bright and sunny as the docks outside. The inn has an upscale gourmet restaurant with a fine wine list. In the guest rooms you'll find not only the expected amenities such as television and telephone, but

drinkup

Before Prohibition, North Carolina produced more wine than any other state in the country. Settlers cultivated scuppernong grapes more than 400 years ago in the settlement of Sir Walter Raleigh, the Lost Colony.

also Oriental carpets, fine furnishings, and hand-tiled bathrooms. Rates, which are surprisingly moderate given the luxurious atmosphere, vary seasonally and include a buffet breakfast and a wine and cheese reception in late afternoon.

The distinctly local *Endless Possibilities* (4711 Croatan Hwy.; 252-715-3870; www.facebook.com/endlesspossibilities.ragweavers.com), a charity-based organization to raise funds for the Outer Banks Hotline Crisis Intervention and Prevention Center, is also a source of inspiration, education, and woven pieces for visitors. Endless Possibilities opened in 2002, selling fiber art to raise money for the hotline and also teaching volunteers to weave. Many of the weavers have come from difficult relationships and homes and find their work here part of rebuilding their lives. Visitors are invited to sit at a loom and try it themselves. A volunteer will help take the weaving off the loom and tie the knots to finish it. Other woven pieces, handbags, rugs, wall hangings, and scarves are for sale as well. Shop hours vary seasonally. Call ahead.

The other community on Roanoke Island, *Wanchese* (named for another Indian who took off for England), doesn't seem to know it is surrounded by tourists. Most of the people of Wanchese fish for a living. Driving on NC 345 South to the village, you pass modest homes—many with a boat in the yard—battered vans, worn pickups, and lots of churches, flowers, and pets. Signs in some of the yards invite you to buy hand-carved duck decoys, driftwood, wood crafts, and nursery plants. All the people you see in the community will talk to you pleasantly and seem to enjoy your watching them work on the docks. At least one family maintains a "shedder" operation for harvesting soft-shell crabs as they shed their shells.

Fisherman's Wharf Restaurant (4683 Mill Landing Rd.; 252-473-6004; fishermanswharfobx.com), a large, unpretentious restaurant on the wharf, surrounded by pilings, wild stands of Queen Anne's lace, and rolls of chicken wire, specializes in broiled and fried seafood and Wanchese crab cakes at modest prices. From your table you can watch the same fishing fleets that probably caught what you're eating. This is a family business, established in 1974 by Malcolm and Maude Daniels to provide good food in a family atmosphere at a reasonable price, and to provide employment opportunities for local residents, and operated now by their 15 children. Serves lunch 11 a.m. to 3 p.m. and dinner from 3 to 9 p.m., Mon through Sat. Closed Sun.

From Manteo, a short drive across the bridge on US 64/264 takes you to Bodie Island (which isn't really an island anymore but a location along the northern section of the Outer Banks), where it's worth stopping to see the Bodie Island Lighthouse, operating since 1872. Aside from Coquina Beach, a good beach for swimming and fishing, you won't find many attractions here. A turn to the south, however, takes you to Hatteras Island, home of the tallest lighthouse in America, the *Cape Hatteras Lighthouse.* When the Cape Hatteras Lighthouse was built in 1870, it stood thousands of feet from the Atlantic Ocean. But erosion gradually brought the sea closer and closer. Experts said the lighthouse would fall into the ocean if it were not somehow protected. After lengthy controversy about what to do and how to do it, Congress authorized nearly $12 million to move the lighthouse away from the shoreline, preserving it as a historic structure.

In June 1999 the old lighthouse was moved 1,300 feet inland, barely an inch at a time, while North Carolinians watched reports of the progress on the Internet and on nightly television news.

Now the lighthouse stands 3,000 feet from the ocean at high tide, about the same distance as when it was first built, and is open for visitors. If you're up for climbing more than 260 steps, you can stand on a balcony at the top to survey the area.

What used to be the lighthouse keeper's home is now a visitor center where you can check out exhibits about local history and pick up a map for a self-guiding nature trail that begins nearby.

In the summer season the lighthouse is open every day from 10 a.m. to 4 p.m. In the off-season it closes earlier. The visitor center is open from 9 a.m. to 5 p.m. daily except Christmas. Token admission fee. This area is undeveloped because the protected Cape Hatteras National Seashore comprises Hatteras, some of the southern end of Bodie, and Ocracoke. Here you can see natural beaches and their attendant wildlife, seashells as they wash ashore and accumulate, and vegetation dwarfed and gnarled by salt and wind but not threatened by macadam. For more information on the area, write the Superintendent, Cape Hatteras National Seashore, Route 1, Box 675, Manteo 27954, or call (252) 473-2111; hatteras-nc.com/light/.

It's a different story turning north from Bodie Island. You drive through the kind of beach-strip conglomeration of motels, restaurants, gas stations, fast-food chains, and beach shops that typifies most popular beach areas. As a follower of unbeaten paths, you might choose to skip it, unless you're interested in seeing the *Wright Brothers National Memorial* (800 Colington Rd. at Kill Devil Hills), which marks the spot where Wilbur and Orville Wright first got off the ground in powered flight on December 7, 1903. The visitor center here has full-size copies of the brothers' glider and their first plane. The brothers' workshop and living quarters have been re-created, too. Open daily from 9 a.m. to 5 p.m. Closed Christmas Day. Admission is $7 per person, children ages 15 and younger free (252-473-2111; nps.gov/wrbr).

Just south of Kill Devil Hills, on the US 158 Bypass in Nag's Head, *Jockey's Ridge State Park* (252-441-7132; jockeysridgestatepark.com) makes a good place to stop, play in the sand, and get some exercise. This is the highest sand dune on the East Coast, where prevailing winds generally range from 10 to 15 miles an hour. Kite flying here is just about perfect. Hang gliding is popular, too. The park has a picnic area and a shelter, as well as swimming and fishing on the sound, but no camping facilities.

Enjoy a more rural setting at *Nags Head Woods Preserve* (701 W. Ocean Acres Dr.; 252-441-2525; outerbanks.com/NagsHeadWoods). This is a 1,400-acre maritime forest with more than 5 miles of hiking trails. More than 300 different plant species, some of them rare, grow here. Fifty species of birds breed in the preserve as well as a variety of reptiles, amphibians, and mammals. The preserve is a project of the North Carolina Nature Conservancy. The preserve is open daily from dawn to dusk. Visitors are asked to sign in at the visitor center.

Once you get this far north on the Outer Banks, it makes more sense to keep driving north on US 158 across the bridge onto the mainland than it does to backtrack. Following US 158, you can pick up US 17 South at Elizabeth City. *Elizabeth City* merits at least a brief stop, if only because it is at the site of a canal dug in 1790 with the unlikely name of Dismal Swamp Canal. A Coast Guard installation nearby and the local shipyard make this clearly a working, rather than a vacationing, area. The town, however, has a number of interesting historical buildings that are easy to check by taking one of several available walking tours (Elizabeth City Office of Economic Development, 606 E. Colonial Ave.; 252-338-3981; www.cityofec.com).

The *Museum of the Albemarle* (252-335-1453; museumofthealbemarle .com), about 3 miles south of town on US 17, provides information on what is known as the Historic Albemarle Area, along with displays of artifacts and exhibits related to local history. (Colonists first revolted openly against the English monarchy here.) The exhibits tell the story of the area's people from the time of its Native Americans. Open Tues through Sat from 10 a.m. to 4 p.m. Closed Sun, Mon, and all state holidays. Admission is free, although some special exhibits do charge admission, and donations are welcome.

Returning Home

Dorothy Spruill Redford, a descendant of the Somerset slave families, published a book titled *Somerset Homecoming: Recovering a Lost Heritage* (Doubleday, 1988). In it she details the research it took to identify and find descendants of the Somerset families; describes contacting them; and tells about the huge, emotional reunion or, more accurately, first meeting ever, they held on the plantation. Redford includes much plantation history in her book as well.

Another interesting spot in Elizabeth City is the ***Historic Main Street District,*** one of four National Register Historic Districts in Elizabeth City. It has the largest number of brick antebellum commercial buildings in the state. The early 19th- and 20th-century storefronts are now home to specialty shops, restaurants, art galleries, and antiques shops. Free brochures for a self-guided tour of the district are available at the Museum of the Albemarle.

And you don't have to have a boat to enjoy the ***Mariner's Wharf*** (252-335-4365) on the Intracoastal Waterway waterfront, where boats are offered free dockage for 48 hours. The "Rose Buddies" greet each boat with a rose and a welcome to Elizabeth City. These are not town workers, just local people who like to be friendly and helpful.

The next community along US 17, Hertford, the Perquimans County seat (population only about 2,000), is on the Perquimans River, which feeds into Albemarle Sound. It's worth a stop to visit the ***Newbold-White House*** (151 Newbold-White Rd.; 252-426-7567; newboldwhitehouse.com), a colonial Quaker homestead, believed to be the oldest house in North Carolina, probably built about 1730. The house has been restored, preserving much of the original handwork of the brick chimneys and walls and some of the woodwork. Though not the original, the furnishings are authentic period pieces. Open April 1 through October 31, from Thurs through Sat 10 a.m. to 4 p.m. Admission is $5; students with ID, $3.

You can learn a lot about the character of the area by taking two tours here, the ***Historic Hertford Walking Tour*** (252-426-5657), Hall of Fame Square, Church Street, and a self-guided driving tour of the ***Old Neck Rural Historic District*** (252-426-7567). See visitnc.com for more information.

The walking tour takes you by old waterfront homes and the 1828 Perquimans County Courthouse and into a district of antiques stores and cafes. The Historic Hertford District is listed on the National Register of Historic Places. You can also get a free map for the driving tour of Old Neck Rural Historic District, New Hope Road, and Old Neck Road. The driving tour runs through a National Register Historic District and into the countryside, past old plantation homes.

As an alternative plan if you are pressed for time, you may decide to skip the northern Outer Banks and go back from Roanoke Island on US 64, which takes you across the Alligator River and through the ***Alligator River Refuge*** (it's not clear whether the refuge protects people from alligators or the other way around), where you'll find lots of wildlife, picnic areas, and boating access. Either way, make your next stop Edenton, the first capital of colonial North Carolina. From US 64, take NC 32 North. On US 17, keep going about 15 miles west from Hertford.

Capital Country

Although **Edenton** is in no way backward, it has managed to retain the calmer and slower pace that we associate with earlier times and has done an outstanding job of preserving its historical sites and promulgating the facts.

Blackbeard lived here, even though he hung out in Bath and maybe left his treasure there. This would have been good pirate country. It was a busy port town in the 18th and early 19th centuries. During the Revolutionary War, supplies were shipped from here to Washington's army farther north.

Edenton had some of the earliest female political activists, too. In 1774, 51 women gathered in the courthouse square to sign a declaration vowing not to drink English tea or wear English clothing.

To steep yourself in colonial and Revolutionary War history, you have a choice of a guided or self-guided walking tour or a trolley tour. Pick up a walking-tour map or join a guided tour for a modest fee at the **Historic Edenton Visitor Center** (108 N. Broad St.; 252-482-2637; edenton.com). A free audiovisual presentation gives you some orientation in the area's history. The Barker House (ca. 1782) was the home of Thomas Barker, a colonial agent in England, and his wife, Penelope, one of those ladies who boycotted English tea and clothing.

Call the visitor center also to arrange a guided walking tour of Historic Edenton. It takes a couple of hours. The tour includes four interesting buildings: Chowan County Courthouse, one of the oldest in the country, built in 1767; the Cupola House, noted for its elaborate Georgian woodwork inside; the James Iredell House State Historic Site, built in 1773, home of the first attorney general of North Carolina; and St. Paul's Episcopal Church, built in 1736. You may also purchase tickets to go into individual buildings apart from the tours.

In addition to the walking tours, you can take a guided trolley tour, which goes into the outskirts of town as well as through the downtown. Walking tours leave several times a day. They include time inside some of the homes. The cost of tours is moderate and varies according to their length and the number of homes visited. The visitor center is open from 9 a.m. to 5 p.m. Tues through Sat. (edenton.nchistoricsites.org). You'll know you're at the visitor center when you see the flag with a teapot flying in the doorway.

When you study North Carolina history, much of it seems to be about war campaigns, documents, and declarations. Two plantation tours in the area give you a more personal look at history on the day-to-day level.

Hope Plantation, about 20 miles west, in Windsor on NC 308, 4 miles west of the highway bypass, re-creates rural domestic life in northeastern North Carolina during the colonial and Federal periods. The plantation belonged to

Governor David Stone, who also served in the state House of Commons and later as a US senator. Stone owned more than 5,000 acres, planted mostly in wheat and corn. The plantation had all the mills, shops, and work areas necessary to be self-sufficient.

The two homes on the plantation, one dating from 1763, the other from about 1803, are examples of architecture that combines medieval English, Georgian, and neoclassical traits, reflecting the changing needs and knowledge of North Carolina colonists. Touring them, you see examples of how they might have been furnished, based on research about the plantation. The project continues to develop, with a reconstruction of the kitchen on its original foundation, restored outbuildings, and historically authentic vegetable and flower gardens. Visitor center hours vary seasonally, as do tour hours. Closed Thanksgiving Day and Dec 20 through Jan 4. Admission is $11 for adults, $10 for senior citizens 65 and over, $6 for students and children 18 and younger. For full information, write to the plantation at 132 Hope House Rd., Windsor 27983, or call (252) 794-3140; hopeplantation.org.

The second plantation also deserves much wider attention. ***Somerset Place*** (2572 Lake Shore Rd., Creswell; 252-797-4560; nchistoricsites.org/somerset/main.htm), a 19th-century coastal plantation near Creswell, belonged to Josiah Collins, a successful merchant who came to Edenton from England in 1774. He and other investors formed the Lake Company, which acquired more than 100,000 acres of land next to Lake Phelps. They dug (or, more accurately, had slaves dig) a 6-mile-long canal through an area known as the Great Alligator Dismal, to join the lake to the Scuppernong River and drain the swamps. When things were going well, gristmills and sawmills produced rice and lumber to ship down the canal in flatboats. But the flooding it takes to grow rice bred mosquitoes that made the slaves sick, so eventually the plantation grew corn and wheat instead.

Collins bought out his partners in 1816, and at his death passed the property on to his son. Later, Josiah Collins III took over. He turned Somerset Place into one of the state's largest plantations, working more than 300 slaves by 1860. Most North Carolinians didn't own slaves; Collins was one of only four planters in the state with more than 300.

The great fascination in visiting Somerset Place lies in the uncommonly detailed records the Collins family kept, especially about the black people on the plantation. The records detailed not only births, deaths, and marriages but also jobs and skills. Thus today we know that the cook was Grace and that one slave, Luke Davis, had only one job, cleaning carpets. We know that two sons of Collins III were playing with two slave boys one winter when all four boys drowned in the canal.

Additional information comes from the accounts of Dr. John Kooner, a physician who used to stay at the plantation for several weeks at a time, treating the slaves and the Collins family. He described an elaborate African dance that slaves Collins had imported directly from Africa apparently taught to the rest of the slave community. They performed it every year at Christmas, beginning at the great house, snaking to the overseer's house, and ending up at the slave quarters. Everyone on the plantation participated, either as a slave dancer or a spectator.

One of the most interesting and important aspects of research at Somerset Plantation is the ongoing archaeological study and excavation there, aimed at learning more about how the early African-American slaves lived and struggled to preserve their own culture and beliefs. In the absence of written records, such artifacts as pottery suggest that the slaves kept up their West African crafts and that later a Creole culture developed on the plantation.

Archaeological exploration has turned up the remains of slave houses, a hospital and chapel, and the plantation's formal garden, as well as the original brick boundary walls.

This kind of priceless information continues to come to light at Somerset Place, where personable and knowledgeable guides work hard to pass it on. You won't experience a routinized, canned tour here.

Ultimately, the Civil War did in the plantation. The Collins family died elsewhere, and today the site is run by the state.

Somerset is open April 1 through October 31, Mon through Sat from 9 a.m. to 5 p.m., Sun from 1 to 5 p.m.; November 1 through March 31, Tues through Sat from 10 a.m. to 4 p.m., Sun from 1 to 4 p.m. Closed Mon during winter when hours are shorter. Closed Thanksgiving day and from December 20 through January 4. All hours may vary, so call ahead. Admission is free, but donations are welcome. At Creswell, the turn for the plantation is marked with a sign.

It's a quick drive from here to the office and main parking lot of ***Pettigrew State Park*** (2252 Lake Shore Rd.; 252-797-4475; ncparks.com/visit/pett/main .php), bordering on Lake Phelps. Actually, Somerset Place State Historic Site lies within the park, too. And a hiking trail from the parking lot takes you to the Somerset Place buildings in about 5 minutes. The trail continues to the Pettigrew cemetery. Another part of the trail, known as the "Carriage Trail" because the Collins family used to like taking carriage rides along the route, leads to an overlook from which you can tread a boardwalk through the cypress woods. Some families like to settle in a picnic area in the park, then walk over to the historic site, rather than starting out at Somerset Place.

A park entrance and parking lot are 9 miles south of Creswell, off US 64 on NC 1166. One of the park's main draws is fishing—largemouth bass, yellow perch, and panfish are plentiful. The lake is also good for shallow-draft sailboats, canoeing, and windsurfing. The park forest has a variety of deciduous trees, along with wildflowers and lower shrubs, all in enough variety to keep nature travelers with botanical interests happy. As for wildlife, a variety of waterfowl, owls and other birds of prey, and lots of woodland animals, including deer, frequent the area. Pettigrew has a few campsites but no hookups.

Finally, you can inspect some displays of prehistoric Indian culture, including dugout canoes, that will help give you a sense of the area's history over a long period of time. The park is open from about dawn to nightfall, varying with the season. Call ahead to check hours for your visit. Park officials warn that GPS is not a reliable guide to finding the park office. Admission is free.

Places to Stay in the Northern Coast & Islands

BEAUFORT

Beaufort Inn
101 Ann St.
(252) 728-2600
(800) 726-0312
beaufort-inn.com
A well-established, friendly place on the waterfront.
Inexpensive to moderate

Inlet Inn
Corner of Queen and Front Streets
(252) 728-3600
(800) 554-5466
inlet-inn.com
This place has great balcony or window-seat views.
Inexpensive to moderate

Langdon House
135 Craven St.
(252) 728-5499
langdonhouse.com
A B&B in a house dating back to 1732, opened by the late Jimm Prest and run since his death by his wife, Lizzette Prest, maintaining their tradition of hospitality.
Moderate

Pecan Tree Inn
116 Queen St.
(252) 728-6733
(800) 728-7871
pecantree.com
A nicely maintained B&B set amid beautiful gardens.
Moderate

KILL DEVIL HILLS

Best Western Ocean Reef Suites
107 Virginia Dare Trail
(252) 441-1611
bestwestern.com/oceanreefsuites
Moderate to expensive

KITTY HAWK

Beach Haven
4104 Virginia Dare Trail
(252) 261-4785
(888) 559-0506
beachhavenmotel.com
A small, peaceful place to stay.
Inexpensive to moderate

MANTEO

Tranquil House Inn
405 Queen Elizabeth St.
(252) 473-1404
tranquilinn.com
A three-story waterfront
facility.
Moderate to expensive

MOREHEAD CITY

Hampton Inn
4035 Arendell St.
(252) 240-2300
(800) 467-9375
hampton-inn.com/hi/
moreheadcity
Moderate

NEW BERN

Aerie Inn
509 Pollock St.
(800) 849-5553
(252) 636-5553
aeriebedandbreakfast.com
This long-time favorite is in
an 1882 Victorian house.
Moderate

OCRACOKE

Edwards of Ocracoke
226 Back Rd.
(800) 254-1359
edwardsofocracoke.com
A family owned and
operated business
with comfortable
accommodations and a
place outside to clean fish.
Moderate

Places to Eat in the Northern Coast & Islands

BEAUFORT

Aqua
114 Middle Ln.
(252) 728-7777
aquaexperience.com
Emphasizes Spanish-style
tapas and top quality
wines.
Moderate

Blue Moon Bistro
119 Queen St.
(252) 728-5800
bluemoonbistro.biz
This place has a
sophisticated menu and a
great wine list.
Moderate to expensive

Net House
133 Turner St.
(252) 728-2002
hisitoricbeaufort.com/
Hospitality/Nethouse.htm
A great place for really
fresh seafood.
Moderate

The Spouter
218 Front St.
(252) 728-5190
spouterinn.net
Try the soft-shell crabs or
house crab cakes.
Moderate to expensive

KILL DEVIL HILLS

Flying Fish Cafe
2003 Croatan Hwy.
(252) 441-6894
http://flyingfishcafeobx.com
You can't beat pan-fried
Carolina crab cakes here.
Expensive

Port-O-Call Restaurant
504 S. Virginia Dare Trail
(252) 441-7484
When you want generous
portions and, maybe, a
break from seafood.
Moderate

MANTEO

Fisherman's Wharf Restaurant
4683 Mill Landing Rd.
(252) 473-6004
www.fishermanswharf/obx
.com
A family restaurant
emphasizing broiled
and fried seafood and
Wanchese crab cakes.

1587 Restaurant
405 Queen Elizabeth St.
(252) 473-1587
www.1587.com
In addition to the usual
seafood, chicken, and
red meats, you'll find a
vegetarian menu.
Moderate to expensive

MOREHEAD CITY

Sanitary Fish Market and Restaurant
501 Evans St.
(252) 247-3111
sanitaryfishmarket.com
This restaurant is kid
friendly.
Moderate

NEW BERN

Annabelle's Restaurant
310 Dr. ML King Jr. Blvd.
(252) 633-6401
Offerings here include such Southern favorites as fried green tomatoes and hot crab dip as well as shrimp, burgers, and salads.
Moderate

OCRACOKE

Howard's Pub and Raw Bar Restaurant
1175 Irvin Garrish Hwy.
(252) 928-4441
howardspub.com
A popular, clattering place serving everything from hand patted burgers to raw oysters.
Moderate

The Southern Coast & Islands

Along the Grand Strand

Like most of this country's coastal areas, the beaches of North Carolina attract plenty of tourists, but some have so far managed to avoid the near honky-tonk atmosphere of the better-known places such as Myrtle Beach, just below the North Carolina–South Carolina border.

Close enough to the border to confuse anyone who misses the North Carolina Welcome Center on US 17, the community of *Calabash* has been known for generations as the "Seafood Capital of the World." In the early years, a couple of families in what was just a fishing village set up tents and later enclosed buildings to sell the local catch, cooked "Calabash style." That meant then, and still means today, seafood very lightly battered and fried, almost like tempura. The stuff has become wildly popular in the area, and though the town now has all kinds of restaurants and tourist shops, you can still order Calabash-style seafood in many restaurants. One that's been around since the 1950s is *Ella's of Calabash* (1148 River Rd.; 910-579-6728; www.ncbrunswick.com/ellas-of-calabash-calabash), open every day but Christmas from 11 a.m. to 9 p.m. The restaurant began

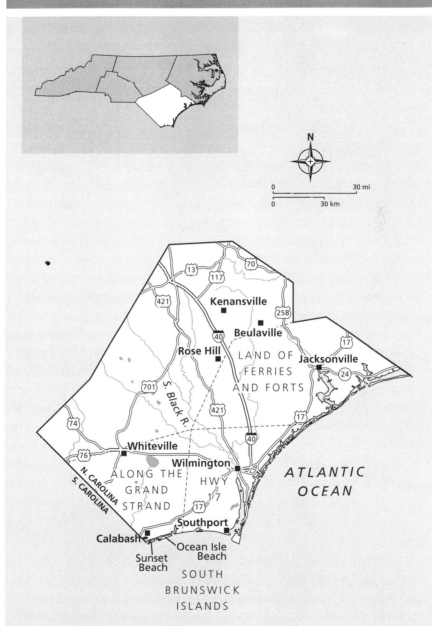

goodnight,jimmy

If you're old enough to remember Jimmy Durante, you may recall that he started closing his radio and TV shows by saying, "Good night, Mrs. Calabash, wherever you are." Local people swear it's because he ate in Calabash and liked it so much that he acknowledged it with those words for Mrs. Calabash, whoever she was.

as a single-room restaurant set up to offer the day's fresh catch to tourists and local people. It's still run by later generations of the same family and remains a preferred restaurant by residents up and down the coast. Although the building now is larger and spiffed up and offers a variety of entrees besides fried fish, the Calabash-style seafood is still the big draw.

In addition to fried fish, some Calabash restaurants offer an oyster roast, which is a huge kettle full of oysters steamed just until they open, a shucking knife to prod the oysters from their shells, a bowl of the steaming broth, a dish of melted butter, a roll of paper towels, and a wastebasket for your discarded shells. These are rock oysters, not the kind you get when you order oysters on the half shell—neatly arranged on a bed of ice. Rock oysters come in clumps, with large, medium, and small

ANNUAL EVENTS
IN THE SOUTHERN COAST & ISLANDS

HOLDEN BEACH

Day at the Docks
(late March)
(910) 842-3828

NAGS HEAD

Nags Head Independence Day
Fireworks
(252) 441-5508

OCEAN ISLE BEACH

Annual NC Oyster Festival
(mid-October)
(800) 426-6644

SHALLOTTE POINT

Annual Flounder Tournament
(early June)
(910) 579-3757

SOUTHPORT

NC Fourth of July Festival
nc4thofjuly.com

WILMINGTON

NC Azalea Festival
(early March)
(910) 754-7177

Riverfest
(early October)
(910) 452-6862
wilmingtonriverfest.com

Talkin' the Talk

In North Carolina what we say is sometimes just the opposite of what we mean, but other North Carolinians get the point. For instance, when a comment begins, "Bless his heart" or "Bless her heart," it sounds as if you're about to say something nice, but it's actually a signal that what's coming next is critical: "Bless his heart, his elevator doesn't go all the way to the top." Or "Bless her heart, she can't even boil water in a microwave." On the other hand, we show affection with the seemingly negative statement, "She's a mess." Or, even more affectionately, "She's a real mess."

And when someone says something with which we agree, we don't say so. Instead we say, "You got that right."

It all makes perfect sense. You just have to know the code.

oysters all stuck together. Eating them, you usually just skip those no bigger than your thumbnail, start with the largest ones first, and work your way down to the smaller ones. It's messy and fun and good, if you like oysters.

As Calabash has grown, a variety of other restaurants have moved in, offering everything from German to Italian cuisine. Some of them make it, some don't. But your true local experience is in an older seafood restaurant.

In summer Calabash is busy, attracting tourists from Myrtle Beach as well as from the beaches to the north, so the best time to visit is in the slower seasons.

South Brunswick Islands

Driving north on US 17 just over 10 miles takes you to the beginning of the *South Brunswick Islands.* Sunset Beach, Ocean Isle Beach, and Holden Beach differ from one another as much as the siblings in most families. Part of the chain of barrier islands off the coast that stretches both north and south, the South Brunswick Islands have no boardwalks and relatively little commercial development except for beach houses and a few small grocery stores.

In the fall of 1989, Hurricane Hugo accentuated an interesting phenomenon along Holden Beach, Ocean Isle Beach, and Sunset Beach. The hurricane didn't do any more damage than any good storm does, breaking up some docks, flooding some first-floor rooms in cabins, and lifting off a piece of roof here and there. But it changed the beaches, hastening an erosion process that was already obvious, moving sand and dunes from the east and depositing them farther west. As more storms have hit the area, the changes continue. This means that the beachfront at Holden Beach grows noticeably more narrow with each storm, as does the east end of Ocean Isle's beachfront, leading to such black-humor jokes as the one suggesting that the way to get cheap oceanfront property here is to buy third row and wait. Meanwhile, the beaches on the west end of Ocean Isle Beach and those on Sunset Beach are growing visibly broader. It takes regular dredging to keep the waterway between Ocean Isle Beach and Sunset Beach open because the currents continue to dump sand there. Beaches have broadened so much at Sunset Beach that when you stand at water's edge, you can't see the first-row cottages behind the dunes. It sounds like good, forward-thinking planning; actually, it's nature.

This shifting creates some problems for developers and homeowners but does not in any way spoil the pleasure of visiting any of the islands. Indeed, if you're interested in the ecology of coastlines, try to find a copy of *The Beaches Are Moving* by Wallace Kaufman and Orrin H. Pilkey Jr., published by Duke University Press in 1979. The book is rich in historical data and information about how tides, storms, and so on work. Even though it focuses on beaches along both the east and west coasts and doesn't talk specifically about the South Brunswick Islands, it describes, explains, and predicts coastline activity. Browsing through the book while you stay in the South Brunswick Islands is like having your very own little nature model to study as you read. It's great fun and genuinely instructive.

Access to **Sunset Beach** used to be via a one-lane pontoon swing bridge across the Intracoastal Waterway. A swing bridge differs from a drawbridge in that the movable part of the bridge swings to the side rather than lifting up to allow tall ships to pass under. The thing was slow. A volunteer firefighter from the early days remembers that it took three minutes to open the bridge, which was a long time if a fire call came to the Sunset Beach Fire Department on the mainland. Sometimes traffic backed up because the bridge was open to allow ships through, a problem especially during the months of heavy tourism. In the 1980s, there was talk of replacing it with a more modern bridge, but many residents resisted, delaying such a project until 2008, when a company from

AUTHOR'S FAVORITE PLACES
IN THE SOUTHERN COAST & ISLANDS

Sunset Beach	Poplar Grove Plantation
Southport	Wrightsville Beach Museum of History
Historic Wilmington District	Cedar Point

Spanish Moss

Not Spanish. Not moss. This gray-green epiphyte thrives almost anywhere in the South where warm air and high humidity are present.

Legend has it that an Indian princess cut her hair on her wedding day, as was traditional, and hung it over an oak tree. But the newlyweds were killed the day they married and buried under the same oak. The princess's hair turned gray, started to grow, and has been spreading among the trees ever since.

Southerners have been trying to figure out a use for Spanish moss for generations. In Louisiana it was used to stuff mattresses in the 1800s. Those that survive are decidedly stiff and crinkly. More recently it's been bagged as a decorative item for florists, but it's only pretty as long as it's exposed to moisture in the air. Take it inland and it turns gray and brittle and crumbles.

My college roommate, back in my Pennsylvania days, kept a bunch, tied with pink ribbon, hanging on a nozzle in the shower room. It did very well there until somebody stole it.

If you want to take Spanish moss home with you, keep it damp as you travel. At home, hang it in a steamy place, such as a shower stall.

Lynchburg, Virginia, won a contract to build a new high-rise bridge, which opened in 2010. Some old-timers still wish things were as they had been, but others see advantages to the new bridge. It's not only efficient; it also gives drivers new views from higher space of the marshes. Plans are in the works to relocate the saved old bridge-tender's house. So far, Sunset Beach remains a place with only a few paved roads and sidewalks, no high-rise condos, and no pink giraffes, waterslides, or beachfront grills. What the island does have is glorious, wide, flat beaches and clean white sand. From most of the beach area, you can't see any buildings at all. The beach homes, most of which are available for rent, sit hidden behind the dunes.

Just south of Sunset Beach, by water, not by road, lies *Bird Island.* It is one of the last undeveloped, privately owned barrier islands on the East Coast. It is a popular place for birding and just spending time in a spot that people have not managed to change. It used to be that the only way to get to that island was to swim, take a boat, or wade across at low tide, making sure to get back to Sunset before high tide. That has changed with recent storms, and now you can walk across any time, regardless of the tide, on sand that's been deposited here.

On Sunset Island, *the Sunset Inn* (9 N. Shore Dr.; 910-575-1000 or toll-free 888-575-1001; thesunsetinn.net) is one place to stay where the innkeepers,

A Little Beach Music & a Seaside Shuffle

The Shag is a dance popular along the coast with origins going back at least to the 1940s, with a surge in popularity at Carolina beaches in the 1960s. Today it's a popular recreation all along the coast. Depending on their state loyalties, shaggers pinpoint either Atlantic Beach, North Carolina, or Myrtle Beach, South Carolina, which is barely an hour from the North Carolina–South Carolina border, as a place where shagging really got going. The music to which one shags ranges from old-time swing to the twist. Shaggers now take lessons, join clubs, and maintain websites. If you're interested in the history and how-to, a good place to start is beachshag.com, but some native Carolinians simplify it: "Just imagine that you're dancing barefoot in the sand with a beer in one hand, kick back, and have a good time."

Dave Nelson and Andrea Ward, fully appreciate the beauty of the island and have taken maximum advantage of it. This 14-room inn has the comfort of new construction with the relaxed feeling of an old style. Except for rental houses and an older motel, it is the only place to stay on Sunset Beach, and the location is prime, with views of the salt marsh and the Intracoastal Waterway. Just a few steps take you to the ocean. One of the most popular rooms in the house is the Bird Island room.

Because Sunset Beach is not heavily developed, it has an air of calm and closeness to nature that has long since been lost from other beaches in the area. The Sunset Inn not only fits in quietly, but it also helps to prevent inappropriate kinds of development by occupying commercial space that otherwise might have gone to waterslides or souvenir shops. Each room has a private bath, TV, small refrigerator, wet bar, and private screened porch. Breakfast is served buffet-style. Andrea emphasizes that it is not "kid friendly." It seems a shame to use the feature, but the inn is equipped for Wi-Fi connection.

More appropriate for families with children, the houses on the island can be rented through *Sunset Properties* (419 S. Sunset Blvd.; 866-976-8204; sunset properties.travel) or *Sunset Vacation* (401 S. Sunset Blvd.; 910-579-5400 or toll-free 800-331-6428; sunsetvacations.com).

The next island north is *Ocean Isle Beach.* To get there, drive north on US 17 about 5 miles and turn right onto NC 179 South, which takes you directly to the Odell Williamson Bridge, across the Intracoastal Waterway. This island is more fully developed, with sidewalks, all paved roads, some cluster homes on the west end, and more traditional beach homes on the east end. Also on the east end, a series of paved and natural canals, where homes have docks, can accommodate boats or just provide pleasant off-ocean outdoor lounging space.

Some people live on the island year-round, but many of the accommodations are used by the owners part of the year and rented to vacationers the rest of the time. You can arrange to rent a place to stay through several agencies, each handling different properties. Three of these are: **Cooke Realtors** (1 Causeway Dr.; 910-579-3535 or toll-free 800-622-3224; cookerealty.com); **R. H. McClure Realty, Inc.** (24 Causeway Dr. Southwest; 800-332-5476; www.mcclurerealty vacations.com); and **Williamson Realty** (119 Causeway Dr.; 910-579-2373 or toll-free 800-727-9222; williamsonrealty.com). The private homes are mingled among those used strictly for vacation and rental. It's a nice mix, and especially if you do not stay in beachfront properties, you can learn a lot about the island from local people and form friendships that continue past your visit.

The **Museum of Coastal Carolina** (21 E. Second St.; 910-579-1016; oceanislebeach.com/museum-of-coastal-carolina) is a great diversion for children. The museum of natural history concentrates on the Carolina coast, with dioramas and Civil War artifacts, as well as Native American artifacts and a fine collection of seashells and fossils. The museum is open from 10 a.m. to 8 p.m. Mon through Thur, 10 a.m. to 5 p.m. Fri, and 10 a.m. to 1:30 p.m. Sat. Admission is $9.50 for adults, $8.50 for senior citizens and students, $7.50 for children ages 3 to 12.

Ocean Isle Inn (37 W. 1st St.; 800-352-5988; oceanisleinn.com) has 70 rooms on the waterfront. Facilities include an outdoor swimming pool and sundeck, an indoor heated pool and hot tub, and the use of boats, rafts, and canoes. The inn serves a complimentary continental breakfast.

Heads Up! Heads On!

If you've never seen shrimp with their heads and legs on, you're in for a surprise, because they look like squirmy, swimming critters, not the neat, pink C-shaped bits surrounding a cup of cocktail sauce.

Local shrimpers sell some of their catch by the sides of most of the roads in the coastal area. They may set up in a crude shelter or off the back of a truck or simply sit there in lawn chairs. They keep the shrimp iced down in coolers.

When you buy shrimp this way, the price per pound is lower than in markets because the shrimp still have their heads on. They seem so loosely attached you can't help but marvel that they haven't come off during some underwater activity! You can pop the heads off easily.

If you have any worries about the freshness of the shrimp, just ask to smell them. If they smell briny, they're fine. If you catch a whiff of ammonia (which has never happened to me at a roadside stand), don't buy them.

A Birdie at the Beach

Sand makes great beaches. It also makes devilish sand traps. It takes another golfing enthusiast to understand why you'd go to the beach and spend the time playing golf, but if you do, you'll be in good company. New golf courses spring up faster than dandelions.

North Carolina has approximately 600 golf courses dotted across the state, designed by such masters as Donald Ross, Tom Fazio, Arnold Palmer, Rees Jones, and Jack Nicklaus.

North Carolina golf courses have hosted the Ryder Cup, the US Open, the US Senior Open, the US Women's Open, and regular PGA tour events.

For a free copy of the *North Carolina Golf Guide,* a comprehensive listing of courses in the state, call (800) VISIT-NC or check the website: visitncgolf.com.

Standing on the west end of Ocean Isle Beach, you can see Sunset Beach. It looks close enough to wade to, which old-timers remember doing before erosion and currents changed the shape of the islands. Standing on the east end of Ocean Isle Beach, you see **Holden Beach,** also seeming almost close enough to wade to. Without a boat, though, getting to Holden Beach requires a drive of about 15 minutes. Richard Mubel once wrote for the *Brunswick Magazine* that Holden is a place where "old meets new, where tradition bisects progress and where history intersects the path of the future." He's talking about the contrasts between the back side of the island, along the Atlantic Intracoastal Waterway and the Lockwood Folly River Inlet, and the oceanfront. Shrimpers and anglers descended from families who settled the area still work along the waterway and inlet, as well as in the open sea, but the oceanfront is strictly a vacationland of white beaches and summer cottages. Holden is a family beach, not a party beach, with between 8 and 9 miles of oceanfront sand. One of its notable features is that it is a sea-turtle nesting place and a bird habitat, and when it comes to nightlife, you can stay up late during hatching season, May through October, to watch the tiny turtles come up out of the sand and head for the ocean. Most people who come here stay either in cottages or condos. For information about rental agencies, of which there are many, visit hbtown hall.com. One well-known agency is **Alan Holden Vacations** (128 Ocean Blvd. West; 910-842-6061 or toll-free 800-720-2200; holden-beach.com).

Campgrounds also serve the island: **Green Oaks Campground** (3342 Holden Beach Rd. Southwest; 910-842-2844; visitnc.com/listing/green-oaks -campground) and **Holden Beach Pier Campground** (441 Ocean Blvd. West; 910-842-6483; visitnc.com/listing/holden-beach-pier-campground-rooms).

Holden Beach RV Park (2650 Liberty Lane Ln. Southwest; 910-842-1809; www.hbrv.net) accommodates RVs.

If you enjoy local festivals and if you lo-o-o-o-ve seafood, try to schedule your Brunswick Islands trip for the third weekend in October, during the annual ***North Carolina Oyster Festival.*** This festival began as a small oyster roast in the late 1970s. Every year the party got a little better, and in three years it got itself proclaimed the official oyster festival of North Carolina. It takes a couple hundred community volunteers to run the event, which now includes a beach run, a bullshooting (tall-tale-telling) contest, and the North Carolina Oyster Shucking Championship. This contest is no small potatoes. It has produced not only a national oyster shucking champion but also the top female oyster shucker in the world. With all that shucking going on, it stands to reason somebody's got to be doing some eating. That's where you come in. Steamed oysters, fried oysters, oysters on the half shell, boiled shrimp, fried flounder, and of course the ubiquitous hush puppies are available in abundance. In addition to the food and contests, the festival features two days of live music that includes beach music (shag), Top 40, country and western, and gospel. Also artists and craftspeople display their wares for sale. For further details and firm dates in any year, call (800) 426-6644; ncbrunswick.com.

From the Ocean Isle Beach area, if you drive north for about an hour or less on NC 130 to US 701, you'll come to ***Whiteville. The Madison House*** (101 N. Madison St.; 910-640-2132; whitevillenc.com/madison house) is the only bed-and-breakfast in town. Innkeeper Yvonne Ellis says the Madison House and Whiteville are the best-kept secrets in North Carolina. She'd like that to change. Yvonne, who was born here, says Whiteville, the county seat of

Let's Pedal!

Ocean Isle Beach is a great place to take your bicycle. The streets are paved, which makes for easy riding, and traffic is heavy only during the standard coming and leaving day, Saturday. The island is about 12 miles long, end to end, a nice ride on nearly flat planes. It's also fun to ride up and down the canal streets, looking at the houses and their kitschy names. My favorite for years was the stoned crab. The house had a picture of an out-of-kilter crab with a silly grin. New owners, with a less 1970s sense of humor, painted out the letter "d," and now the house is just the stone crab.

You'll find several places where you can take a bike down onto the beach, too. Riding there is good at low tide, when the sand is damp and hard. Sand that the water doesn't reach, even at high tide, is soft and hard to manage, better for walking. For a perfect early-morning workout, you can ride on the beach, then park the bike and walk for a while.

Columbus County, has small-town ambience and city sophistication. Unfortunately, many people know it only as a town they pass on US 701 on the way to the beach, but the area has enough natural attractions to warrant staying for a while, including Lake Waccamaw, the Lumber River, and the *North Carolina Museum of Forestry* (910-914-4185; naturalsciences.org). The Madison House is a beauty—a Victorian of nearly 7,000 square feet, it features a fireplace in the parlor and two kitchens, one of which is a full commercial kitchen. Yvonne and her husband, Jack, have a background in the restaurant business. In addition to preparing breakfasts, they cater special events, and often can provide not only breakfast but also dinner for their guests.

Jack Ellis has a passion for restoring old cars, which fascinates some guests and sometimes becomes part of the inn's service, providing special transportation for a special occasion. The inn has 5 rooms, furnished in understated elegance with antiques and warm colors. Three have private baths, while two share a bath, and each has wireless Internet access. There's also an outdoor swimming pool. Jack and Yvonne ended up with this house in September 2001 because the people who were selling specifically wanted them to have it. "It was perfect," Yvonne says. "All we had to do was move in." So the Ellises are happy; Yvonne thinks their guests are, too. "If they're not happy, they're fooling us."

US Hwy 17

The Brunswick Isles are served by businesses in the town of *Shallotte,* a few miles inland on US 17. This is the place to stop when you need to do laundry or pick up a bicycle pump from the hardware store or get a prescription filled in a good-size pharmacy. You could say it's a place devoted to practical issues, like what to do with the kids on a rainy day at the beach. In an addition old-timers would never have imagined, *Planet Fun* (349 Whiteville Rd.; 910-755-2386; http://planetfuncenter.com) advertises itself as "Brunswick County's largest entertainment center." Inside this sprawling building you'll find all kinds of games with planet-inspired names. Constellation Alley Bowling, Space Quest 2-Story Laser Tag, Ocean Quest Cosmic Mini-Golf. The Asteroids Arcade Redemption Center boasts "the largest selection of redemption and video games in the area." If you were longing for a lava lamp, this would be the place to find it! You wouldn't even have to leave the building to eat. The Starz Grille sells everything from crab legs to pizza, and offers a Sunday buffet as well as take-out service. As you might expect, this is not a quiet place. A parent might take respite at the Lowe's Home Improvement Center next door—a definite playground for lots of adults. Planet Fun says hours fluctuate, but you can generally expect to find the place open from mid-morning to late night 7 days a week.

Another restaurant to check out in Shallotte is ***The Purple Onion Cafe*** (4647 Main St., 910-755-6071; purpleonioncafe.com). The atmosphere here is quite different. Breakfast choices range from the standard Southern favorites such as grits, sausage, and biscuits to more urban choices like bagels with cream cheese and croissant sandwiches. If you order the Big-Onion Breakfast, which includes eggs, sausage, bacon, grits, home fries, pancake, and toast or biscuit, you could probably skip more meals for two days. But there is lunch, featuring homemade breads, a soup of the day, and lots of salads. Breakfast is served 6:30 to 11 a.m. daily, lunch 11 a.m. to 4 p.m., Mon through Sat and to 2 p.m. Sun. From their bakery you can buy homemade pies, cookies by the dozen, fresh-baked breads, and cakes, including the Southern classics red velvet cake and Sun Drop pound cake, by the slice or whole.

If you should ask around town, "Where do the locals eat?" the answer would be ***Duffer's Bar & Grill*** (4924 Main St.; 910-754-7229; duffersbarand grill.com). They started as a pub in a strip center in 1997. It became so popular the owners knocked out a wall and expanded into the next unit of the strip center. The added space allowed them to have a dining area on one side and a bar area on the other, thus making it family friendly. Duffer's remains unassuming, with the kind of paper menus carrying small ads for local businesses on the back, and reminding you their food is prepared as it is ordered, so "relax and enjoy your meal." Although you can certainly order salads, you might question how light the food is otherwise, since it includes such sandwiches as a shrimp po'boy and seafood dinners that can be grilled, fried, or blackened. Duffer's has all ABC permits and offers wine and beer by the glass as well as the bottle. For kids, there are chicken tenders as well as such as PB and J and grilled cheese. Open Mon through Thurs 11 a.m. to 9 p.m., Fri and Sat to 10 p.m.

From Shallotte, driving north on US Hwy 17 brings you to ***Southport,*** on the western bank of the Cape Fear River, where the river joins the Atlantic Ocean. The harbor accommodates yachts, charter boats, and fishing piers. The town, rich in military and maritime history, was first called Smithville after Benjamin Smith, who became governor of North Carolina, but in 1887 the name was changed to Southport. To get into town from US 17, turn right onto NC 211. Shortly you'll be driving into what is obviously still a real fishing village with stores and gas stations and marinas, although growing numbers of tourist-oriented shops are opening. Many of the homes in Southport are listed on the National Register of Historic Places. The old 12-bed ***Fort Johnston Hospital,*** dating back to about 1852, has been moved and turned into a private residence; the ***Old Brunswick Jail,*** dating back to the early 1900s, now houses the Southport Historical Society. In *Keziah Memorial Park* you'll find a tree that the Cape Fear Indians bent over as a marker when it was just a sapling. It may be more than 800 years old. Half a century ago children could crawl under its arch.

The *A. E. Stevens House,* circa 1894, is noted as the home built for Mr. Stevens and his betrothed. She changed her mind and married his best friend. They built a house across from Mr. Stevens, who remained a bachelor the rest of his life. There's lots more, equally human and interesting, all mapped out on a 1-mile, self-guided walking tour called *Southport Trail.* You'll find a nice assortment of restaurants, antiques shops, and specialty stores in the area, too. Their names and sometimes their proprietors may change from year to year, but they're always fun. A shopping guide with a map, as well as the free self-guided walking-tour brochure of Southport's historic sites, is available at the visitor center (202 E. Bay St.; 910-457-7927; cityofsouthport.com). Open Mon through Sat 10 a.m. to 4 p.m., Sun 1 p.m. to 4 p.m.

Southport used to be the special province of people with boats and people who fish. Even those who docked their boats in Southport and lived inland didn't expect much in the way of elaborate accommodations or shopping. This is all changing—that's the good news *and* the bad news. As specialty shops and antiques shops open, more tourists come in, making the place not quite so off-the-beaten-path as it used to be. But the good news is that you can find more places to stay and eat.

Lois Jane's Riverview Inn (106 W. Bay St.; 910-457-6701; loisjanes.com) is a small bed-and-breakfast in an 1891 home. It was carefully restored in 1995, and the house retains much of its original character and furniture. One of the guest rooms, called "Lois Jane's Room," is furnished and decorated as she kept it in her lifetime, right down to a collection of Wedgwood plates on the wall.

BETTER KNOWN ATTRACTIONS
IN THE SOUTHERN COAST & ISLANDS

WILMINGTON

Battleship *North Carolina*
(910) 251-5797
battleshippnc.com

Cape Fear Museum
(910) 798-4350
capefearmuseum.com

CAPE FEAR COASTAL BEACHES

Wrightsville, Carolina, Kure
(800) 222-4757
capefear.nc.us

Guests gather around a table in the crimson dining room to share breakfast and conversation. The inn is directly across from the river.

Another small B&B is *the Brunswick Inn Bed and Breakfast* (301 E. Bay St.; 910-457-5278; brunswickinn.com). Here you'll stay in spacious rooms in a Federal-style mansion dating back to about 1896. The place has wonderful views of the water, and each room has a working fireplace. A home-cooked gourmet breakfast is included in your daily room rate.

A popular excursion from Southport takes you to *Bald Head Island* by ferry. Only a few hundred people live here, and future plans for the island call for tightly limited new construction. The first lighthouse in North Carolina was built on this island. *Old Baldy Lighthouse and Smith House Museum* (910-457-7481; baldheadisland.com) commemorate the island's history. Admission to the lighthouse and museum is $6 for adults, $3 for children 3 to 12. The two facilities are open Tues through Sat 9 a.m. to 5 p.m., Sun 11 a.m. to 5 p.m. To get to the island, take the passenger ferry from Deep Point Marina (1310 Ferry Rd.; 910-457-5003) in Southport. Ferries leave at the top of the hour and cost $22 for adults and $11 for children 3 to 12.

North of Southport via NC 133, *Brunswick Town State Historic Site* marks the first settlement in the Cape Fear area. Here you can study the remains of the colonial port town of Brunswick and the earth mounds of Fort Anderson that the Confederate Army built about 100 years later. Some of the old foundations have been excavated and are uncovered as archaeological exhibits. The mounds have survived pretty much intact since the Civil War and actually make a good spot from which to see the older ruins. A visitor center on the site has slide presentations and exhibits about the colonial town and the artifacts excavated from the ruins. This is one of those well-managed sites where you can learn about both colonial life and the Civil War and get a sense of the continuity from one time to the other. Brunswick Town is open Tues through Sat 9 a.m. to 5 p.m. Admission is free (910-371-6613; nchistoricsites.org).

After this, the easiest thing to do is return to US 17 to drive on up to *Wilmington.* People who live here call Wilmington the best-kept secret in North Carolina. They're of two minds as to whether that's good or bad. The thriving, historic community has a full share of entrepreneurial types who've done much to revitalize waterfront areas and old downtown buildings. They welcome tourists and new businesses. Some of the old-timers would rather the community's cultural and historical attractions not become too well known, lest all the new traffic spoil the ambience.

In 1989 Wilmington, which was settled before the Revolutionary War and was the last Atlantic port open to blockade runners during the Civil War, celebrated its 250th anniversary.

There are two buildings in the area worth seeing inside. The beautifully restored *1770 Burgwin-Wright House* (224 Market St.; 910-762-0570; burgwin wrighthouse.com) stands at the corner of 3rd and Market Streets. It was built in 1770 on the foundation of the abandoned Wilmington City Jail. One reason the owner chose this site and kept the foundation was because it had a tunnel running down to the water, so he could get to the boats without going outside. Open Tues through Sat 10 a.m. to 4 p.m. Closed on major holidays. Admission is $12 for adults, $6 for children 5 to 12. The *Zebulon Latimer House* (126 S. 3rd St.; 910-762-0492; latimerhouse.org) is one of the few remaining examples of a town house of the time. The same family inhabited it from its completion in 1852 until the historical society took it over in the 1960s. About 60 percent of the furnishings are the family's original belongings. Three of the four floors are open, so you can see everything from beds to china. The house also has archives and a library for those who want to study further, with a researcher available on Tues and Thurs. The house is open Mon through Sat from 10 a.m. to 3 p.m. Closed on major holidays. Admission is $12 for adults, $6 for children 5 to 12.

Both the Burgwin-Wright House and the Zebulon Latimer House have gardens, largely maintained by volunteers, within the confines of their original brick, masonry, and stucco walls, planted with flora that would have been typical of the area and such homes in the 1800s.

Another pleasant way to see the Wilmington District is to take a *Spring-brook Farms* sightseeing tour (910-251-8889; horsedrawntours.com) by horse-drawn carriage, with a costumed driver who narrates as you pass the historic sites. At Christmas a nice touch is that you ride in a closed reindeer-drawn carriage, snuggled in a lap rug, for a tour narrated by Santa. Tours leave from the corner of Water and Market Streets. Hours vary with the season, weather, and day of the week. To plan a tour, call ahead. If no one is there, you can still learn current tour hours by listening to a recording. Reservations are not necessary. Sometimes tours may be arranged for different times by appointment. Rates are $12 for adults, $5 for children under 12.

Perhaps the most unlikely tour possibility is *Cape Fear Segway Tours* (106 N. Water St.; 910-251-2572; capefearsegway.com). You may recall that the Segway was introduced some years ago on *Good Morning America* before the vehicle had a name. They simply called the device "it." One rides the Segway standing up, holding on to handlebars that control it. It's come into use in some North Carolina cities as a way for parking-patrol people to cover more ground and presumably write more tickets than they could on foot. Riding takes a little practice. President George W. Bush lost his balance during his first trial at the White House. But in Wilmington, visitors can book a tour that begins with a period of instruction and practice before setting out to see the city. Tour groups are small—6 or 7 people—with guides who know the area and, in many cases, have acting backgrounds, which makes them good at entertaining as well as informing. Your choices include a waterfront tour ($45) that lasts about 1.25 hours, a 2-hour tour of the historic district ($55), a tour of set locations for the television shows *Dawson's Creek* and *One Tree Hill* ($45) taking about 1.5 hours, and an "advanced" tour traveling farther south than the others ($60). This one requires previous Segway experience since it covers a lot of ground with varied topography. You'll need to book in advance because the groups are small and the tours are popular, especially in summer.

Of course some places deserve a full-attention visit, not just a tour stop. The Daughters of the Confederacy are responsible for creating the oldest history museum in the state. In 1898 they announced their intention to establish a "creditable museum of confederate relics." The **Cape Fear Museum of History and Science** (814 Market St.; 910-798-4350; capefearmuseum .com) was the result. For years it was moved from place to place, looking for a home. Since 1992 it's been housed in a large structure built just for the museum.

Not all the exhibits are about the Civil War. One comes from a tad before the Civil War—the reproduction of the 20-foot-long Wilmington ground sloth, believed to have lived 1.5 million years ago. The creature had fur and hand-shaped appendages with claws, and it stood 15 feet tall. The original was found during construction on a dam basin at Randall Parkway, Wilmington, in 1991. The state gave the original to the North Carolina Museum of Natural Sciences in Raleigh, which in turn created the reproduction of urethane foam and steel for the Cape Fear Museum. Experts say the creature was not a dinosaur, but an ice age mammal.

The Michael Jordan Discovery Gallery features natural history of the upland forests, bottomland, and maritime forest in interactive exhibits for children and also includes some artifacts from Jordan's years growing up in Wilmington.

Yet another part of the museum shows one-third-scale wood carvings of bride figures by Frank Haines, with costumes researched and sewed by Elizabeth Haines. The brides range from Pocahontas to Queen Nefertiti.

But all that doesn't mean the museum has abandoned the Civil War. Along with military artifacts and representations of the Wilmington waterfront as it was in 1863, you'll find a diorama of the second battle of Fort Fisher in 1865.

The museum is open Mon through Sat 9 a.m. to 5 p.m. and Sun 1 to 5 p.m. Admission is $6 for adults, $5 for senior citizens, military, and college students with valid ID, and $3 for children ages 3 to 17. Children under 3 are free.

If you are traveling with children, or with grown-up model railroad nuts, go to the **Wilmington Railroad Museum** (505 Nutt St.; 910-763-2634; www .wrrm.org), which spells out a major part of the town's history. Although Wilmington is known now for being the state's main deepwater port, railroading used to be Wilmington's major industry. In 1840 the Wilmington and Weldon Railroad, with 161 miles of continuous track, was the longest in the world. About 1900 it merged with several other rail lines to become the Atlantic Coast Line Railroad, with headquarters in Wilmington. But in 1960 the company moved the whole shebang to Jacksonville, Florida. Unlike enterprises that move away these days, though, Atlantic Coast Line did not leave its employees in the lurch but took all 1,000 of them, along with their families, to Florida.

The museum depicts the history not just of the Atlantic Coast Line but also of railroading in the Southeast, through a variety of exhibits. The red caboose in the children's corner is a draw for kids and can be booked for birthday parties. For more historical viewing, the museum also has a 1910 Baldwin steam engine; a Seaboard Coastline Railroad caboose; and a Richmond, Fredericksburg, and Potomac Railroad boxcar. Other displays include everything from railroaders' gear going back more than 100 years to illustrations of ghost stories about train disasters. For the hobbyist, large layouts of Lionel and HO-gauge model railroads are enough to send you to the nearest model railroad store. The museum is open Mon through Sat 10 a.m. to 5 p.m., Sun from 1 to 5 p.m. Apr through Oct; the rest of the year, it's open Mon through Sat 10 a.m. to 4 p.m., but hours may change, so call ahead to check. Admission is $8 for adults, $7 for senior citizens and military, $4 for children ages 2 to 12. Children under 2 are free. All children must be accompanied by an adult inside the museum.

One attraction locals know well and tourists often miss is the **Louise Wells Cameron Art Museum** (3201 S. 17th St.; 910-395-5999; cameronartmuseum .com), at the intersection of Independence Boulevard and the 17th Street Extension. It's remarkable especially for an important collection of the original color prints of Mary Cassatt, the 19th-century American artist who worked with the Impressionists in France. This museum is community-supported and does not operate on government funds. For a long time the museum housing the collection, St. John's Museum of Art, comprised three historic buildings on Orange Street. But while the museum collections grew, the buildings wouldn't stretch any farther, and only about 11 percent of the museum's holdings could be displayed at once, so supporters raised funds for a new building, with a new name, in a new location. St. John's Museum of Art closed the last day of December 2001. The new Louise Wells Cameron Art Museum, designed by architect Charles Gwathmey, has 42,000 square feet, about triple the earlier space, and it sits on a campus of almost 10 acres.

Like St. John's, it is the only accredited art museum in the region and has, in addition to the Cassatt work, a permanent collection featuring 200 years of North Carolina art and temporary exhibitions that change regularly. The facilities include an extensive gift shop, a cafe, and a sculpture garden. A series of Confederate defensive mounds that were built near the end of the Civil War on the property provide a new dimension the old museum didn't have. The museum galleries open at 11 a.m. Tues through Sun and close at 5 p.m., except on Thurs when they're open until 9. Admission is $8 for adults, $5 for students, and $3 for children ages 2 to 12. The museum has a lively schedule of educational opportunities for children, all designed to be fun. One that seemed unlikely was "It's All About the Uke," an afternoon devoted to learning about the instrument, and a sing-along led by a local musician Zach Hanner—aka Dat Howlie Boy—whose specialties include bluegrass and Hawaiian music. The ukulele has captured lots of fans around the Wilmington area.

The North Carolina Ukulele Academy (203 Racine Dr.; 910-538-3419; alohau.com) caters to these enthusiasts and creates new ones. Who knew ukuleles came in so many different sizes: soprano, concert, baritone. Or so many different models: plastic, bamboo, electric, electric-acoustic. And you can buy a ukulele here for less than $50, up to far more than $200. Kent Knorr, founder of the academy and shop, loves the uke, especially for kids, because it's simple to learn, small enough to be carried easily, and gives everybody a chance to share music. But Knorr teaches adults, too. The enthusiasm is contagious. A stop here could put a whole family in a good mood and send you home with a new hobby. Open Mon and Tues 11 a.m. to 5 p.m.; Thurs, Fri, and Sat 11 a.m. to 5 p.m.

When it comes to bed and board, you'll find Wilmington full of good restaurants representing many ethnicities, but at least one stop should be at **Chandler's Wharf** and the **Cotton Exchange** on the Cape Fear River. These two complexes of restored historical warehouses and buildings now house a variety of specialty shops and restaurants rather than maritime activities. They are near where the River Walk meets the Cape Fear Bridge. Among the restaurants in this area, *Elijah's Oyster Bar* at 2 Ann Street (910-343-1448; elijahs .com) and the *Pilot House* at the same address on the waterfront (910-343-0200; pilothouserest.com), serve lunch and dinner.

For places to stay, Wilmington has a healthy number of hotels and motels, as well as about 20 bed-and-breakfast facilities. Two of these stand out as special, each with easy access to the historic district. *Front Street Inn* (215 S. Front St.; 914-762-6442 or 800-336-8184; frontstreetinn.com) is a 12-room hostelry in a beautifully restored brick building that used to house the Salvation Army of the Carolinas. When Richard and Polly Salinetti, the owners of the Front Street Inn, decided there should be more to retirement than golf, they set off in search of the perfect bed-and-breakfast inn. It took them six months to find Wilmington and five minutes to fall in love with the Front Street Inn. The inn was established more than a decade ago by a craftsman and a decorator who knew how to take advantage of the building's 14-foot-high ceilings, large window casings, and maple floors, creating an atmosphere of light, humor, and zest, with rooms so different from one another they almost defy description. The Georgia O'Keefe Suite, for instance, is filled with art gathered from sources ranging from thrift shops to galleries. In the Jacques Cousteau Suite some walls are painted by local artists. In the breakfast room, color, plants, and big windows complement buffet offerings that feature seasonal ingredients and might include anything from smoked salmon to homemade granola and yogurt. From the Sol y Sombra ("Sun and Shade") Bar you can choose from an assortment of beverages including wine, beer, and champagne. The place also has an exercise room and a game room. The inn is close to the historic district and good restaurants. For those who can't leave business behind, wireless, dial-up, and DSL Internet connections are available. The Salinettis bring the laid-back approach of maturity, along with a lively dose of humor, to their undertaking. "You can mention old," Richard says. In a conversation with Richard while I was working on this update, we established that I am six months older than he. "You made my day," he said.

I said, "At our age, why aren't we spending our time sitting on a veranda sipping champagne?"

"We couldn't last fifteen days," he said.

At 114 S. 3rd Street, **Rosehill Inn Bed and Breakfast** is the kind of place other innkeepers visit for a night out. Built in 1848, the neoclassical revival house has a fireplace of Italian marble and rosewood and a beautifully refinished pulpit staircase. Throughout the house, especially in the 6 guest rooms, bright colors figure prominently in the decor (910-815-0250 or 800-815-0250; rosehill.com).

The people of Wilmington love a party, and there's no better one than **Riverfest,** which celebrates the city's history and its location between the Cape Fear River and the Intracoastal Waterway. Riverfest always happens the first weekend each October along Front Street and in the historic downtown district. The first Riverfest, in 1979, was the scheme of a group of Wilmingtonians looking for a way to revive Front Street and the downtown after retailers moved to a mall and shopping centers. That first party comprised a few concessions, trolley rides, and fireworks. People liked it so much the town did it again the following year and has continued ever since, adding new entertainment each year. You can expect to find more than 150 craft vendors, three stages of entertainment, a variety of races and contests, and exhibits, all set in the mood that comes with longtime, ongoing success (wilmington riverfest.com).

Land of Ferries & Forts

Just a few miles away from the historic port of Wilmington, you come to a series of beaches: Wrightsville, Carolina, Wilmington, and Kure. For folks seeking out-of-the-way places, the beaches don't offer much secluded charm, but they can be fun, with enough amusement and entertainment to please the kids without doing in Mom and Dad, if you avoid the peak summer season. A number of historical and marine attractions are especially important and interesting.

Wrightsville Beach is 12 miles east of Wilmington. It operates as a year-round island resort and has plenty of motels and some nice, casual, moderately priced seafood restaurants.

The *Wrightsville Beach Museum of History* (303 W. Salisbury St.; 910-256-2569; wbmuseum.com) is one of those grassroots enterprises that reflects its own small area in unique detail and just makes you feel good with its honesty. The museum is in the fourth-oldest cottage on the island and does two things. First, it provides a good example of what beach cottages in the area used to be like, furnished just with odds and ends left over from permanent homes. And it houses a variety of permanent and changing exhibits that tell you about the history, geography, and culture of Wrightsville Beach.

For instance, the kitchen remains pretty much intact, with white ceramic tile, a white porcelain kitchen sink, and an assortment of cooking utensils typical of the early 20th century. The bedroom and bathroom are simple, functional places, appropriately furnished and pieces are donated. Photographs show how other rooms might have been furnished with stuff collected here and there. A 12-foot model of Wrightsville Beach in about 1910 shows the Lumina Pavilion, where couples danced to the music of Benny Goodman, a bathhouse for changing into beachwear, and a trolley, as well as sections of beach and the boardwalk. The model is still a work in progress, and the museum solicits additions and contributions to it.

Changing exhibits may include anything from the history of surfing to a retrospective on lifeguards to photographs from the collection of a local news photographer. The exhibit of women's bathing suits from the early 1900s on, a summer event each year, makes you yearn for a simpler, more modest time. The museum gives attention to the history of the barrier islands, the beach, the Civil War, and 1954's Hurricane Hazel. An oral history video shows area residents recalling life as it used to be in Wrightsville Beach. This is the one enterprise for which the author of this book would volunteer if she lived anywhere close.

The museum is open from 10 a.m. to 4 p.m. Tues through Fri, noon to 5 p.m. Sat, and 1 to 5 p.m. Sun. Closed on major holidays. Admission is free.

Driving south from Wilmington on US 421 for a little less than 20 miles takes you to the beaches on ***Pleasure Island.*** This area is highly commercial and built up, but if you stick it out to Kure Beach, you'll find two attractions worth taking time to see if you're interested in the naval aspects of Civil War history and in marine life.

On US 421, 3 miles south of Kure Beach, is ***Fort Fisher National Historic Site*** (910-458-5538; nchistoricsites.org/fisher). The fort stood up under heavy naval attack during the Civil War, and some of the 25-foot earthwork fortifications that protected the Cape Fear River and the port of Wilmington from Union forces remain. Reading about such parapets is one thing; looking at them and musing on how they must have been built before the days of bulldozers is a more vivid experience, intensified by such touches as a reconstruction of the gun emplacement and a history trail. There's also a museum that displays Civil War artifacts and offers an audiovisual show, models, and dioramas on the history of the fort. If you travel with a picnic cooler, you'll enjoy the picnic area on the site. Admission is free but donations are appreciated. From Memorial Day through Labor Day, open Tues through Sat 9 a.m. to 5 p.m. and Sun noon to 5 p.m.; closed Mon. Off-season hours are Tues through Sat 9 a.m. to 5 p.m.; closed Sun and Mon and most major state holidays.

When you get this far south on the island, you will have two choices: You can take the Fort Fisher Ferry to Southport, which brings you close to the Brunswick Islands, from whence you began driving, or you can backtrack up the island and take the bridge across to Wilmington, another starting point. At first glance the obvious way to avoid the dilemma of decision would be to begin by taking the ferry from Southport to Fort Fisher, then drive north on the island, and finally cross over to the delights of Wilmington. You may indeed decide to do it that way, especially if you're not traveling during the peak summer months. But you need to know that the ferry crossing takes an hour. For current schedule information when it's time to decide, phone (800) BY-FERRY or check the website: ncferry.org.

For a committed off-the-beaten-path traveler, a drive of about 75 miles up I-40 from Wilmington to Duplin County is worth a day, or several days. This area is full of history, pretty country, and nice people. It's away from the inevitable development along the shore but still part of the coastal plain. NC

24/50 takes you into Kenansville, a town of a little over 1,000 people graced with many restored antebellum houses as well as three antebellum churches. *Liberty Hall Plantation* (409 S. Main St.; 910-296-2175; libertyhallnc.org) is the restored 19th-century ancestral home of the Kenan family, who date back to the time of the Revolution. The Kenan family's influence and their philanthropic activities are still strong in the town. The plantation includes 12 support buildings, in addition to the mansion, and a visitor center and gift shop. It is open Tues through Sat 10 a.m. to 4 p.m. Closed on major holidays. Admission is $5 for adults.

Next to Liberty Hall is *Cowan Museum,* the restored 1848 Kelly-Farrior House, a Greek revival structure filled with more than 2,000 household and farming artifacts from this rural area. Other buildings on the property include a furnished log cabin and a one-room school. Open 10 a.m. to 4 p.m. Tues through Sat. Closed Sun and Mon. Admission by donation (910-296-2149; cowanmuseum.org).

Directly across from the plantation and museum stands *the Murray House Country Inn* (201 NC 24/50; 910-296-1000; murrayhouseinn.com). Murray House Country Inn is a restored 1853 Greek revival mansion listed on the National Register of Historic Places. Its guest rooms, all with private entrances in a newer carriage house, are furnished with a mix of antiques and good reproductions and connected to the main house with formal gardens. The rooms have become popular with business travelers because they are quiet and comfortable. Breakfast is served in the main house, and rates include a tour of the home. Lynn and Joe Davis bought the house specifically to prevent its deterioration. "It took us a year to get the guy to sell," Lynn Davis recalls. They bought and restored the place in 1990 and opened as a bed-and-breakfast in 1994. "It just seemed like the right thing to do with the house," Lynn says. A visit here would be a rich experience for anyone interested in architecture and history. Lynn grew up in Kenansville and knows a lot about the town, its old families, and its architecture. Since opening the bed-and-breakfast, the Davises have been working to create a "New Urbanist Village" here, based on the principles of traditional village development as opposed to the ubiquitous suburban sprawl. This is definitely a work in progress.

One of the best established restaurants in the area is *Country Squire Restaurant,* between Kenansville and Warsaw, a few miles to the north, at 748 NC 24/50, (910-296-1727; countrysquireinn.com). The restaurant serves lunch and dinner. The extensive menu ranges from soups, salads, and burgers to steaks and prime rib. The Squire has a standing offer to anyone who can consume a 72-ounce steak in an hour. The meal costs $85, but if you eat it in an hour, it's free. There are rules about what you must eat besides the meat, including tomato juice, celery sticks, salad, and side dishes, and you must sit at a table alone. You may not leave the table after the steak is served until you are finished or the time limit is up, and the meat may not be cooked more than medium well-done. The restaurant has all ABC (liquor) permits and a big wine list, which may make staying at either the adjacent *Vintage Inn Motel* or a country guest house appealing after dinner (910-296-1831; countrysquireinn.com).

A little to the south of Kenansville, in Beulaville, *Tarkil Branch Farm's Homestead Museum* (1198 Fountaintown Rd.; 910-298-3804; tarkilfarms museum.com), in a restored 1830s homestead, shows you what early farm life would've been like for families living in rural North Carolina in the 1800s. The museum has period furnishings in the home, nine outbuildings, and old farm equipment. Wagon tours and a hiking trail are available. The museum is open Sat from 9 a.m. to 5 p.m. If you call ahead, it may be possible to arrange a tour Tues through Fri. Admission $5, children under 10 free. The folks here recommend wearing comfortable shoes and clothes because the tour includes all the outbuildings and the home on the property and takes about 2 hours.

If you're interested in North Carolina wineries, you may want to schedule a trip on your way back to Wilmington to *Duplin Winery* (505 N. Sycamore St.; 800-774-9634; duplinwinery.com), about an hour's drive from the coast. The winery is in Rose Hill, on US 117, about halfway between Wilmington and Goldsboro. Or take exit 380 from I-40. The winery conducts tours and tastings and, of course, sells its wines. Duplin Winery is especially well known for its Magnolia, a soft dry table wine; its Hatteras Red; and its scuppernong dessert wine. This has become the largest winery in the South. The winery has added a bistro specializing in foods prepared with local, fresh ingredients. The winery is open Mon through Thurs 11 a.m. to 6 p.m., to 7 p.m. Sat. Lunch is available Mon through Sat. from 11 a.m. to 3 p.m. Free tours are available Mon through Sat 10 a.m. to 4 p.m., and free tastings Mon through Sat 5 to 6 p.m.

From Wilmington the best way to head north is to drive on US 17 for a while. Stretches of it are annoyingly full of strip-city areas where traffic is heavy and slow. One interesting stop, right on the highway shortly after you leave Wilmington, is the *Poplar Grove Plantation* (910-686-9518; poplargrove.com). This is a nonprofit operation supported by the Poplar Grove Foundation. It has an unusual history in that it not only survived the Civil War, but also became economically successful again by growing peanuts. The original plantation operated in the tradition of the

sweet, sweet

The word *scuppernong* is an Indian word meaning "sweet tree." Scuppernong is one of the oldest grapes in America, and a favorite among Carolinians, who like things sweet.

times, as a self-supporting agricultural community with more than 60 slaves. The manor house burned down in 1849 and was rebuilt the following year where it now stands. When you visit the plantation, guides in period costume lead you on a tour of the manor house—a three-floor Greek revival building—and the outbuildings, describing what daily life on the plantation was like.

The outbuildings include a tenant house, smokehouse, herb cellar, kitchen (plantation kitchens were always in separate buildings), blacksmith shop, and turpentine and saltworks display. With or without a guide, looking at these buildings dramatically brings home some realities of history. A visitor looking at the small, roughly finished, uninsulated tenant house said, "It's hard to imagine that a whole family actually lived in here." Another visitor, seeing the mock hams, sausages, and bacons hanging in the smokehouse, wondered what the real thing would have been like in such hot weather and said, "It's a wonder everybody didn't die of food poisoning."

Open Mon through Sat 9 a.m. to 5 p.m., Sun noon to 5 p.m. Admission is $12 for adults, $10 for active military and for senior citizens, $6 for children ages 6 to 15. Last tour begins at 4 p.m. Closed Easter Sunday, Thanksgiving Day, and Christmas week through January.

Continuing north on US 17 takes you through some very local, untouristy areas, such as Holly Ridge. If you want more of a sense of the area, shortly after you pass Holly Ridge turn left on Verona Road, and following the signs, head toward Haws Run. You'll go by some pretty little houses with lovingly tended gardens, then an abandoned trailer park, and finally, many occupied mobile homes on the way back out to US 17. This detour of only a few miles gives a view of what many small North Carolina communities near the coast are like—not all beach and boats.

Then you're into the area around Jacksonville, which is shaped and colored by *Camp Lejeune Marine Base.* Traffic is fairly heavy, and the area bulges with the kind of commercial development that surrounds military bases: motels, restaurants, arcades, shopping centers, and the like. But even though driving through such a section isn't as relaxing as spinning along a country road, it's tremendously instructive and sometimes funny. Most of the people you see in the vehicles are heartbreakingly young men with perfect posture and haircuts so short you can almost see their scalps from the next automobile. Often they're in pairs or groups, and often they're towing boats or hauling bikes. The progression of the establishments and signs you pass along the road tells a story: Foxy Lady, New Ink Tattoo Shop, a motel sign that proclaims WELCOME MR. NUNNERY, Real Value Diamond Outlet, an assortment of churches, and the Maternity and Newborn Store. The base's influence sometimes surfaces in interesting ways. The first name of a man who once was a newspaper editor in the Piedmont region was "Lejeune." His mother named him that because it's where he was conceived.

Here's information of a more dignified nature. Camp Lejeune is one of the most complete training centers in the world and covers 110,000 acres. You may wish to stop at the Beirut Memorial, honoring those killed in Beirut and Grenada. It is outside the gate of Camp Johnson on NC 24. You can't get onto the base without a pass, and you can't get a pass without a driver's license and registration certificate. The information center at the main gate on NC 24 is open 24 hours a day (910-451-5655; lejeune.usmc.mil/mcb/index.asp).

From Jacksonville you could logically continue up US 17 to New Bern, or you could travel east on NC 24 toward the ocean to check out the Bogue Banks and then go on to Morehead City, Beaufort, and Atlantic, and ferry across to the Outer Banks. Better yet, if you're not hurrying, avoid this section of NC 24, which runs along another edge of the marine base, and continue north about 15 miles more on US 17, where you pick up NC 58. It runs southeast along the side of the Croatan National Forest and is a much more pleasant drive to the coast. **Cedar Point** is a nice place to stop for a picnic or a rest and perhaps a hike along the Cedar Point Tideland Trail. You'll find camping areas and picnic tables in the shade along the water. Nearby is Cape Carteret, a little town that's probably pretty much solved its crime problem by locating its liquor store right next to the police station and town hall.

Places to Stay in the Southern Coast & Islands

HOLDEN BEACH

Gray Gull Motel
3263 Holden Beach Rd.
At the bridge
(910) 842-6775
graygullmotel.com
A quiet, clean accommodation with a picnic area.
Inexpensive

OCEAN ISLE BEACH

Ocean Isle Inn
37 W. 1st St.
(800) 352-5988
oceanisleinn.com
This resort-style inn has both ocean and sound views.
Moderate

SOUTHPORT

The Inn at River Oaks
512 N. Howe St.
(910) 457-1100
theinnatriveroaks.com
A small, older, family-owned inn, renovated in 2005.
Inexpensive

Lois Jane's Riverview Inn
106 W. Bay St.
(910) 457-6701
loisjanes.com
An inn with the feel of a fine family home.
Moderate

SUNSET BEACH

The Sunset Inn
9 N. Shore Dr.
(910) 575-1000
(888) 575-1001
thesunsetinn.net
At this peaceful place on the island, pets are not permitted and children really are not appropriate.
Moderate

WILMINGTON

Front Street Inn
215 S. Front St.
(910) 762-6442
(800) 336-8184
frontstreetinn.com
This is an inn with lively decor in a historic building.
Moderate to expensive

Rosehill Inn
114 S. 3rd St.
(910) 815-0250
(800) 815-0250
rosehill.com
Luxurious accommodations with Victorian accents in an 1848 home.
Moderate to expensive

WRIGHTSVILLE BEACH

Blockade Runner Beach Resort
275 Waynick Blvd.
(910) 256-2251
blockade-runner.com
Resort is the operative word here; lots to do on nicely kept grounds.
Moderate to expensive

Places to Eat in the Southern Coast & Islands

CALABASH

Captain Nance's Seafood Restaurant
Riverfront
(910) 579-2574
Ask for the catch of the day if you want fish caught locally.
Moderate

Ella's of Calabash
1148 River Rd.
(910) 579-6728
ellasofcalabash.com
Try something fried in their tempura-like batter.
Moderate

SHALLOTTE

Duffer's Bar & Grill
4924 Main St.
(910) 754-7229
duffersbarandgrill.com
It's where the locals eat, and it's kid friendly.

The Purple Onion Cafe
4647 Main St.
(910) 755-6642
www.thepurpleonioncafe
.com
Famous for huge breakfasts and great fresh baked goods.

SOUTHPORT

Thai Peppers Restaurant
115 E. Moore St.
(910) 457-0095
www.thaipeppersnc.us
Thai food and sushi get rave reviews.
Moderate

WILMINGTON

Elijah's
2 Ann St.
Chandler's Wharf
(910) 343-1448
elijahs.com
Crab cakes are a favorite.
Moderate to expensive

Riverboat Landing
2 Market St.
Chandler's Wharf
(910) 763-7227
riverboatlanding.com
Ask about the catch of the day.
Moderate to expensive

Index

About the Author

Sara Pitzer is a transplanted Yankee who has been roaming and writing about the South since 1983. She can't go back north, where it's cold and people talk too fast. In 2006 she received the Charles Kuralt Award from the North Carolina Travel Industry Association. Sara lives in the woods with a yard full of birds and a house full of pets.

Acknowledgments

Craig Distl helped me visit many of the places I've written about and suggested new attractions for this edition. Leah Hughes also provided much useful information. Many friends suggested new places for me to tell you about, and the great IT people at Innovative Solutions, as usual, provided the electronic wizardry it takes to produce a manuscript via computer these days. Thanks.